Economics in the Long Run

The

University

of North

Carolina

Press

Chapel Hill

& London

NEW

DEAL

THEORISTS

AND

THEIR

LEGACIES,

1933–1993

Economics
in the Long Run

THEODORE ROSENOF

HB
87
.R67
1997

The paper in this book meets the guidelines for permanence and durability
of the Committee on Production Guidelines for Book Longevity of the
Council on Library Resources.

Library of Congress Cataloging-in-Publication Data

Rosenof, Theodore.

Economics in the long run: New Deal theorists and their legacies, 1933–1993
/ Theodore Rosenof.

p.   cm.

Includes bibliographical references and index.

ISBN 0-8078-2315-5 (cloth: alk. paper)

    1. Economics—History—20th century.   2. United States—Economic
policy.   3. New Deal, 1933–1939.   4. Keynes, John Maynard, 1883–1946.
5. Hansen, Alvin Harvey, 1887–   .   6. Means, Gardiner Coit, 1896–   .
7. Schumpeter, Joseph Alois, 1883–1950.   I. Title.

HB87.R67   1997

338.973'009'04—dc20   96-24647

                                                              CIP

01 00 99 98 97   5 4 3 2 1

FOR PAT, CHUCK, & LIZA

Contents

Acknowledgments

As a historian, I wish to thank two evolutionary economists for reading and critiquing an earlier version of this book. Frederic S. Lee read what became the first ten chapters; he then referred my work to Warren J. Samuels, who read that version in its entirety. I am also grateful to my friend Lewis Bateman and his staff at The University of North Carolina Press for shepherding the manuscript through the evaluative process and to the Press's two anonymous readers for their critiques and suggestions for revision. I am indebted to Pamela Upton for guiding me through the complexities of modern electronic editing, to Barbara Kelly for word processing, and to Nancy Malone for copyediting. Thanks are also due the Mercy College interlibrary loan staff for efficiently providing me with books and articles over the years, to the Mercy College Faculty Development Committee for help in defraying expenses, and to the staffs of the Harvard University Archives, the John F. Kennedy Library, the National Archives II, and especially the Franklin D. Roosevelt Library. Permission to cite materials from the Alvin H. Hansen and the Joseph A. Schumpeter Papers was granted courtesy of the Harvard University Archives. Finally, I express my deep appreciation to my wife, Pat, and children, Chuck and Liza, to whom this book is dedicated, for their patience and support over the lengthy course of research and composition.

Economics in the Long Run

Introduction

The essential argument of this study is twofold. First, it is my contention that "long-run" or "evolutionary" concepts of economics, advanced during the New Deal Era to explain the Great Depression and out of vogue during the post–World War II boom, have reemerged since the early 1970s with the onset of a new era of long-run or "secular" economic dilemmas. It is my second contention that division within the camp of evolutionary, heterodox economists in and about the New Deal impeded a unified challenge to orthodoxy not only in the 1930s and early 1940s but also with implications and ramifications stretching into subsequent decades. A corollary point is that the long eclipse of a divided evolutionary economics also served to delimit interpretations of the New Deal's nature and to narrow understanding and utilization of its legacy.

Decades before the New Deal Era, American institutionalist economists broke with what they considered the abstractions of orthodoxy in order to explore the changing complexities of the "real world." Keynesian heterodoxy emerged out of the rather abstract traditions of British economics. But John Maynard Keynes, contemptuous of orthodoxy's comfort in the belief that in the long run the Great Depression would cure itself, nonetheless had an evolutionary or historical vision or perspective that underlay his short-run analysis and public policy prescriptions. Gardiner C. Means, active in the New Deal almost from its inception, contributed significantly to institutionally or structurally based analyses of the Great Depression and to the early New Deal's groping for institutional or structural solutions to it. Means, too, based his analysis on a long-run perspective, that of the "corporate revolution." Alvin H. Hansen, best known as the pioneer American Keynesian, was actually much more than that. Steeped in Continental economic theory before his Keynesian adherence, Hansen developed an evolutionary view of the economy based on the changing pattern of external or "exogenous" stimuli. Melding Continental with Keynesian theory, Hansen, active in the later New Deal, set forth his concept of secular stagnation and his proposed solution of secular public investment. Finally, Joseph A. Schumpeter, a longtime rival of Keynes, fought a rearguard action against long-run theories oriented toward the New Deal or government intervention, positing his alternative based on the internal or "endogenous" regenerative power of the "capitalist engine" itself.

These Great Depression–based, New Deal Era evolutionary theories were all, in one way or another, discredited, distorted, or largely ignored during the secular post–World War II boom. Institutionalism was widely dismissed as embarrassingly out of date in the age of the sophisticated "new economics." Gardiner Means, a figure of magnitude in the 1930s, appeared much diminished after 1940. His contributions, once considered seminal, now paled in comparison with the impact of Keynesianism. Secular Keynesianism, however, was abandoned in favor of the "neoclassical synthesis," that is, the marriage of short-run Keynesian policy prescriptions to essentially orthodox economic theory, resulting in a mechanistic formula for "fine-tuning" an economy deemed essentially healthy. Alvin Hansen, hailed as an "American Keynes" at the height of his prestige, was subjected during the postwar boom to ridicule over his theory of secular stagnation and maintained his reputation only as the senior American expositor of Keynes and as the mentor of influential neoclassical synthesis Keynesians. Schumpeterianism now likewise seemed in considerable measure a matter of historical rather than contemporary economic relevance and interest.

The postwar boom came to an end with the troubles of the early 1970s. The new era brought forth problems not remediable by the fine-tuning wisdom of the boom's 1960s apogee. Inflation became rampant and stagnation reappeared, not in the form of a cataclysmic Great Depression but by way of minimal growth and sluggishness interrupted by bouts of severe recession and only brief, ephemeral leaps into semblances of a boom. Over the course of the 1970s, the problems of inflation and stagnation—joined together as "stagflation"—proved beyond the scope or grasp of conventional neoclassical synthesis Keynesian formulas. From the perspective of the period after 1973, the 1930s took on the look not of a time before economists and policymakers achieved sufficient economic understanding to fine-tune but rather of a period of shared economic confusion and turmoil. Now, once again, voices were heard proclaiming that the economy faced both short-run and long-run or secular problems. In this context, theories and analyses based on or related to those of the 1930s reappeared. Structural interpretations reemerged to explain "secular" inflation. The search for a secular version of Keynesianism received impetus. And versions of Schumpeterianism were set forth, while long-run theorists undertook to explain economic phenomena beyond the reach of short-run analysis.

It is my additional contention that heterodox economics after 1940 was shaped and weakened by fissures in evolutionary theory and policy dating back to the late New Deal, particularly the fissure that saw Means on one side and Keynes and Hansen on the other. The early New Deal had proceeded in part in the spirit of Means. The depression was interpreted in terms of structural maladjustments and imbalances, and the perceived solution centered on new structural mechanisms to achieve readjustment and renewed balance. Keynes and Hansen skirted structurally based analyses and solutions in favor of those focused on exogenous phenomena. Seeing lack of inducement to invest rather than structural malfunctioning as the key to the Great Depression and public investment as the key to its solution, Keynes and Hansen emphasized what came to be called "macroeconomics," whose "microeconomic" underpinnings they largely neglected. For his part, Means sharply rejected a Keynesian analysis not based on structure. Keynes and Hansen seemed to triumph, but it proved to be a Pyrrhic victory. For the eventual triumph was that of neoclassical synthesis short-run Keynesianism, and it was this version of Keynesianism that proved unsuccessful in the 1970s, discrediting Keynesianism generally.

The failure to achieve synthesis during the late New Deal between the structural approach of Means and the exogenous approach of Keynes and Hansen contributed to the emergence of neoclassical Keynesianism during the postwar boom and to the debacle of the 1970s and thereafter. Despite the efforts of Keynes and especially of Hansen to root their theories historically, in the climate of the boom the now conventional version of Keynesianism lacked not only a focus on structure but also a sense of history, of evolution, of the long run. The divorce between structurally based institutionalism and Keynesianism and the stripping from Keynesianism of its historical dimension undermined the ability of what now passed for Keynesianism to meet the reemergent secular problems of the post-1973 era.

The division and eclipse of evolutionary economics, coupled with the triumph of the neoclassical synthesis, served in turn to shape and somewhat distort and obscure understanding of the nature and legacy of the New Deal. "The New Deal order is dead," wrote Gary Gerstle and Steve Fraser, editors of a 1989 series of essays on the subject.[1] There were, however, different New Deals, or "intended" New Deals.[2] The New Deal legacy, as it came to be understood during the decades of the post–World War II boom, represented only part of the set of economic ideas and public policies engendered during and after the 1930s. Nonetheless, by the 1950s and 1960s it came to be seen as the economic whole. The durable New Deal was deemed the neoclassical Keynesian synthesis with which the post-1945 boom was associated. The New Deal legacy was one of fiscal policies designed to ensure a demand-based optimum macroeconomic climate. It was against the inadequacies of this version of the New Deal tradition, its failure to combat stagflation successfully, that criticism welled up in the 1970s, culminating in the intellectual and political repudiations of the 1980s.

But it was not the New Deal tradition that was dead. It was the New Deal qua neoclassical Keynesianism that had died. In the 1970s and 1980s, views of New Deal economic futility, irrelevance, and obsolescence were really views of neoclassical Keynesian futility, irrelevance, and obsolescence. There were long-run versions of what the New Deal meant, intended, or, as a legacy, still promised, and these, hitherto eclipsed and not always recognized as such, reemerged as the postwar boom and neoclassical Keynesianism faded. These long-run theories and policies provided a connection between the "intended" New Deals of the 1930s and secular problems and proposed solutions of the 1970s, 1980s, and 1990s. It is also true that the long-run versions of the New Deal legacy could, like the discredited neoclassical Keynesianism, be seen and dismissed as variants of failed governmental economic intervention. Here the legacy sought was pre–New Deal.

The neoclassical Keynesian collapse not only led to a heterodox revival but also engendered a resurgent orthodoxy. It had taken the devastation of the Great Depression to inspire powerful challenges to orthodox theory, most notably that of Keynes. Orthodoxy had held that the economic "system" or "mechanism" was inherently self-correcting, that downturns were necessarily followed by cyclical upswings, that institutional "imperfections" or external "shocks" were mere aberrations, and that government intervention would only impede and delay normal and natural readjustment and recovery. The Great Depression undermined such assumptions and led to the New Deal's enhanced role for government. For nearly a half century, pristine pre-1929 orthodoxy had been discredited and held at bay. Now it burst loose again in reaction to the theoretical and policy failures of the 1970s.

If the Great Depression inspired a challenge to orthodoxy and if the boom decades created—or cobbled together—a synthesis of pre-1929 orthodoxy and elements of 1930s heterodoxy, the more recent period, with the demise of the neoclassical synthesis, has witnessed a struggle for the succession between a 1930s-based heterodoxy and a pre-1929-based orthodoxy. Proposed structural planning to combat inflation and via "industrial policy" to counter stagnation failed to be implemented in the middle and late 1970s and was swept aside in 1980 by the juggernaut of "Reaganomics," based in good measure on 1920s policy proposals. A Schumpeterian revival in the eighties fed into Reaganomics in one version but called for a more vigorous public sector in another. With the fading of the Reagan boom and the onset of recession in the early 1990s, a renascent interest in public investment, recalling Alvin Hansen's advocacy and the legacy of New Deal–constructed infrastructure, was expressed by economists, policymakers, and President Bill Clinton, only to face the policy challenge, especially after 1994, of a renewed orthodoxy.

Despite their differences and whatever the limits to their heterodoxy, the economists on whom I focus in this book shared a long-run or evolutionary approach to economics, placed economic analysis in historical time, and moved beyond concepts of static equilibrium. If orthodox economics grounded itself on Newtonian physics, determined to discover "universal axioms" valid across time, then heterodox, evolutionary economics was akin to "neo-Darwinian" biology, searching for "homologous patterns" and seeking to account for changes over time.[3] As the institutionalist Thorstein Veblen once put it, the basic question was "not how things stabilize themselves in a 'static state,' but how they . . . grow and change."[4] Evolutionary economists believed that changed conditions—due to technological advances, structural development, demographic trends, geographic expansion, business innovation, policy climates—brought changes in the economy. Hence, they argued, the economic system was not a timeless phenomenon operating according to timeless laws but evolved along with and reflected the disruptions and discontinuities of historical change, as illustrated, for example, by the upheaval of the 1930s, the problems of the post-1973 era, and even, in long-run perspective, the boom decades between.

PART ONE.
THE NEW DEAL ERA

The Great Depression of the 1930s was an event of cataclysmic proportions, affecting not only the United States but also Europe and the wider world. Economists had been accustomed to previous depressions, or "panics," as they were earlier styled, but the crisis of this decade was a disaster of far greater magnitude than any that had gone before. It was the depth and persistence of the economic collapse which caused some analysts to conclude that this depression was in some basic respects different and that it was of epochal significance compared with its predecessors. It was this response to the Great Depression which resulted in interpretations that viewed the crisis in long-run or secular terms.

There were at the time, and continued to be thereafter, disputes as to whether the depression originated in America and spread outward or whether essentially European developments, linked to the impact and aftermath of World War I, also afflicted America. But there could be no question as to the depression's extraordinary worldwide consequences. With the collapse of international trade, nations moved increasingly toward solutions to the crisis based on domestic policy, relegating international cooperation to the sidelines, especially after participants failed to reach agreement at the 1933 World Monetary and Economic Conference in London. Most dramatic, the depression led to the rise and triumph of Nazism in Germany and hence to the Second World War.

Within the United States there existed a wide array of interpretations of the depression. To some analysts, it was essentially part of the "natural" or "cyclical" rhythm of a capitalist economy, now aggravated by "outside" or "external" factors. The culprits here included the destructive effects of World War I, disastrous monetary decisions by the Federal Reserve Board, and the devastating impact of the 1930 Hawley-Smoot tariff. All these were blamed for turning a cyclical decline into a secular catastrophe. This was true, in its own fashion, of President Herbert Hoover's analysis. Rejecting a secular view of the depression's origins, Hoover, during his administration and throughout his long life, continued to insist that flaws in the domestic economy were relatively minor, European developments jolted the basically healthy American system, and it was the election of 1932 and the ensuing New Deal that undermined business confidence and caused the depression to persist. The Hoover administration's antidepression policies, accordingly, were mild: initially it urged business to maintain wage standards and purchasing power and then insisted on government budgetary rigor so as to encourage the business confidence that would lead to renewed private investment and consequent recovery. The more innovative Reconstruction Finance Corporation was accepted by Hoover only with great reluctance.

The continued descent of 1932 belied Hoover's expectation and assurance of a timely return to "normal" conditions. Similarly, it contradicted the prevailing wisdom of the 1920s that "business cycles" were merely oscillations within a rhythmical pattern and led to an early readjustment via the economic "mechanism." The way was now open to heterodox concepts and proposals, such as those advanced during the 1932 campaign by Franklin D. Roosevelt's "Brains Trust." Along with an array of other approaches, including work relief spending and monetary manipulation, the basic thrust of the early New Deal was structural. Despite the passage of reciprocity treaties, it was also domestic. The collapse of international cooperation and world trade in the early 1930s was not to be rectified until victory in World War II. The key initiatives of the early New Deal, the National Recovery Administration (NRA) and the Agricultural Adjustment Administration (AAA), were consistent with the institutional diagnosis that the economy's underlying problems were structural in nature and that only structural reorganization and planning could resolve them. The NRA, it was anticipated, would lead the way to recovery through intra-industry agreements (or "codes") that would set "fair" wage and hour standards, increase workers' purchasing power, and stimulate reemployment. Simultaneously, AAA would undertake to "adjust" burgeoning agricultural production through agreements with farmers in the basic commodity areas—a domestic focus as distinct from the proposals of the 1920s to stimulate exports. This, it was anticipated, would increase farmers' prices and incomes. Although the AAA was a qualified success, with agricultural recovery under way by the mid-1930s and with farmers increasing their purchases from industry, the NRA did not work as New Dealers had hoped. Code authorities, essentially dominated by the leading corporations of each industry, engaged too often in restrictive practices, with price increases canceling out wage hikes. Despite much initial hoopla, disillusion set in, brickbats were hurled by antitrusters, and many came to see the NRA as a millstone around the administration's neck. The question was whether to revamp the NRA or abandon a structural planning approach. As it turned out, dispatched by a Supreme Court decision in 1935, the once ballyhooed NRA was never resurrected (although pieces of it were, notably labor and wage-and-hour legislation). Other policies, particularly work relief spending, nonetheless helped to bring about a steady, if limited, recovery by the mid-thirties and led to Roosevelt's electoral triumph of 1936.

In the wake of 1936, preoccupied with court reform and persuaded that recovery would now be self-sustaining, Roosevelt reduced "emergency" work relief spending. Disaster ensued. The limited recovery of 1933–37 became the sharp recession—within the depression—of 1937–38. While critics blamed New Deal policies for the collapse, the administration remained in intellectual confusion and policy disarray for months, split among those who stressed business confidence and budgetary restraint (shades of the hapless Hoover), those who stressed structural problems and structural solutions (whether a new, improved planning mechanism or an antitrust effort), and, increasingly, those who stressed public spending. With the association of the business confidence formula with Hooverian futility and structural planning formulas with the unlamented NRA, the administration's spenders carried the day. Work relief spending, after all, was linked to the 1933–37 recovery, and its curtailment to the 1937–38 recession. But spending's conceptual underpinnings were changing: whereas earlier spending was designed for the "emergency"—to "prime the pump," in the lexicon of the time—public spending was now increasingly viewed as a permanent addition to an economy suffering from "secular stagnation." Further, the structural accompaniment to spending was no longer that of planning but rather an antitrust revival that continued into the early 1940s.

Spending was of overwhelmingly greater importance for the future, but it was eclipsed in the public eye for a time by the antitrust crusade of Thurman Arnold, the flamboyant former law school dean and best-selling author. Hailing originally from Wyoming, making his way to the citadels of the Northeast via West Virginia, Arnold first achieved national re- known with *The Symbols of Government* (1935) and *The Folklore of Capitalism* (1937). Satirizing the "folklore" of laissez-faire capitalism while outlining a public philosophy for the emergent New Deal, Arnold dismissed the antitrust tradition as an antiquated and opportunistic hobby of politicians. Shortly after, he became head of the Antitrust Division of the Department of Justice. Arnold, however, was no old-fashioned moralist denouncing bigness per se. He was a legal craftsman attacking "bottlenecks" in the operation of the modern economy. Antitrust could thus be seen as a pre-1929, preplanning, and indeed archaic structural solution, but it could now also be seen as a useful public policy tool in a world of large corporations: it would seek to discipline rather than to dissolve them, analogous in its own way to the concepts of Gardiner Means. As such a tool antitrust could complement more comprehensive macroeconomic approaches. Arnold was no economist, of course, and his own run wound down and eventually folded with American involvement in World War II. Large corporations that were producing for the national defense, it was argued, should not be "harassed" by this late-blooming New Dealer. Here, as elsewhere, as Roosevelt put it, "Dr. New Deal" had to give way to "Dr. Win-the-War."

Antitrust had experienced its last hurrah at center stage. Bursting forth in the late nineteenth century, prominent in the policy debates of the Progressive Era of the early twentieth century, it continued post-Arnold in a distinctly secondary role, with antitrusters performing as technicians in comprehensive conceptual and policy frameworks set by others. In broader ways as well, the New Deal had intellectual and policy roots in earlier progressive reform, most basically in the idea that government should be used to address economic and social problems not remediable through and even exacerbated by the private economy. The Progressive Era, which had arisen in part out of the depression of the 1890s, second only to that of the 1930s in severity, withered on the impact of World War I and the apparent prosperity and "normalcy" of the 1920s. As the economy plunged after 1929, however, a more critical and reform-minded attitude reemerged. Afflicted by the depression and building on the progressive reform legacy, Americans became more willing to modify inherited social and economic ideas and policies. The depression thus provided the political opportunity for New Dealers not only to address the immediate emergency but also to effect permanent improvements. Out of this came social security old-age pensions, unemployment compensation, and federal bank deposit insurance. Moreover, a basic belief deeply embedded by the depression experience took lasting hold: never again should government stand by passively and allow society to sink into an abyss such as that of 1929–32. The return of boom times brought some return of pre-1929 euphoria. Old ideas made a partial comeback. But the basic idea of security stuck.[1]

1.
The Focus on Structure

nstitutionalism was rooted in late-nineteenth- and early-twentieth-century intellectual challenges to economic orthodoxy and was reflected particularly in the work of Thorstein Veblen, among others.[1] Its emphasis on the importance of structure in terms of analysis and proposed solutions was evidenced in the pronouncements of its formulators. Walton Hamilton, who in 1919 proclaimed an "institutional economics," stressed the need to study "those neglected institutions which exercise a controlling influence over our economic life."[2] In 1932 John Maurice Clark declared that institutionalists did not believe in abstract choices "between pure competition and pure monopoly, or between pure private business and pure socialism."[3] This attitude of openness appeared to fit the upheaval of the Great Depression and the promise of reform offered by the forthcoming New Deal.

Institutionalists also advanced the "Veblenian dichotomy," the basic notion that whereas technology produced economic advancement, business, concerned with profit, often restrained growth via its control over the productive process. That is, although "industry" brought forth production, "business" held it back when profit was not in sight.[4] Institutional economists of the early depression years reflected this influence when they maintained that the crisis was primarily due to corporate decisions based on considerations of profit and loss. Focused particularly on the role of the large corporation in relation to the economy as a whole, they held that institutions, as distinct from "external" forces, and the economy's basic structure, as distinct from "accidental" factors, explained the collapse. They adhered to the proposition that large-scale business had in good measure replaced small-scale competition as the preponderant organizational feature of the modern industrial economy and that, along with its positive benefits, business concentration had created excessive private economic power that required a larger offsetting role for government.[5] They were characteristically suspicious of proposals for "planning" that emanated from corporate business, proposals that were, they feared, geared to restriction rather than to expansion—in Veblenian terms, to "business" rather than to "industry." Instead, institutional economists favored structural planning with a larger public input, planning designed to cause individual corporate decisions to be made in a way consistent with overall economic stability and growth.[6]

Structurally oriented economists prominent in the early New Deal, ensconced particularly in the Roosevelt administration's Department of Agriculture and National Resources Committee, included Rexford G. Tugwell, Mordecai Ezekiel, and Gardiner C. Means, among others. These economists accepted the idea that technological advance required large-scale industrial organizations. They therefore stood steadfastly in opposition to the antitrust tradition. They also believed, however, based on their study of the economic system in terms of its interconnected operation as a whole, that certain features of the management of large corporations had introduced disruptive changes into the economy, especially by way of price and wage policy. Excessively high prices and low wages, whatever their perceived immediate benefit to individual firms, contributed to a failure of demand and a downward economic spiral. The depression, to them, was not simply a sudden occurrence but was rooted in long-run institutional and structural changes in the economy, and its solution required major changes in public policy and government's role. The development of "private planning" geared to narrowly conceived interests of particular firms now required the corrective use of public planning.[7]

In 1931, on the eve of publication of *The Modern Corporation and Private Property*, the most influential study in this tradition, coauthor Adolf A. Berle wrote that the crux of the economic problem lay in "the great corporate structure."[8] He later noted of imbalances between the economy's productive capacity and its follow-through that in this regard the observation of the "cynical economist . . . Veblen" was "a plain statement of a plain fact."[9] Former Veblen associate and future New Deal economist Isador Lubin maintained in 1932 that what was now required was "a national public policy to control the general balance of production and consumption."[10] To Ezekiel, creation of "effective planning and coordination" to ensure that "the great centralized industries" made "sound" decisions constituted "a major challenge to the New Deal."[11] And to the Department of Agriculture's Louis Bean, the central need was to coordinate the policies of the component groups in the economy—to create overall and "composite" rather than "scattered" and "individual approaches to recovery."[12] Here were the central economic preoccupations of the early–New Deal analysts: the role of the large corporation in relation to the depression and the need for new public policy so as to coordinate economic forces that such corporate development had rendered market procedures incapable of accomplishing.

Berle and Means's *Modern Corporation and Private Property*, published in 1932, put the case with force and impact. The authors held that with the separation of ownership from management and control in the large corporation, the notion of "individual initiative" as a driving economic force no longer had a core validity. Further, the trend toward greater concentration and an ever more central role for the large corporation appeared likely to proceed a good deal further. Nor could competition among a few large corporations serve as an effective regulator of economic activity. In this setting, with enormous power in the hands of a relatively few private firms, some form of counteracting public control would be necessary.[13] Berle, the senior author, had originally intended to focus the book primarily on the legal relationship between property-holding stockowners and power-controlling managers rather than on the related economic implications. A lawyer with economic interests, Berle hired Means to aid with the statistical industrial research. It was Means who developed the data that illustrated the concentration of corporate power and who fashioned the basic economic arguments in the book.[14] Means later claimed that the book's "main thrust" concerned "the effect of the modern corporation on the working of the economy as a whole" and the need for new "public policies" reflective of the modern corporation's emergence and significance. Market principles applicable to a highly competitive small-scale economy, Means reaffirmed, were not applicable to an economy that was increasingly characterized by competition among a few large corporations.[15]

The publication of *The Modern Corporation and Private Property* at the depth of the depression guaranteed the book its attention and relevance. Legal scholar Jerome Frank compared it to Adam Smith's *Wealth of Nations* for its conception of "a new economic epoch."[16] Another reviewer saw in the book's message "the logic and the philosophy of the New Deal."[17] Berle became a member of Franklin D. Roosevelt's "Brains Trust" during the 1932 campaign, and in mid-1933 Means noted with justified satisfaction that the book's conclusions had been widely circulated and had, "to an important extent, entered into national policy."[18] So it seemed in 1933, when the central focus was very much on economic structure; when many within the Roosevelt administration held that corporate price and wage policies had disrupted the smooth functioning of the economy, leading to depression; and when the widespread feeling was that new public structures were needed to provide overall coordination to the economy, thus ensuring withdrawal from the depression and future economic stability. The actual unfolding of the early New Deal, however, particularly as embodied by the National Recovery Administration, was jarring to thinkers in this vein. Too much private control and too little public, too much restriction and too little expansion: these hardly constituted their vision of what planning should be about. As put by George B. Galloway in May 1934, NRA "planning" was restrictionist, "shrewd" in a narrow "business" sense but hardly "genuine economic planning" as proponents conceived it.[19]

A common criticism of institutionalism was that it remained too static and descriptive, despite its claim to an evolutionary perspective. The study of institutions per se, critics asserted, could not account for a dramatic collapse such as that of the Great Depression. Dynamic, noninstitutional factors also had to be called into account, something seemingly beyond the institutionalists' ken. Institutionalism thus chipped away at orthodoxy's assumptions, the conclusion ran, but failed to fashion an adequate alternative theory as comprehensive and inclusive as its rival purported to be.[20] In 1975 the Keynesian Paul Samuelson condescendingly characterized early New Dealers as "Veblenian planners as innocent of the intricacies of modern macroeconomics" as those they opposed.[21] Writing, ironically, as the post–World War II Keynesian consensus he had helped to shape was falling into tatters, Samuelson did not give equivalent play to institutionalist insights into the nature of corporate structure and power.

Institutionalists, through structural planning, tried to alter the system from within. Believing that disaster had resulted from institutional malfunctioning, from corporate decision making that had had an adverse impact macroeconomically, they endeavored to fashion new and rearranged institutions that would cause macroeconomically beneficent corporate decisions to be made. In Tugwell's terms, a "connective tissue" was needed to meld together the component parts of the economy, thus enabling them to function as a harmonious whole. Given the proper planning, with effective public control, business would not sabotage industry by "destroying its own market" through price and wage policies in the narrow immediate interest of individual firms but calamitous to the economy as a whole.[22] Like Tugwell, other early planners tried to buck the disillusionment wrought by the NRA, presenting over the remainder of the decade what they considered genuine planning schemes. Mordecai Ezekiel, in particular, pushed plans for coordinated, structurally based macroeconomic expansion of production.[23] His audience, however, appeared inoculated against further experiments along these lines by memories of an NRA gone awry. With the decline of the institutionalist and structural planning approach and in the wake of the NRA, Keynesianism promised the easier route of impacting the economy from without. Through fiscal policy, an environment could be created that would be conducive to the effective functioning of the system. Assured of a secure environment, business, in effect, would see no need to sabotage industry. Macroeconomic policies would lead to harmonious microeconomic decisions.[24]

In his 1964 study of Thorstein Veblen, which was published at the apogee of what had become orthodox Keynesianism, Douglas Dowd held that Veblen's analysis was "remarkably close" to that emanating from Keynes's *General Theory*. But Veblen, he wrote, focused not on why new investment took place but on production restriction within a given state of investment. Veblen thus lacked "an adequate theory of consumption and investment," Keynes's seminal contribution.[25] In 1982 Peter Temin, not unlike Samuelson with his strictures of 1975, took the early New Dealers to task for trying "to solve a macroeconomic problem with microeconomic tools," that is, for dealing with the various component parts of the economy as if "the economy was . . . the sum of its parts" and as if dealing with all the parts was the same as dealing with the whole. The effective "integration" of economic policy geared to the whole was the accomplishment of Keynes.[26] But, as was commonly argued by the time Temin wrote, a shortfall of orthodox Keynesianism was its relative inattention to structure and power and to component parts—its missing elements in the process of public policy integration. And there were, after all, structural as well as Keynesian concepts of integration—of dealing with the economy as a whole. Indeed, structural planners' criticism of early–New Deal policy focused on its ad hoc, piecemeal, segmented nature, when what was called for was a systematic, holistic, integrated approach.[27] Thus if institutionalists may be faulted for the incompleteness of their analysis in terms of nonstructural phenomena, orthodox Keynesians may be faulted for their failure to consider and incorporate structural elements more fully. The schools themselves remained segmented rather than integrated, chronologically successive—with one giving way to the other as a preponderant influence over the course of the New Deal Era—rather than synthesized as a comprehensive and inclusive long-run heterodox challenge to orthodoxy.

2.
Keynesianism as
Long-Run Economics

nitially predominant in New Deal economic analysis, the structural approach was challenged and eventually displaced by another long-run perspective: that originating with John Maynard Keynes. Born in Britain in 1883, the son of an economist, Keynes had the greatest impact of anyone on economics in the twentieth century. Keynes was a legendary figure: brilliant, quick, and possessed of flair and supreme self-confidence. A practitioner of the "dismal science" of economics, he enjoyed and patronized the arts. A member of the famed "Bloomsbury Group," he had an affair with painter Duncan Grant and later married Russian ballerina Lydia Lopokova. Keynes was reared in the established tradition of Alfred Marshall, yet he founded a "new economics." A master of theory, he was geared to policy and used his gift for polemic to advance his cause.

Keynes came to prominence with *The Economic Consequences of the Peace* (1919), his blistering attack on the Treaty of Versailles, which was followed by his public policy advocacy of the 1920s and what was meant to be his masterpiece, *A Treatise on Money* (1930). But the spread of the Great Depression plunged Keynes into the rethinking that led to his epochal *General Theory of Employment, Interest, and Money* (1936). Like institutionalists, Keynes in his own fashion undertook to examine the economy as a whole, to provide a "general theory" of the economy's nature and performance. Also like institutionalists, Keynes held that what worked as a part of the system might not work for the system as a whole, that what served the interest of individual firms might not serve the well-being of the economy in toto. There was no necessary adjustment mechanism intrinsic to the system to equate the parts and the whole. Out of Keynes's work evolved the modern distinction between "microeconomics" and "macroeconomics."[1]

Keynes also shared with institutionalists a historical dimension that he applied to economic performance. But whereas institutionalists focused above all on how economic structure changed through time, Keynes focused primarily on the changing environment in which the system operated, on forces external or exogenous to the economic mechanism itself, including not only technology but also geography and demography. Thus although he was overwhelmingly concerned with the immediate crisis, a concern manifestly understandable and justifiable in the midst of the Great Depression when writing his *General Theory*, and although his disparaging comments about the long run in which "we are all dead" are among his most quoted, Keynes did place his short-run analysis in a long-run or secular perspective. The short run was in some measure a product of the long run and inseparable from it. Specifically, exogenous conditions for nineteenth-century capitalism were, to Keynes, more favorable to growth and progress than were exogenous conditions in the twentieth century. Along with technological development, geographic expansion and population growth were deemed of great import in inducing that investment which underlay economic progress during the earlier epoch. The problems of contemporary capitalism were due in some measure to less favorable exogenous conditions.[2]

What Keynes provided essentially was what his great rival Joseph Schumpeter called a "vision"—a long-run perspective in which he placed his more detailed analysis. In this sense Keynes's vision posited a concept of discontinuity in capitalist development. What was assumed to be the "norm" for capitalism in the nineteenth century was actually unique to that period. That is, nineteenth-century, laissez-faire capitalism was not valid for all times and places but functioned as it did because of the particularly favorable conditions of the century—technological advance, expansion into new lands, and rapid population growth. The norm for the nineteenth century, however, was just that: a norm for a discrete period. That norm was now altered, upset by the havoc of World War I, and, evident even before the Great Depression, in the stagnant industries of the 1920s British economy, industries whose problems appeared to be long-run or secular rather than short-run or cyclical, which further helped shape Keynes's discontinuity perspective. A new "norm" had thus emerged, requiring new assumptions and policies diverging from the old. The nineteenth-century vision of automatic economic progress would now have to give way to one in which progress had to be consciously shaped and stimulated. This new norm was what some were to label "secular stagnation."[3]

How central secular stagnation was to Keynesianism as a whole has long been a matter of debate. Some have seen the stagnation thesis as constituting the very core of *The General Theory*.[4] Others have stressed that Keynes only occasionally alluded to stagnationist phenomena in that work—that hints and suggestions, obiter dicta, did not constitute an overall theory.[5] Schumpeter, in particular, stressed the theme of centrality, seeing in Keynes's early writings, such as *The Economic Consequences of the Peace*, "the origin of the modern stagnation thesis" and "the embryo of the *General Theory*." *The General Theory* itself was "the final result of a long struggle" to develop the stagnationist vision.[6] But however central stagnationism was to Keynesianism, it remained for Keynes a perspective or vision rather than a well-developed theory. Keynes biographer Robert Skidelsky summed it up well, saying that the degree to which Keynes accepted a full-fledged secular stagnation thesis was "open to question," but a "consciousness of changed conditions was . . . the departure point of Keynesian economics." In this sense *The General Theory* was indeed an effort to build on "Keynes' perception of historical discontinuity."[7]

The General Theory did not provide much in a secular stagnationist mode that was specific, substantive, and explicitly developed. Along stagnationist lines, the passage cited most often was the one in which Keynes wrote of the nineteenth century's satisfactory level of employment being due to, among other things, "the growth of population and of invention" and "the opening-up of new lands."[8] More fully developed within *The General Theory* was the psychological notion of confidence and uncertainty, which was, however, not unrelated to perceptions of "hard" secular stagnationist realities. The modern capitalist, according to Keynes, lacking the favorable environment of the nineteenth century and its consequent state of ebullience, was highly sensitive, easily rattled, overwhelmed by uncertainty, and unwilling to venture forth except in a spurt of high confidence. "Animal spirits," buoyed by feelings of optimism, were subject to passivity when captured by a spirit of pessimism.[9] The link between psychology and reality at the activating level came by way of investment. According to Keynes, the key to the economic problem lay in the "weakness of the inducement to invest."[10] Investment depended on expectations and on confidence, and there was no way under modern conditions for laissez-faire capitalism to assure such a state of confidence as would guarantee investment sufficient to avoid wide swings in employment.[11] The result was that "the economic system in which we live" could continue "in a chronic condition" of low-level "activity for a considerable period without any marked tendency either towards recovery or towards complete collapse." Keynes concluded that "the environment and the psychological propensities of the modern world must be of such a character as to produce these results."[12]

The environment as linked to psychology thus produced the lack of investment leading to a tendency toward chronic stagnation. Outlined and suggested in the lengthy and prolix *General Theory*, aspects of Keynes's secular perspective were developed in a more focused manner in an early 1937 article. Given as the Galton Lecture before the Eugenics Society and published in the *Eugenics Review*, "Some Economic Consequences of a Declining Population" further allowed Keynes to provide a long-run context for the short-run analysis of *The General Theory*.[13] In this article, Keynes foresaw a continuance in the decline of population growth in contrast with the robust population growth of the nineteenth century. Linking long-run demographic trends to psychology and investment, Keynes held that population expansion tended to promote optimism, because businesspeople foresaw ever increasing markets, whereas with relative population decline the contrary was true. Further, Keynes argued, in terms of "hard" secular stagnation criteria, in accounting for "the causes of the enormous increase in capital during the nineteenth century . . . , too little importance . . . has been given to the influence of an increasing population." As Keynes saw it, "An increase in population increases proportionately the demand for capital."[14] Commenting on this Keynesian theme, British economist J. R. Hicks avowed that "the expectation of a continually expanding market, made possible by increasing population, is a fine thing for keeping up the spirit of entrepreneurs. With increasing population, investment can go roaring ahead."[15]

Keynes's stagnationist vision thus provided a framework for his *General Theory*. The economic threat, unless offset, was one of impending stagnation or underemployment equilibrium: the economy could come to rest at a chronically low level of activity.[16] Here Keynes departed from conventional business cycle theory—that is, the idea that the economy fluctuated with ups and downs and the notion that a swing in one direction would necessarily lead to a swing in the other. Rather than fluctuations or business cycles, Keynes now focused his analysis on a perceived long-run tendency toward stagnation and chronic underemployment.[17] Moreover, unlike cycles, the tendency toward stagnation was not self-correcting within or through the mechanism of the economic system itself; a necessary inducement to invest did not automatically spring from the inner nature of the system. The economy could not simply be conceived of as a self-adjusting mechanism; it was not in toto a mechanism at all but a process evolving through time. Depression could not be understood simply in terms of "frictions" within the system, mechanical maladjustments; it had to be understood more fundamentally in terms of the age and environment in which the system qua mechanism existed. Price, including the rate of interest, was no longer viewed as the essential equilibrating and self-adjusting element of the mechanism. Rather than adjusting through price or interest rate, an economy approaching low-level equilibrium adjusted—or, more appropriate, maladjusted—through lower output and lower employment—a result of lower investment.[18]

What was to be done, according to Keynes, to offset underemployment equilibrium lacking a stimulus from within? Just as past external or exogenous forces had stimulated the economy in the nineteenth century, so too would new external or exogenous forces stimulate the economy now, new forces requiring an enhanced role for government, one that departed from the previous century's laissez-faire. Part of the solution involved consumption; more fundamental was investment. While the failure of the inducement to invest led to stagnation, the economy was also depressed by the lack of propensity to consume. Hence, in addition to an emphasis on investment, Keynes called for government policies to increase the propensity to consume by way of income redistribution. Increased consumption would in turn serve to stimulate investment.[19] Given the key role of investment, or lack thereof, in causing stagnation, a direct push toward greater investment was also needed to bring about adequate effective demand.[20]

Monetary policy was not adequate to induce investment in an economic state characterized by conditions of stagnation, including expectations so low that increased investment could not be roused by lower interest rates. In earlier works, such as his *Treatise on Money*, Keynes had seen interest rates as playing a key equilibrating role: lower interest rates would bring forth the necessary greater investment. By the time of *The General Theory*, however, although Keynes still saw a role for lower interest rates as an inducement to invest and believed that they could help maintain investment once stimulated, he no longer believed that they would suffice. Expectations could reach so low a state that no change in the economic mechanism per se—no adjustment within that mechanism, such as lower interest rates—could jolt the inducement to invest from its stupor. Hence only an external force, one outside and distinct from the system as mechanism, could play that role, bringing about the needed investment to drive the economy out of a low-level equilibrium.[21]

That external force would have to be an enhanced economic role for government. It would center more specifically on government fiscal policy, more precisely on government spending, and still more precisely on government investment. For just as chronic stagnation could not be explained in terms of business cycle theory, so too would government spending have to be geared not to a cycle but to a chronic investment deficiency.[22] What was needed to offset paralyzingly low expectations of capitalists and to offset the lack of inducement for private investment was public investment.[23] As Keynes put it in *The General Theory*, the responsibility now for determining total investment could not "safely be left in private hands," hence "a somewhat comprehensive socialisation of investment" would constitute the "only means" of approaching full employment.[24] It would provide "the environment which the free play of economic forces" required to unleash full production.[25] Use of public investment to create a favorable environment in which the economic mechanism could operate obviated the need to intervene more overtly in that mechanism. By providing that favorable environment through control of "the aggregate amount of resources" in which the economic system as mechanism would function, government would "have accomplished all that is necessary."[26] Government would have done what was necessary, that is, to create a positive environment for the exercise of "individual initiative," to offset "the odds loaded against" the capitalist under conditions of low expectations and stagnation.[27] Public investment, in short, would create the necessary environment in which the private economic system or mechanism could successfully operate. Here was the upshot of Keynes's "general theory."

But this general theory, commentators were quick to adduce, left out some critical ingredients. Although Keynes was well aware of the vital role of technology in long-run economic growth, for example, this role was assumed rather than developed as an integral part of his theory. As Alvin H. Hansen put it, Keynes took "real factors . . . largely . . . for granted. The psychological . . . aspects are indeed at points well treated," Hansen elaborated, "but . . . the dynamics of technical progress . . . are passed by almost unnoticed."[28] Allan Gruchy, a leading institutionalist of the post–World War II era, held that Keynes emphasized psychological elements at the expense of the technological and institutional factors so key to Thorstein Veblen and his successors.[29] Gruchy here pointed to what critics considered another lacuna in Keynes's general theory: the relative lack of attention to economic structure. This was not without irony, for Keynes undertook to explain stagnation apart from a conventional stress on institutional or structural "frictions." But in so doing, it was argued, he simultaneously gave insufficient attention to more deeply rooted structural sources of the economic malady.

In this regard Keynes himself set the stage for what was later to be dubbed the "neoclassical synthesis," that is, the marriage of Keynesian macroeconomic policies to pre-Keynesian microeconomic theoretical assumptions. Keynes declared that once the proper economic environment was obtained by way of public investment, the economy as mechanism would thereafter function satisfactorily. There would be no need to interfere significantly with the mechanism itself, that is, with prices or microeconomics as distinct from macroeconomics.[30] Once the proper environment was set, the classical theory came "into its own again from this point onwards," Keynes wrote.[31] This was not, of course, without its appeal, political and otherwise. The government would have to assure a favorable overall environment. But government would not be deemed a structural part of the system. Nor would it get deeply involved with the intricacies of prices and wages. It would act from outside to shape an environment, not from inside to plan the details of the system or mechanism.

Keynes, then, did not devote great attention to factors of economic structure, institutions, or organization—key preoccupations of institutionalists. Formally, in *The General Theory* he assumed "perfect competition," which may be ascribed in part to the continuing hold on him of the Marshallian tradition in which he was intellectually reared. Perhaps more fundamental, it may also be ascribed in part to his emphasis on economic environment as the key factor explaining the lack of inducement to invest. If an exogenously based lack of investment was the key determinant, then structural or institutional considerations were not. If environment was the crux, then mechanism was not.[32] As Alfred S. Eichner, a leading "post-Keynesian" of the 1970s and 1980s, put it in a letter to the contrary-minded Gardiner C. Means, Keynes believed that the level of investment, not price policy, was "the more fundamental problem" in explaining unemployment.[33]

More specific, the theories of "monopolistic competition" and "imperfect competition" associated with Edward Chamberlin and Joan Robinson, respectively, were not incorporated into Keynes's *General Theory*, even though these developments in theory were under way simultaneously with Keynes's and, more remarkable, even though Joan Robinson was a close associate of Keynes, who was a reader of her book for her publisher.[34] To be sure, the basic malady to Keynes's mind was rooted in the economic environment as distinct from structure or organization, and imperfect competition related to the latter. Keynes focused intensely on his central argument and was not to be distracted. As his associate and biographer R. F. Harrod later recalled, at the time of the appearance of *The General Theory*, Keynes "did not take an interest in any ideas except his own."[35]

Beyond this, however, Keynes apparently did not want to confuse or muddle the essential point he was making. He assumed perfect competition not because he believed it was the norm, far from it, but rather as a way of meeting his theoretical foes on their own ground. Traditional theory had acknowledged that institutional or structural "frictions" could impede or obstruct the smooth functioning of the economic system. To have incorporated imperfect competition would have opened the door to an "imperfectionist" interpretation of his theory, that is, to an interpretation focused on conventionally acknowledged "frictions." By assuming perfect competition, Keynes endeavored to evade and avoid this complication and thus to cut to the very core of traditional theory.[36]

Traditional theory in effect assumed a favorable environment, taking that of the nineteenth century to be the eternal norm. Keynes used the notion of a changing environment, or altered exogenous conditions, to challenge orthodoxy. Environment, psychology, and investment were Keynes's key concepts, not institutions, structure, or price.[37] Still, there were clearly ways in which institutionalist emphases corresponded to those of Keynes. If an unfavorable economic environment could lead to lack of investment and a low-level equilibrium, so too, in the institutional analysis, could structural rigidities wrought by the rise of the large corporation. To acknowledge the latter was not necessarily to negate the former, whatever the conscious strategy of Keynes in the 1930s. Indeed, it has been argued, an institutionalist microeconomics would have complemented and completed Keynesian macroeconomics, giving it a more valid and appropriate microeconomic foundation than that provided by outdated Marshallian assumptions. An institutionalist microeconomics would have augmented rather than detracted from Keynes's concept of underemployment equilibrium.[38]

Thus while Keynes's relative neglect of institutional factors did make intellectual sense—he could confront traditional theory on its own grounds without the distraction of "frictions"—and while it did make political sense—providing an improved environment might well have seemed politically more acceptable than tinkering with a mechanism—the skirting of institutional elements also had its drawbacks. Already apparent in the 1930s and 1940s and disastrously evident by the 1970s was the cleavage it helped to create among those geared to economic change in the earlier period and its contribution to a disunity and attendant weakness of challenges to traditional theory in the latter era. The foremost analyst of institutional factors in the 1930s, Gardiner C. Means, found himself relegated to the sidelines in *The General Theory*. Means's price concepts, although not disputed by Keynes, were nonetheless placed outside the central framework of Keynesian analysis.

3.
Gardiner C. Means
and the Corporate
Revolution

G ardiner Coit Means had the origins of an American Brahmin. Born into a Congregationalist minister's family in Windham, Connecticut, in 1896, he was also the grandson of Congregationalist ministers and traced his ancestry back to early New Englanders. Growing up in Massachusetts and Maine, he attended Exeter Academy, after which he enrolled at Harvard, where he majored in chemistry. He enlisted in the military on American entry into World War I and was assigned to officers' training camp at Plattsburgh, New York; there he met the young Adolf A. Berle. Receiving his commission, Means was transferred to a military aeronautics school on Long Island, where, one day, his plane went into a tailspin at two thousand feet. He skillfully managed to widen the spin, however, and so was thrown from the plane when it crashed, unconscious but only bruised. He ended his wartime service stationed in Texas. Following his discharge, Means joined the Near East relief effort to aid Armenians in Turkey, working there for a year and a half. On returning to the United States, he studied at the Lowell Textile Institute and then launched his own textile business. He again enrolled at Harvard, now as a graduate student in economics, receiving his master's degree in 1927. That year he also married Dr. Caroline F. Ware, a specialist in economic and cultural history.[1]

Means's nonacademic activities considerably influenced his intellectual development. Turkey's preindustrial economy reflected, he believed, the economics of Adam Smith, given its small-scale competition and bargaining over prices. But with its production of a specialty item, his own textile business operated quite differently. Means could set and maintain his prices over a period of time. By the time he returned to Harvard, Means felt he had reason to be skeptical of traditional theory. The economics he was taught at Harvard, Means thought, related for the most part to the time of Adam Smith or to the conditions of Turkey rather than to the highly organized economy in which he operated his business. At Harvard, however, he also took a course with W. Z. Ripley on the corporation and industry. This course and Ripley's writings meshed with Means's own evolving view of the nature of the modern economy.[2] Means was granted his Ph.D. by Harvard in 1933, but not without difficulty. His dissertation, "The Corporate Revolution," was divided into two sections: a statistically based factual part demonstrating the growing role of the modern corporation, and a theoretical part, in which he discussed the implications of this enhanced role for orthodox theory. In granting Means his degree, the doctoral committee accepted the first part of his dissertation but rejected the second. The theoretical section was thus deleted from the approved manuscript.[3]

In the meantime, Means had renewed his acquaintance with Adolf Berle. Berle had been searching for a collaborator with economic expertise, and Berle's and Means's wives, who had known each other at Vassar, facilitated the new partnership.[4] Like Means, Berle was the son of a minister, but their personalities were quite different. Berle was flamboyant, whereas Means was relatively staid. Berle could be mercurial; Means was characteristically steady. Berle's writing style was supercharged; Means's was more conventional. If Berle was the "star," Means nonetheless shared in the acclaim granted *The Modern Corporation*. Often described as "unassuming," albeit stubborn and persistent, Means was no braggart. Hence it was apparently the rather brash Berle, not the more placid Means, who at a 1932 Columbia University seminar compared *The Modern Corporation* to Adam Smith's *Wealth of Nations*, much to the outrage of at least one observer.[5]

In his dissertation and in early articles, as well as in his coauthored *Modern Corporation and Private Property*, Means outlined the broad perspective that was to govern him for the rest of his long career. In the modern economy, he wrote in his dissertation, competition no longer played its traditional role, with the market increasingly replaced by administration. In such an economy, he held in articles of 1931 and 1932, production was to a very important extent undertaken by large, not small, units and was characterized by concentrated control rather than by market competition. Adam Smith's economics, accordingly, would have to give way to more relevant concepts of analysis.[6] Means was thus quite correct in his recollection that by the time he joined the Roosevelt administration in 1933, he was "keenly aware" that economic activities "were subject to a high degree of administrative decision-making."[7]

Most particularly, Means dealt with the role of price in the modern corporate economy, with the emergence of a pricing power held by large corporations. This pricing power was what Means was to call the ability to "administer" prices. The rise of the large corporation, the decline of competition, and the concentration of control: all meant a diminishment of the role of the market in price determination. The corresponding growth of the corporate power to administer prices had major consequences for the economy as a whole. Microeconomic decisions, rather than impacting macroeconomically through market forces, now had direct macroeconomic consequences.[8]

The rise of the large corporation, including the separation of formal ownership from effective control, also meant, according to Means, that investment decisions had been separated from savings decisions and that the two would not be meshed automatically. But this aspect of his thought—one akin to Keynesian concepts—was never significantly developed by Means beyond his dissertation effort, and it never became an integral part of his macroeconomic theory. More vital to him was the structural impact of the large corporation on the economy, notably the disruption of the market mechanism wrought by corporate predominance. It was this element of his work that Means developed at great length in the future.[9]

In his emphasis on structure, Means's work meshed with that of the institutionalists. He did not evolve intellectually out of the institutionalist school. Harvard was hardly a bastion of Veblenians, nor did Means read much of Veblen or think of himself as an institutionalist. Indeed, he sometimes pronounced himself "irked" to be so classified. He stressed that his own interest in institutions was explicitly related to macroeconomic theory and that theory, in his view, was not a strong suit of self-professed institutionalists. In fact, Means's emphasis on price policy reflected orthodox theory's stress on the importance of the market mechanism. Means essentially retained traditional theory's focus on the role of market and price but argued, based on his study of the modern corporation, that the centrally important market and price mechanism no longer operated as traditional theory held it would. Means, however, also acknowledged the complementariness of his work and institutionalism, agreeing that his analysis of the modern corporation and its impact related very well to the characteristic institutionalist emphasis on the role of the evolving and changing economic structure.[10]

His reputation established by the highly positive reception granted *The Modern Corporation and Private Property*, in the early summer of 1933 Gardiner Means enlisted in the New Deal. Recruited by Rexford Tugwell, whose views of the modern economy jibed with Means's own, Means first served as an economic adviser to Secretary of Agriculture Henry A. Wallace. He left that position in 1935 to join the Industrial Section of the National Resources Committee (later the National Resources Planning Board) and in the early 1940s worked in the Bureau of the Budget. Within the Department of Agriculture, he joined the like-minded Tugwell as well as fellow New Deal planners Mordecai Ezekiel and Louis Bean. As Wallace's economic adviser, Means was to focus not on agriculture per se but on the industrial economy as it related to agriculture. In this regard he also became a member of the Consumers' Advisory Board of the National Recovery Administration.[11] This assignment and his subsequent positions in Washington provided Means with an opportunity to develop his economic concepts further, as well as to influence public policy at a critical juncture in its history. Over the course of the decade, he continued to develop his central idea of a "corporate revolution" in American economic development and to sketch a new framework of economic planning to supplement and in some measure to substitute for the disrupted market mechanism.

Means's vision was based first on the impact of technology on the economy and its structure. It was technological change, he believed, that underlay the growth of the large corporation. Technological advance had caused large units to develop, and the modern economy required large units to function. There could be no going back.[12] The transformation of a premodern into a modern economy was also the transformation of a predominantly competitive, small-scale agricultural economy into an increasingly concentrated, large-scale industrial economy.[13] Along with the perplexing difficulties of a modern, concentrated industrial economy, Means held, came enormous benefits—greater efficiency, mass production and distribution, and a higher standard of living. Corporate concentration was irreversible, and reversal was not desirable.[14]

With concentration came administration. The modern economy, Means believed, while retaining a sector, including agriculture, in which market forces predominated, nonetheless was increasingly characterized overall by large corporations' exercising of control over the market. Traditional economists treated instances of concentration and control as "special cases," exceptions to the rule of a market-based competitive economy. To Means, the special cases had become more general, and the previous rule had become more nearly the exception. Theories, concepts, and terms associated with the old, chiefly competitive economy no longer had general applicability. Now, new theories, concepts, and terms—ones centering on concentration, control, and administration—were needed to understand the changed economic structure and its impact on economic activity. Market concepts would hereafter be encompassed within this "broader" theoretical framework.[15] This was Means's effort, like that of Keynes, to subsume the old theory within the new. The movement from market dominance to increasing administration was, Means concluded, "the crucial difference between the assumptions of the classical economists and the actual functioning of our present economy."[16]

Means was aware that particular groups of large corporations rose and fell over time, but he believed that the increased role of large corporations as such was an enduring part of the modern economy.[17] The growth of large corporations, the increasing dominance of administrative as distinct from market forces, had a basic and pervasive macroeconomic impact. Corporate administration undertaken in the interest of a firm or industry had far-ranging consequences. Whereas the market had provided a rough coordination of the economy in earlier times, the mixture of market and administered forces now could lead to economic imbalance and instability.[18] Thus administration, although a result of technology and an integral part of the modern economy, was now also exercised as an unbalancing and a destabilizing force. While thinking in terms of the firm, Means wrote, "corporation managements" necessarily impacted on "the condition of the entire nation. Their influence thus is more extensive than the scope of their responsibility or the scope of their consideration." This growth of administration was "the essential . . . basis of present economic difficulties." It had made the American economy "subject to increasingly serious depressions."[19]

In Means's analysis, this disruptive impact came above all by way of what he termed "administered prices." The basic and most famous statement of Means's administered prices thesis came in a memorandum to Secretary Wallace that was published in early 1935 as a Senate document entitled *Industrial Prices and Their Relative Inflexibility*. Means originally intended to provide a statistical analysis of the behavior of wholesale prices in agriculture and industry, demonstrating the differences in behavior of prices in the competitive agricultural vis-à-vis the administered industrial sector and showing that new mechanisms would now be needed to create and maintain economic balance. The early versions of these mechanisms—the National Recovery Administration and the Agricultural Adjustment Administration—soon passed from the scene; the part of the study related to these agencies receded in importance, but the part dealing with price behavior had a lasting impact.[20] As to price behavior, Means recalled, his findings "were much more startling and in conflict with the classical analysis than even I had expected."[21]

Means considered administered prices, like other aspects of a modern corporate economy, a result of technological advance and economic progress.[22] Administered pricing had grown along with the movement from a competitive agricultural to an increasingly concentrated industrial economy. In the modern economy, administered pricing had developed to the point where it, rather than market-determined pricing, characterized large areas of industry.[23] The fact that the "bulk of prices" were "not established in free markets" constituted "an essential structural characteristic of the American economy."[24]

The administration of prices meant, according to Means, that coherence between microeconomic decision making and macroeconomic results was shattered. What Keynes had found in environment and investment, Means found in the breakdown of the automatically adjusting market mechanism. With a perceived decline in demand, according to Means's analysis, corporations with the ability to administer prices—that is, to set and maintain prices within a discretionary range—characteristically found it in their interest as firms to hold prices essentially at or near current levels and to cut production and employment instead. Regardless of the negative macroeconomic effect, a given company could be more certain of selling a set amount at a set price than of selling more at a downwardly flexible price in the face of falling demand. The decision so to administer prices was thus entirely sound and rational from the standpoint of the interest of the individual company. As long as all companies in a concentrated industry administered prices along these lines, their basic stability, albeit at lower levels of production, could be maintained.[25] The problem was that the growth of administered prices "diverted" the drive for "immediate self-interest" from acting as a force for economic readjustment into a force often acting to exacerbate economic maladjustment.[26] The traditional notion that the interplay of self-interests via the market would lead to a general interest was now undone by the ability of corporations to administer prices and thereby in some measure to control the market. In view of administered prices, the conclusion of "traditional economics"—that the exercise of self-interest resulted in "an effectively functioning economy"—now would more nearly have to be reversed.[27]

Means's central point was that the ability to administer prices upset the traditional equilibrating role of the market mechanism. According to Means, the market mechanism was supposed to operate, and to a greater or lesser extent had operated, as an overall coordinator of the economy in the era when the economy was largely competitive and price-driven. The market mechanism had provided an automatic adjustment mechanism. If demand declined, for example, prices would also fall, thus maintaining real demand. Maladjustment, forces of disequilibria in the economy, would thereby be corrected. Administered prices now obstructed and essentially rendered ineffective this self-correcting market mechanism. Administered prices did not automatically decline in the face of reduced demand, and thus real demand was not maintained; instead, initial maladjustments were aggravated. Flexible market prices correlated with a flexible market mechanism and a flexible, self-adjusting economy. Administered prices were relatively inflexible, hence obstructing the market mechanism and permitting a low-level economic state to develop and continue in the absence of any corrective coming from outside the framework of the market mechanism.[28]

Administered prices thus disrupted the working of the market mechanism and made existing maladjustments worse. Maintaining prices in the face of falling demand while decreasing production and employment caused mass buying power to drop and demand along with it. The downward spiral continued as the ramifications of administered prices spread through the economy. Rather than a high-level equilibrium restored through price flexibility, a low-level equilibrium was created through price inflexibility combined with production and employment flexibility. Further, those parts of the economy still characterized by market pricing—such as agriculture—suffered doubly. Prices went down on what farmers produced, while the prices of industrial goods they needed remained relatively rigid.[29]

Therefore the microdecisions of corporate price administrators had macroeconomic effects—decisions made at the firm and industry level had great impact on the overall economy. Means looked at administered prices primarily in terms of their macroeconomic effect, basically considering his analysis of administered prices a contribution to macroeconomic theory. The existence of widespread administered prices, he held, "shattered" the traditional theory that pivoted on the equilibrating function of the market mechanism.[30] As Means put it in 1934, classical economists had assumed that supply and demand were equated by a flexible price, whereas under price administration, production and demand were equated at a given price.[31]

Means argued that relatively inflexible administered prices explained the exceptional severity of the Great Depression. Market prices dropped as demand declined, but administered prices remained relatively rigid, with production and employment reduced instead.[32] Had the traditional market mechanism operated, had administered price inflexibility not developed as a result of long-run structural change, no Great Depression would have occurred. The economic decline would have been temporary and would have corrected itself through the market mechanism.[33]

It was the long-run development, growth, and spread of administered prices, then, that accounted for the extraordinary scope of the 1930s depression. Administered prices, Means acknowledged, had long existed, but heretofore they had not been so pervasive as to prevent the market mechanism from performing the function of adjustment and correction. Now, by obstructing adjustment and by magnifying and exacerbating the initial downward movement, they plunged the economy further into the abyss.[34] Administered prices did not directly initiate depression but made "the economy more susceptible to violent fluctuation in activity." They turned "an initial small fluctuation of industrial activity into a cataclysmic depression." Large areas of pricing "had become so inflexible that the economy lacked resiliency. . . . Levels of depression never before reached were broken through." Lacking now the market mechanism of readjustment and recovery, depression threatened to stabilize.[35] Due to the breakdown of the market mechanism, stagnation loomed.

In Means's analysis, therefore, the Great Depression was in good part the long-run result of the rise of concentrated industrial business with its attendant administered prices. Corporate concentration underlay administered pricing. In general, allowing for exceptions, the more concentrated industries became, the more relatively inflexible administered prices appeared. It was not "monopoly" with which Means was concerned but the administered price decisions made in areas of the economy that lay between classic monopoly and classic competition.[36] Nor, in looking back, did Means believe that organized labor was significant in creating rigid wage rates as part of the inflexibility underlying the spread of depression in the early 1930s. Organized labor was a minor factor at that time in the great industries; wage rates as well as prices were administered by large corporations as part of a concerted policy.[37]

Means's disassociation of his concept of administered prices from "monopoly" was partly due to the fact that he was focused on what became known as "oligopoly"—industries dominated by a few large corporations. Additionally, Means's work was used in the political arena to attack "monopoly" by the forces of "antitrust" ideology, a persuasion that he did not share. Moreover, the use of the term "monopoly" was seen by Means as an evasion of the issue; he viewed the rise of corporate concentration and administered prices as a thrust at the very citadel of traditional economic theory so heavily based on the centrality of a functioning market mechanism. To Means, the rise of concentration and administered pricing obstructed the working of that vitally important market mechanism. This changed economic reality required the fashioning of a new overall theory of which classical theory would be a part—a part relevant to the remaining competitive sector, a truncated element of a newly evolved whole. What distressed and annoyed Means was the way traditional theorists, in keeping with their treatment of "monopoly," similarly characterized concentration and administered pricing as exceptions to the norm, special cases, "frictions." Seeing concentration and administered pricing as the essence of a new norm, Means strenuously objected to their incorporation into the "friction" category of traditional theory, their acceptance as special cases or exceptions only. To Means they constituted a new norm that challenged classical theory at its core. "Exceptions" would delay the "normal" workings of the economy; to a considerable extent, a new norm rendered the market mechanism inoperable.[38] This new norm transcended the traditional and mutually exclusive categories of "monopoly" and "competition." Administered prices, Means acknowledged, were set within limits prescribed by the market, but not to the extent that would force sharp price reductions in the face of a sharp curtailment of demand.[39] The time had come, Means wrote to John Maynard Keynes in 1935, to think "of the economy as one part-way between perfect price flexibility and perfect inflexibility with different parts of the economy tending toward one or the other end of the scale." Under such conditions, traditional dogmas "built on the assumption of flexible prices" would have to be "rebuilt" in the light of new realities.[40]

Means, while acknowledging the significance of the "monopolistic competition" and "imperfect competition" theories of Edward Chamberlin and Joan Robinson, also somewhat distanced himself from them. These theories were useful, Means held, in that in abstract terms they posited the existence of an area in between classical competition and classical monopoly. He would have used the term "imperfect competition" in connection with his administered prices thesis, he later wrote, had the term been more widespread at the time of his original analysis.[41] On the other hand, Means downplayed any close connection between his administered prices thesis and the studies by Chamberlin and Robinson, declaring that these studies did not depart sufficiently from classical theory and that actual business behavior was not reflected in them. They did not rest on a concept of administered prices.[42] Thus he denied that his administered prices thesis accorded "with the theories of 'monopolistic' or 'imperfect' competition." He found "nothing in either theory to explain price-insensitivity to a general recession drop in demand and nothing to prevent the operation of the classical unemployment mechanism." He "never regarded them as even attempting to deal with the macroeconomic problem."[43]

Means's administered prices thesis became quite influential within the Roosevelt administration, dovetailing with such analyses as those of Rexford Tugwell and Mordecai Ezekiel. Its impact was limited, however, by the fact that support for structural planning, which Means favored and toward which he believed his analysis pointed, was on the wane by the mid-1930s and also by the fact that it was latched onto by political antitrusters to lambaste big business in a way that Means found disagreeable and archaic.[44] Support for Means's administered prices thesis also came from the wider intellectual community. Historian Charles A. Beard wrote to Means that *Industrial Prices and Their Relative Inflexibility* went "to the center of things," challenging the notion that there was a "'normal' course of things" to which the country could return. Popular economist Stuart Chase congratulated Means for "one of the most significant economic generalizations of our times." And from John Maynard Keynes came a letter of praise and agreement: "I think that your distinction between market prices and administered prices is one of first-class importance and very illuminating. I have been aware of the point in a dim sort of way, but had not crystallised it, as you have. Nor had I realised how sharp and important a division there is in practice between the two."[45] Means was understandably pleased with the positive reception that *Industrial Prices and Their Relative Inflexibility* received, coming so soon after the phenomenal success of *The Modern Corporation and Private Property*, and expressed hope for an even wider impact. A Senate document, he noted, did not have the same appeal as a book. He and his wife, Caroline F. Ware, he reported, had "been trying to write the same thing in a more extended book form," though neither of them had "a flair for writing. . . . For the present, the job seems to be to get the Senate Document talked about."[46]

For Means, the corporate revolution and administered prices meant a need for new forms of economic planning. The whole shift from market control to increased administrative control created imbalances in the economy that only new forms of planning and coordination could correct. Corporate administration—in effect, private partial planning—upset the equilibrating function of the market mechanism; corporate administration served the perceived interest of the corporation, not the economy as a whole. The existence of private planning for private interests by way of its impact on the overall economy in turn necessitated some form of public planning for the more general interest. This new planning would not negate traditional "rights" of private businesspeople. But whereas earlier private businesspeople had the right to operate within the constraints provided by market controls, now in those areas where the market had ceased to function as an overall coordinator, they would operate their firms within the constraints provided by the institutional replacement for the market mechanism.[47]

The most important aspect of private administration that required a form of public planning was, to Means, the power to administer prices. It was this power that upset the operation of the market mechanism; to ensure economic balance it would now have to be integrated into and coordinated within a larger planning framework. To achieve stability, some aspects of "industrial policy" would now have to be placed in the hands of new planning institutions.[48] Such new institutions would reflect the division between ownership and control that was characteristic of the modern corporate sector. For the most part, new mechanisms were needed to exercise control, not ownership. Private ownership of great corporations would continue, but with new agencies exercising the powers of coordination that had earlier been held by the now obstructed and diminished market.[49] Under the new forms of planning envisaged, businesspeople would continue to make decisions for their own firms "to the same extent and within the same limits as in the old economy"; their power remained the same, "whether the limits are set by the market or by some administrative body."[50]

Means's vision of a new planning framework was holistic, that is, he believed that it should provide a context for the overall economy. Planning sectors of the economy "piecemeal" was inadequate; each partial plan, each sector of the economy, had to be understood in terms of interrelationships and the relation of each to the whole.[51] Although aware that the economy was in a continual state of flux because of technological change, organizational shifts, varying consumer tastes, and the like, Means also insisted that there were patterns of structural continuity that made the economy "an integral whole," "a single functioning machine."[52] These connections and this unity had to be kept in mind in devising new planning arrangements, "new techniques of control" providing for an "industrial policy" that would establish a "framework of policy" melding "self-interest" and the "separate elements of national policy" with "the optimum use of human and material resources," all so coordinated as to constitute "a national whole."[53]

One of the basic faults of the Roosevelt administration's early efforts at planning, such as the National Recovery Administration and the Agricultural Adjustment Administration, was precisely, Means believed, that they lacked this holistic coordinating approach to the economy. The NRA and the AAA came into existence as a result of the unbalancing effect that corporate concentration and administered pricing had on the economy. They constituted mechanisms designed to counter that effect by bringing administration into the public realm. But they were at best pioneering efforts, by no means finished products. With each geared to a particular sector of the economy, there was little effort at overall coordination. Sectoral planning under public auspices lacking overall coordination could be as unbalancing as private partial planning. And in the case of the NRA, the new agency was dominated by private businesspeople whose private partial planning had been so important in creating the imbalances that the new mechanisms were created to correct.[54]

A more effective, publicly coordinated planning, Means held, would involve agencies on which business, labor, consumers, and government were all represented. Consumers, for example, traditionally protected through the workings of the market, could now once again be protected through the direct participation of their representatives on the new coordinating mechanisms. Such broad and diverse representation would, Means argued, lead to results roughly akin to those of the obstructed market mechanism, that is, a rough overall balance.[55] As Means put it in a

1934 memorandum, the establishment of "price and production policy" by "group bargaining" under public auspices appeared to be the most promising technique likely to achieve balanced results akin to those of a "true market." Government would mediate, assist the weaker parties involved, and use its authority to reach decisions conducive to overall balance.[56]

Means's planning vision involved an effort to devise nonmarket mechanisms for areas of the economy in which the market no longer functioned effectively, while meshing and coordinating the market with planning in those areas where the market mechanism still did function effectively, all to achieve overall balance.[57] He was trying to fashion a "technique of economic coordination within which the market" could be "employed as a useful tool." Such planning would involve "a synthesis of . . . market and nonmarket . . . phenomena," a "tying together" of market and administration "into a single system."[58]

Providing for strategic planning at key points, Means's concept also called for a simultaneous pattern of decentralization. Like other New Deal planners, he thought not in terms of a rigid plan but in terms of flexible mechanisms that would allow for adjustment of plans in accord with changing circumstances and for implementation of broad decisions designed to create overall balance, while reserving remaining decisions for private business to make within the context of planning's general framework.[59] His planning would be in "a continual process of formulation and reformulation," for no "static plan could" succeed in "a dynamic industrial society." Planning would have to be "as dynamic" as the economy itself.[60] Further, it would "set up traffic lights" rather than engage in a detailed "taking over of industry," such "traffic lights" as those made possible by studies of production and consumption patterns, helping to avoid disastrous disruptions because of misestimates of productive capacity or consumer demand and thus facilitating harmonious adjustment between microdecision making and macroeconomic stability.[61]

In a broad sense, Means's ideas here were comparable with those of Keynes. Each saw government as providing an overall framework within which private business could operate. Each eschewed what he considered excessively detailed planning, leaving that to the private sector. But there was also, of course, a crucial, defining difference. Means focused on economic structure and saw the new framework in terms of new structural or institutional mechanisms. Keynes focused on the investment climate and saw public investment as the key stabilizing or coordinating instrument. Each saw the Great Depression in terms of historic evolution but keyed on different aspects of that evolution: the corporate revolution for Means, and the altered economic environment for Keynes.

Means, like Keynes in *The General Theory*, concentrated primarily not on business cycles but on long-range changes that culminated in the underuse of resources.[62] Means's interpretation of the Great Depression, geared to structural change, alluded only to such long-range changes in the economic environment as population and geographic expansion. As to the immediate background of the depression, Means did argue that a surge in domestic construction and foreign loans facilitating purchases of American goods fueled the economy in the 1920s. But as these sources of economic stimulation declined, the economy, weakened, Means suggested, by the failure of large corporations to pass savings due to technological advance on to workers in the form of higher wages, developed a deficiency in buying power and by 1929 had reached "an unstable condition."[63] Later, Means included monetary contraction as an initiating factor in the economic crisis. But whether in the 1930s or subsequently, Means's central focus was always what turned the decline beginning in 1929 into the Great Depression, not its initial causes—that is, not the short-range or immediate economic context but the structural changes that Means believed had introduced unprecedented rigidity into the economic system. Whatever the immediate origins of the downturn, Means held, only administered prices and inflexibility could explain how an initial decline could turn into massive unemployment, could explain "equilibrium at less than full employment," and could account for the failure of "classical . . . automatic correction" to occur.[64]

In addition to structure, although clearly subordinate to it, Means throughout his long career paid attention to monetary theory. Essentially, Means argued that the development of an economy divided into flexible and relatively inflexible price structures had significant implications for monetary policy. In such an economy, a decrease in the money supply would lessen demand, causing market prices to decline while administered prices remained relatively rigid. Flexibility in administered industry would be exercised through reduced production and employment, aggravating the initial decline in demand. To counter this, Means contended, the money supply should be maintained at a level sufficient to keep market prices on par with administered prices, thus avoiding the disparity in price behavior between market and administered prices along with the attendant implications for production and employment.[65] The goal was not "the maintenance of a stable price level as such," Means concluded, "but rather the maintenance of stability in production and employment."[66] During the 1930s, however, Means stressed that structural maladjustments called first and foremost for structural remedies; hence, although the proper "monetary policy would greatly increase the stability of our economic system," he did "not believe that it would . . . eliminate the need for economic coordination that could come from national planning."[67] Keynes, in his letter commending Means for developing the administered prices thesis, went a bit further in his own inimitable way, advising that the bearing of Means's "theory on stabilizing monetary policy leads one rather far afield."[68]

Means also related administered prices to investment, although this factor, so central to Keynes, was never thoroughly woven into Means's macroeconomic theory. Basically, Means held that, given administered prices, decreased costs made possible by technological advance were not passed on through workers' wages, which led to a deficit of purchasing power. Thereafter the relative inflexibility of administered prices forced a drop in production and employment and thus a further decrease in purchasing power and a lower economic level inhospitable to increased investment. Means therefore linked insufficient inducement to invest primarily to the impact of structural rigidity, viewing it as an effect rather than as an initiating cause of economic decline.[69]

The stress on structure versus environment in Keynes's sense gave a somewhat mechanical quality to Means's thought. Means essentially accepted the mechanistic nature of traditional economic theory—the idea that the economy at its core could be understood as a mechanism—but argued that because of structural change over time, the historic market mechanism no longer functioned satisfactorily. He did not venture forth fully and inclusively into a consideration of what Keynes considered the larger economic environment in which the economy as mechanism functioned. What Means had from this perspective was a macroeconomic theory of the economic mechanism rather than a macroeconomic theory also encompassing the more broadly conceived environment. Put differently, Means had a theory of severe depression and maladjustment—due to the partial breakdown of the market mechanism—rather than a theory that also included growth, which Means apparently assumed as a result of the impact of technology on resources. This said, Means's theory of structure and mechanism led in the 1930s to much the same conclusion as Keynes's theory centering on the environment: severe depression and low-level equilibrium. For Keynes, the price system failed to equilibrate the economy because of the failure of the inducement to invest—that is, lack of adequate investment meant that the economy was equilibrated at a low level via cuts in output and employment. Prices—for example, interest rates—could not compensate in this environment for the lack of inducement to invest. For Means, the economy was also equilibrated at a low level via cuts in output and employment, but because of the failure of the market mechanism to operate—because of the structural inflexibility of the price system per se.

By the end of the 1930s, Means's structural emphasis was effectively displaced in New Deal political economics by a rival's secular theory of the economic environment that was far more developed and complete than the musings of Keynes. If the early New Deal focused largely on structure in the spirit of Means, the late New Deal was deeply influenced by the version of Keynesianism fashioned by the American progenitor of a thoroughgoing concept of secular stagnation: the energetic Alvin H. Hansen.

4.
Alvin H. Hansen
and Continental
Theory

Alvin Harvey Hansen's journey to fame and Harvard took fifty years. Compared with those of Gardiner Means, his beginnings were not auspicious. The son of Danish immigrants, he was born in Viborg, South Dakota, in 1887. Growing up in a rural farm community, he disliked farm chores, preferring school, which in his case was a one-room building in which he crossed rows to sit in on the more advanced lessons. In this pursuit he was encouraged by his grandfather, a well-read former minister. Hence from early on he was more than the "simple farm boy" he liked to call himself in later years. The young Hansen left Viborg for Sioux Falls to attend high school and then became the first youngster from his area to go to college. As a student at South Dakota's Yankton College, a small Congregational institution, Hansen earned money for his tuition and board by waiting on tables and for a time by caring for a local doctor's horse. He earned a bachelor's degree in 1910, followed by work in the Lake Preston, South Dakota, public school system to earn money to proceed with a graduate education, which he pursued at the University of Wisconsin. Receiving a doctorate in 1918, at Wisconsin he was exposed to institutionalism by John R. Commons and Richard T. Ely. Marrying in 1916 and briefly on the faculty of Brown University, Hansen moved to the University of Minnesota, where he remained, building a career and raising two daughters, until called to Harvard in 1937.[1] Persistent and dogged, like Means, he also possessed, in the words of Paul Samuelson, a "nonaggressive manner" and was disinclined "by temperament . . . to blow his own horn." A knowledge of foreign languages facilitated Hansen's deep reading in Continental economic theory. A Guggenheim Fellowship at the end of the 1920s provided for a year in Europe, where he met, in particular, German and English economists. At Minnesota, he moved beyond the academic realm into public affairs, serving as a government consultant and providing studies across a range of economic affairs—a prelude to his federal service during the Roosevelt administration.[2]

Hansen's predepression writings remained for the most part well within the bounds of traditional economic thinking, although some bases were also clearly being laid for his later, long-run theories. His dissertation, published in 1921 as *Cycles of Prosperity and Depression in the United States, Great Britain, and Germany*, set the stage for his lifelong interest in the subject but did not contribute to the basic conceptual underpinnings of his subsequent work. There and in a 1920 article he set forth a monetary theory of business cycles.[3] In a second 1920 article, however, Hansen evinced what were to become long-standing views, stressing that economic activity was inherently dynamic and ever changing.[4] As early as 1924, Wesley Clair Mitchell, the eminent authority on business cycles, commended Hansen for the latter's ability to combine concrete statistical data with general economic theory in his study of the subject.[5] *Business-Cycle Theory*, published in 1927, fully established Hansen's own reputation as an expert in the field. In it Hansen provided a wide-ranging survey of views and also disavowed his earlier monetary interpretation of depression, now stressing "real" factors such as those emphasized by Continental economists Arthur Spiethoff and Joseph Schumpeter. He speculated, moreover, that seriously disturbing forces in the economic environment were perhaps weakening. In an inversion of his later secular stagnation theory, yet pivoting on the same key forces, he suggested that never again would anything comparable with the nineteenth-century exploitation of the resources of

America be forthcoming, nor was it likely that future inventions would be as epochal as the railroad had been to that earlier era. These changes boded "the nineteenth century . . . to become unique" and violent disturbances to be less characteristic of the future.[6] Hansen was hardly a prophet here, two years before the 1929 crash, but his emphasis on resources and technology—the larger economic environment—was part of his evolving secular economic analysis.

With the depression's arrival, Hansen set out to explore its origins, significance, and likely development. In his 1932 *Economic Stabilization in an Unbalanced World* and other writings of the early thirties, Hansen set forth his initial analysis. Essentially, in keeping with the Continental theories he outlined in his 1927 volume, Hansen interpreted the depression in terms of real, wavelike factors, such as dramatic oscillation in the production of capital goods. This depression was not unique, Hansen held, only the latest in a long line of major downturns. Useful in explaining the severity of the crisis, he believed, was the "long wave" theory of Russian economist Nikolai Kondratieff, with whom Hansen had earlier corresponded. As applied now, the new depression could be seen as a "downswing" in a pattern of long cycles lasting forty-five to sixty years. Additionally, Hansen thought, legacies of World War I helped to explain the nature of the present depression, as did institutional rigidities such as the tendency of concentrated business and trade unions to endeavor to maintain prices and wages in the face of a general decline.[7]

As to the depression's solution, in the early thirties Hansen counseled patience. Technological and other disruptive forces caused economic downswings but promoted economic growth in the long run. Efforts to achieve greater stability by way of government intervention would lead only to a more static state, thus undermining economic progress.[8] Meanwhile, in the early 1930s Hansen saw the decline in the population growth rate as a sign in itself of greater stability. Great industries, such as construction, were important factors in economic fluctuations; a lower population growth rate helped to explain the depth of the depression, but it would also contribute to a greater measure of future stability.[9]

Hansen continued into the mid-1930s to probe for the deeper causes of the Great Depression, also focusing on the relation of investment to capital goods and population trends.[10] In a 1933 survey of theories of the business cycle, Hansen, in his discussion of the savings-investment imbalance school, noted that its "outstanding proponent" in the English language was John Maynard Keynes, who had "arrived at his conclusions . . . independently and without close knowledge of . . . the continental economists." This reference was, of course, to the pre–general theory Keynes and was based on *A Treatise on Money*. Also of great import for Hansen's future development was his focus on the question of whether there was an "element of periodicity (if we may apply that word to a recurrent oscillation which varies in length) in business fluctuations, or whether the phenomenon may better be described as a 'Konjunktur,' a fortuitous combination of circumstances."[11]

Despite the severity of the depression and the vigorous activity of the New Deal, Hansen continued after 1933 to reject calls for a governmentally focused solution to the crisis. Essentially, he argued, the only solution was to await the passage of time. Eventually, new stimuli would develop for investment to pull the economy out of depression. Technological advances, perhaps delayed, would nonetheless bring renewed investment and expansion in time. This was far superior, Hansen held, to efforts to force recovery by way of government programs. Foreshadowing his Keynesian phase, he argued that monetary policy would not be sufficiently effective in promoting investment; only external stimuli such as invention could adequately spur the inducement to invest.[12] Nor could public investment do the job. This effort at "artificial" stimulation would merely discourage private investment.[13]

Clearly the Hansen of the early and mid-thirties was far removed in the realm of public policy from the Hansen of the late thirties and the forties—the Hansen who emerged as the nation's leading advocate of public investment. Here, the Keynes of *The General Theory*—plus the impact of the recession of 1937–38—played a crucial role. In basic respects, however, the Hansen of the early and mid-thirties already possessed an outlook that led via Keynes and the recession to the Hansen of the later years. Going back to the twenties and evident in his early analyses of the depression, Hansen was historically oriented; interested in the deeper, long-run trends of economic theory and development; and geared to the very concepts that, crystallized by Keynes and the recession, led to the secular stagnation theory of the late thirties and the forties. Of critical importance, here, was the central impact on Hansen's thinking—rooted in the 1920s, continuing in the 1930s before Keynes, and incorporated thereafter with Keynes—of the Continental school, which formed the essential basis of Hansen's long-run theory. Thus along with the profound changes in public policy advocacy that Hansen underwent and the central importance of Keynes, a basic core continuity existed in Hansen's thought from the 1920s on by way of his adherence to the Continental school, a continuity that helped turn his Keynesianism in the direction of a full-blown theory of secular stagnation.

The Continental school emphasized "real" as distinct from monetary factors in business cycle causation. The Russian Michel Tugan-Baranowsky, for example, stressed the role of the investment rate in his analysis, making consumption a relatively passive factor. The German Arthur Spiethoff, building on Tugan-Baranowsky, pointed to the stimulative effect on investment of technological developments and of the exploitation of new lands and to the "saturation" reached once these investment needs were satisfied. Joseph Schumpeter stressed the irregular "bunching" of innovations as basic to cyclical fluctuations, and others, including Gustav Cassel and Knut Wicksell, developed variants of a Continental kind. (In the English-speaking world, with its different traditions of economics, D. H. Robertson came closest to this mode of thinking.) Thus the Continental school, particularly as espoused by Spiethoff, whose influence impacted most deeply and durably on Hansen, emphasized the environment in which the economy operated, holding that investment was the pivot of the economy and that investment in turn depended on external stimuli such as technological advance and the creation of new markets. Stimulated by such factors, investment was generated and a boom began; as the stimuli tapered off, investment grew sluggish and economic decline set in to await the development of new external stimuli. Overall, the stress was on investment, exogenous factors, the spurts and lapses of a discontinuous process, and objective or real as distinct from monetary or psychological factors.[14] This school of thought pervaded Hansen's own analyses as he sought to explain economic fluctuations in terms of investment-inducing external stimuli.[15]

Hansen consistently emphasized such exogenous forces as technological advancement and its absence, new industries and their exhaustion, geographic expansion and its close, and population trends and movements as the factors underlying shifts in investment that in turn generated overall economic growth or decline.[16] These "initiating" factors, he noted in 1932, "need not themselves run in cycles." Looking back in 1949, Hansen observed that in his 1927 *Business-Cycle Theory* he had stressed real factors, "somewhat against the stream of Anglo-American thinking in the 1920's," and that this "point of view also pervaded" his later books. Shortly after, he wrote that macroeconomics, although associated with Keynes and *The General Theory*, actually began decades earlier with the Continental school, whose contribution remained too little recognized among

"Anglo-American" economists.[17] Hansen was also aware of related strands of thought. The Russian economist Kondratieff, he wrote, had contributed to a growing understanding that what was commonly referred to as the business cycle was actually "a component of many cycles."[18] And he noted the institutionalist Thorstein Veblen's concept of chronic depression as the underlying norm of modern industrial society.[19] Beyond this, of course, Hansen grew up in a country in which technological advance, population growth, and geographic expansion were central elements of national history and heritage. The "frontier school" of American historians, led by Frederick Jackson Turner, flourished at the very time Hansen was coming of age in the still "frontier" state of South Dakota.

As of the mid-thirties, Alvin H. Hansen was, in the later judgment of Paul Samuelson, "an important but not outstanding analyst." The economist Paul H. Douglas, in a 1933 letter to Rexford Tugwell, described Hansen as "hard-headed and intellectually hard-boiled, . . . extremely competent . . . and absolutely reliable."[20] Already Hansen had displayed and was displaying qualities that after 1937 were to make him for a time perhaps the nation's most widely known and influential economist—a lucid writing style, a deep knowledge of the literature, an ability to use economic theory to illuminate current economic problems, and as he approached the age of fifty an openness to changing his mind in important ways, incorporating into his intellectual outlook concepts which in some ways complemented but which in other respects contradicted his own.[21]

Through the years, Hansen had essentially been critical of Keynes. In a 1934 letter, for example, he referred to Keynes's views on public spending as "definitely wrong" and "far too mechanical," though he also characteristically allowed that further study might prove otherwise.[22] As has often been remarked, Hansen's first reaction to *The General Theory* itself was not notably enthusiastic, Hansen concluding that Keynes was not therein providing the basis of a "new economics." In that initial reaction and in other writings of 1936–37 vintage, Hansen continued basic emphases of his earlier work, including the notions that economic downturns had their positive aspects in preparing the economy for fresh spurts of progress, that regenerated private investment and not public investment would fuel a genuine recovery, and that institutional rigidities aggravated the economic crisis.[23] Still, a basic point remains that major elements of Hansen as Keynesian and Hansen as secular stagnationist were in place before *The General Theory* and before the sharp 1937–38 recession. It was these elements, along with the impact of the recession, that led Hansen to embrace Keynesianism. For example, Hansen also held in 1936–37, as before, that some periods were more favorable to investment and expansion than others because of such underlying factors as technological advance and exploitation of new resources.[24] He also made clear that he considered these exogenous forces, shaping the environment in which the economy operated, more basic than institutional factors: "The influence of monopolistic combinations upon depression has long been a subject of study. . . . The presence of monopolistic competition . . . commands attention. . . . Yet I cannot but feel that it has no more than minor significance for cycle theory."[25]

In 1937 Hansen, reflecting the degree of recovery that had occurred since 1933, announced that the nation was now "immersed in the upswing of the cycle."[26] At that point, before the recession, he was still thinking in terms of depression-boom cycles, with the one giving way to the other as favorable conditions for private investment returned. It was the recession, in the midst of depression, that called into question the traditional idea that economic downturns were self-correcting, led to the concept of an extended period of stagnation beyond that of the cycle theory, and suggested that passively awaiting a recovery was inadequate and unacceptable under these circumstances. It was with the 1937–38 recession that Hansen swung around to the notion of a durable underemployment equilibrium, related to new secular forces, which could be assuredly unstuck only by new, unprecedented external stimuli. Here Hansen "melded" the secular aspects of *The General Theory* with his longtime adherence to the Continental school to develop an interpretation of American economic history, a long-run diagnosis of the Great Depression, and a long-run prescription for America's economic future.[27]

Hansen felt that Keynes essentially clinched the case against traditional theory, although the groundwork had been laid earlier by the Continental school's emphases as well as by American institutionalists. In that sense there was no sharp dividing line between pre- and post-Keynes economics, a continuity reflected in the important elements of Hansen's thought that continued into his Keynesian phase. Still, Hansen concluded, only Keynes had provided the comprehensive theory needed to challenge successfully the old theory of economic self-correction. Despite the limits of Keynes's knowledge of works in languages other than English, existing elements of thought had been set forth and incorporated by him into a new seminal pattern, just as Keynes had crystallized Hansen's thinking along a familiar and yet strikingly new path. Keynes's 1937 Galton Lecture article on population, in particular, meshed with Hansen's longtime emphasis on secular trends.[28]

From *The General Theory*, heightened by the impact of the recession, came acceptance of the idea of underemployment equilibrium as distinct from cycles of boom and depression, an indefinitely non-self-correcting rather than a predictably self-correcting state.[29] Thus although Hansen had long thought in terms of secular trends and underlying forces promoting periods of boom and contraction, he had previously thought of the downturns as swings that were predictably correctable via an upsurge in private investment brought about by exogenous forces. Now, by way of the impact of recession within depression and the Keynesian idea of durable underemployment equilibrium, Hansen accepted the concept that the downturn was not necessarily self-correcting in terms of previous historic stimuli or predictably correctable within an assured or acceptable time span, that new kinds of external stimuli might be needed beyond those conventionally assumed, and that now in the Great Depression the downturn might be due at least in part to unprecedented secular trends—the essence of Hansen's theory of secular stagnation.

Hence, Keynes provided the definitive notion of underemployment equilibrium, but Hansen welded this to his longtime adherence to the Continental school's emphasis on the economic environment. As Hansen later put it, "'Secular stagnation' is in fact another name for . . . Keynesian 'underemployment equilibrium.'" Both were based "fundamentally upon the same foundation stones"—analysis of long-run trends of population, natural resources, and technology.[30] Of his generation, it notably was Hansen who in the end embraced Keynesianism, rather than those who, unlike himself, had supported public works spending before *The General Theory*'s full-blown rationale. The shared policy prescription proved less compelling than the Continental theoretical base in terms of conduciveness to Keynesian conversion. Hansen's Keynesianism did bring a marked departure precisely in the realm of public policy by way of his new enthusiasm (despite some initial tentativeness) for public investment as the great key to solving the Great Depression and promoting future economic growth. "The cure for secular stagnation as also the cure for underemployment equilibrium," Hansen later wrote, was "vigorous fiscal policy."[31]

Hansen's pre-Keynesian adherence to the Continental school gave his Keynesianism a secular push and provided a basis for important distinctions, or at least important differing emphases, between Hansen and Keynes. Hansen was not just Keynes's major American advocate, vital as that role was; he also developed and articulated his own analyses and prescriptions in a Hansenian Keynesian mode.[32] Through Hansen, as Richard Musgrave put it, "the Keynesian concept of underemployment equilibrium was . . . extended into a theory of economic stages and development."[33] What Hansen did was to provide a larger, broader, and deeper historical dimension and framework than did Keynes; through attention to the periodicity of the long-run stimuli to investment, Hansen created a Continental-Keynesian synthesis with concrete, historical elements to buttress underemployment equilibrium theory.[34] Whereas Keynes alluded to historical epochs but stressed psychological uncertainty, Hansen as a "hard" secular stagnationist alluded to psychological uncertainty but stressed historical epochs. Finally, although Keynes alluded to technological advance, it was Hansen, drawing on the Continental school (and particularly here on Schumpeter as well as Spiethoff) who made technological advance a well-developed, historically based, and organic part of his overall theory.[35]

It was this secular Keynesian, this Continental school Keynesian, who rose to prominence in America at the end of the 1930s and into the 1940s as a voice for a permanent new fiscal policy in the New Deal in place of the now fading structural planning preferred by early New Dealers such as Gardiner Means. It was this Hansen who became a vocal and influential advocate of his version of Keynesianism in academic circles and a seemingly tireless publicist and popularizer geared to educating the broader public opinion in the country to what he considered the new economic realities. It was this Hansen who, as it turned out, occupied the Littauer Chair in Political Economy at Harvard beginning in 1937 and who, in his fiscal policy seminar, helped train many young economists—some highly influential in time—in the tools of Keynesian analysis. It was also at Harvard that he became a congenial colleague of Joseph Schumpeter, with whom he shared many basic ideas but from whom he sharply departed in his Keynesian phase. Hansen's wider public fame and impact began with his testimony before the Temporary National Economic Committee and continued with service as an adviser to the National Resources Planning Board, where he effectively ousted Gardiner Means as the dominant economic analysis and policy influence, and as an adviser to the Federal Reserve Board chairman Marriner Eccles.[36] In 1939 British economist Nicholas Kaldor viewed Hansen as "the leading authority on business-cycle problems in the United States," by which time Hansen had largely folded the cycle into his secular analysis. *Fortune* declared in 1942 that in the United States Hansen held "a position comparable to that of Keynes" in Great Britain. This was no small accolade for the "genial, quiet," and "mild-mannered" professor who was simultaneously an industrious, determined, and hard-driving public policy advocate.[37]

5.
Alvin H. Hansen and
Secular Stagnation

The Alvin H. Hansen who fused Continental analysis with Keynesianism—the Hansen of the late thirties and the war years—was above all and appropriately associated with the theory of secular stagnation, which was hinted at by Keynes and now comprehensively developed. In keeping with the Continental school ideas that were now melded with those of Keynes, Hansen continued to stress the importance of exogenous forces as the basic, essential stimuli of investment.[1] Also in keeping with the Continental school, he consistently stressed the centrality of investment as the pivot between prosperity and depression; and he now believed, given Keynesian underemployment equilibrium, that the collapse of investment could also mean stagnation.[2] It was not simply a lack of balance between savings and investment, Hansen emphasized; savings and investment could be equated at a "low level." Rather, "the problem of our generation is, above all, the problem of inadequate private investment outlets."[3] Vibrant recoveries were necessarily investment led, he held, a stress likewise derived from the Continental school; a recovery based largely on consumption was consequently anemic and limited. It had "no momentum of its own, . . . no inner power to complete its . . . development."[4] All these points became part of Hansen's stagnationist analysis and bases for his public investment solution.

By the late thirties and into the forties, Hansen, long fascinated by the historical bases of economic development, had become more and more immersed in secular, as distinct from conventional, business cycle perspectives and analysis in the formation of his theory of secular stagnation. Problems of the business cycle he now largely subsumed under this broader secular schema. In long periods of boom, he held, the business cycle operated to produce relatively mild and brief economic declines; in periods of secular stagnation, by contrast, such economic declines became prolonged and painful depressions. During the late thirties and the wartime forties, Hansen believed that the problem of secular stagnation or "long waves" much outweighed in importance the problem of the traditional business cycle. The key difficulty, he believed, was a result of long-run or secular, rather than relatively brief, cyclical factors.[5] Traditional business cycle theory, geared to "recurring wave-like movements of relatively moderate amplitude," could not explain "the devastating collapse of the Great Depression." Traditional business cycle theory, with its "thesis that each phase of the cycle is generated out of the preceding stage," did not fit into an explanation of a crisis that Hansen believed was vitally related to underlying secular forces.[6]

Was Hansenian secular stagnation new and unprecedented, or was the current bout a recurrence of older ones? Was his secular stagnation theory one of trend or period or one of long cycles or waves? Hansen himself believed that economic growth and development came by spurts, adding that with spurts "there must of necessity be a cycle." He also referred to "'long waves' of expansion and stagnation." To Simon Kuznets, the eminent authority on secular economic patterns, it appeared that Hansen accepted "the hypothesis of the Kondratieff 'long waves.'" Former Hansen student David McCord Wright similarly suggested that "secular stagnation may also be the trough of a 'Kondratieff.'" The closest early student of Hansen's secular stagnation concept, the sympathetic Benjamin Higgins, found it not entirely clear from Hansen's own writings whether he considered secular stagnation a theory of trend and period or one of long cycles and waves. In 1946, however, Higgins wrote that in Hansen's view exogenous factors, apart from the Kondratieff cycle, contributed to chronic underemployment levels, and shortly thereafter Higgins distinguished between "the Hansen thesis" and "merely . . . a Kondratieff downswing." On balance, Higgins concluded, secular forces emphasized by Hansen were "trend factors rather than cyclical factors," and thus it seemed probable that Hansen considered his own theory to be one of trend. In any case, Higgins held, for secular stagnation theory "to have an independent meaning of its own, it must be distinguished from all types of cycle theories, and be treated as a theory of long-run trend."[7]

Hansen addressed this issue, albeit more than a decade after he first presented his secular stagnation theory, in discussing the Kondratieff long wave concept as developed and exposited by Schumpeter. Schumpeter, Hansen wrote, regarded "long periods of buoyancy and relative stagnation as part of a genuine wave-like movement. . . . Whether these secular movements are really long-cycles, whose phases stand in an integral relation to each other, is at least debatable and the weight of competent opinion appears to be against Schumpeter." That there were "long periods" of this sort, on the other hand, Hansen found "highly persuasive."[8] This Hansenian statement cohered with economist R. A. Gordon's conclusion that Hansen did "not look on these . . . secular movements as constituting cumulative, self-generating cycles."[9]

Essentially, while he sometimes used cyclical or long wave terminology, Hansen appears to have thought in terms of recurring but discrete periods, similar in basic characteristics but differing in the precise ingredients that made up the constituent elements of progress or stagnation of each. Cyclical notions or pendulum-like mechanical swings are, after all, more consistent with economic theories that are essentially endogenous—that is, emphasize the inner nature of the economic process or system itself—rather than exogenous—ones that emphasize the impact of external forces on that process or system. Hansen very clearly lay in the exogenous camp, firmly from the 1920s on, focusing on and emphasizing exogenous forces—the forces shaping the environment in which the economy operated. An endogenous theory, seeing the system as above all a result of its inner workings, often tends by its very nature to be cyclical. A machine, a mechanism, works in terms of regular movements and patterns. An exogenous theory, such as Hansen's, necessarily left more to chance. Who could say, with mechanical certainty, when technological advances might be forthcoming? Or when new resources might be uncovered? Or what demographic trends might shape the future? Thus although wavelike configurations might exist in Hansen's schema, they would not be wave-like in certitude in any mechanical sense. Put differently, while before 1937 Hansen did see a business cycle in periods of boom and bust, as he delved more fully into long-run secular trends after 1937 and as he developed his secular stagnation as distinct from business cycle theory, he built less on a mechanistic cyclical notion and more on concrete, historical analysis of the different periods of American (and indeed Western) history. That is, the theory of secular stagnation was historically based on an analysis of periods and trends—on Hansen's belief that development was not smooth but "lumpy" and discontinuous. If there were periods that seemed to reflect a pattern of waves or cycles, this pattern was not due to any rhythmic, self-propulsive workings of the system per se but reflected the external impact of the constituent elements of economic progress—periods in which those elements were more or less favorable to boom or stagnation.

As he developed and presented his secular stagnation theory, Hansen outlined historical eras that were reflective of growth or stagnation, but while periods of growth and stagnation recurred, each was also discrete, indicative of the particular elements that made it distinctive. Throughout modern history, Hansen argued, there had been extended periods of buoyant expansion and extended periods of low-level stagnation, each fueled by exogenous elements of economic progress or dampened by their relative lack. The Industrial Revolution itself was, of course, viewed as a period of great growth. Then there was a period of relative stagnation before the exuberant boom of the "railroad age." As that age tapered off, another period of relative stagnation followed, including the severe depression of the 1890s. Thereafter the electrical and automotive era constituted a new buoyant period, followed by slackening and the onset of the 1930s depression. Whole eras of buoyant and great industries were followed by extended periods of difficulty as the stimuli to growth abated and great industries lost their dynamism and went into relative or absolute decline. Each depressed era awaited a new burst of external stimuli to fuel investment for a new buoyant era. To this extent and in this way, the 1930s depression was not unique.[10]

As William E. Stoneman, a scholarly analyst of secular stagnation theory, put it, Hansen "from the outset carefully based his characterizations on historical precedent, appealing particularly to Spiethoff's views of the depressed 1890's." Thus Hansen stated in 1938 that there had been a long period of "secular stagnation" in the late nineteenth century. He declared in 1941 that in some measure the 1930s depression resembled "conditions in the nineties."[11] In a 1945 letter he noted that the term "secular stagnation" stemmed from Spiethoff's "phrase 'Stockung-Spanne' . . . for which a pretty good English equivalent is 'periods of stagnation.'" Although "Spiethoff's periods of secular stagnation" were in time frame "identical to the down-swing of Kondratieff's and Schumpeter's long waves," he (Hansen), "characterized them as periods." The upshot was that secular stagnation was not something "that we may have someday"; it was something that had already occurred "over long periods several times in the past."[12]

Thus secular stagnation was not unprecedented; there had been earlier such eras. But some periods were more epochal than others, and Hansen believed that the 1930s had launched such an epochal era. Stated by Hansen most dramatically, the contemporary era was ushering in a new epoch more strikingly different from what had gone before than any since the time of the Industrial Revolution itself. So put, the Hansen of the late thirties and war years was not seeing in the Great Depression simply a new era of secular stagnation. Rather, he saw an era of secular stagnation with more far-reaching implications than those which had gone before. The nineteenth century, he maintained, had been special; its circumstances of geographic expansion and population growth linked to technological advance had provided rich opportunities for private investment to fuel economic growth; that era was now giving way to a new and quite different one in which ample opportunities for private investment were less evident.[13] Thus despite "prolonged periods of stagnation" in the nineteenth century, this period was unprecedented.[14] Coming at a time when the economy was "undergoing . . . a . . . change no less basic and profound in character than the industrial revolution," the Great Depression was "a unique phenomenon." It was "of a magnitude and duration which has eclipsed all others, not excepting even the deep and prolonged depressions of the seventies and nineties."[15]

This analysis was in a sense analogous to that by Gardiner Means, who argued that the corporate revolution, culminating in the Great Depression, was the most extraordinary change in economic life since the Industrial Revolution. For Hansen, however, the most basic and profound change involved not economic structure but rather the exogenous forces that shaped the environment in which the structure operated. "Forces slowly accumulating over a long period of time" had now "converged" to create unprecedented unemployment.[16] This was Keynes's low-level underemployment equilibrium. Hansen distinguished between "extensive" and "intensive" factors underlying economic growth: extensive factors included geographic expansion and population growth; the basic intensive factor was technological advance. Both extensive and intensive stimuli were strong in the nineteenth century. Now, with the end of American geographic expansion and a decline in the population growth rate, extensive stimuli had significantly weakened, and Hansen was not convinced that the intensive stimulus of technological advance alone was sufficient to attract investment adequate to promote growth along traditional lines.[17] It was the decline of extensive stimuli which presented "a change in our economy for which we have no precedent in the past."[18]

Thus this era, with its Great Depression, was unique because two factors that had existed throughout the nineteenth century were now largely no longer in play: the extensive stimuli of geographic expansion and rapid population growth. The slowdown and virtual disappearance of these extensive stimuli made this era different from any "during the last two hundred years," creating a new environment for the economy.[19] Nineteenth-century "periods of secular stagnation" did not include, as the present period now did, this loss of "the buoyancy . . . springing from the existence of a vast, rich, unexploited continent . . . and the intimately associated phenomenon of a rapid growth of population."[20] His secular depression analysis, with its stress on geography and population, broadened Hansen's earlier emphasis on long periods of boom and bust into his long-run stagnation concept of the thirties. Elements of it were already apparent in his rather critical review of *The General Theory* in 1936. There Hansen wrote that "the frontier for the entire world is largely gone and population is approaching stabilization," this before the recession of 1937 and Hansen's emergence as a full-fledged secular stagnationist Keynesian.[21]

The trek across the continent and rapid population growth, Hansen argued, had historically "fixed the economic pattern" of the country. Capitalists could think in terms of ever-growing markets and outlets for profitable investment. Approximately half the capital outlays of the preceding century, Hansen estimated, were due to population growth and territorial expansion.[22] There remained, Hansen acknowledged, technological advance as an exogenous stimulus to investment and growth, a factor of enormous import, given its contribution to the rise of new industries to replace those in decline, but it now lacked the attendant influence of geographic and rapid population growth. Technological advance would no doubt continue to lead to the development of great industries, but it was just one source of historic stimulation. Moreover, given changed conditions, new industries might require less capital investment than did their predecessors; their emergence in the future, as in the past, would be uneven; and nothing apparent was on the immediate horizon.[23] Hansen concluded that a question remained as to whether technologically induced intensive investment alone could "attain the buoyancy and tempo of earlier periods." Thus, although technological advance remained, the American economy could now "remain as highly dynamic as that of the nineteenth century" only if a substitute were found for earlier extensive stimuli.[24]

Hansen believed he had found such a substitute in public investment. Critics often lambasted Hansen and other secular stagnationists as pessimists who were resigned to a no-growth economy. Hansen and others responded that they were in fact optimists, given the correct remedy to the diagnosed condition. That is, Hansen was not arguing that growth had come to an end but that growth based on a certain set of exogenous forces had stagnated. The key, of course, was not passive acceptance of stagnation but vigorous efforts to develop new stimuli to investment and growth to replace those in decline. The unprecedented nature of this era of secular stagnation required an unprecedented response: massive public investment.[25]

By public investment, Hansen meant something different from and far beyond early New Deal "pump priming," in which spending was designed to provide an initial stimulus, after which private investment would take over. What Hansen had in mind was permanent government spending. Such ongoing public investment would provide a new stimulus to growth, given the secular deficiency of private investment, and would also "compensate" for short-run fluctuations in private investment. The long-run program of public investment to promote overall growth would encompass the compensatory aspect of public spending. Put differently, growth-oriented public investment would attack secular stagnation, and compensatory spending would deal with cyclical fluctuations within the larger secular context. This permanent schema would replace the "hand-to-mouth" temporary character of early New Deal spending.[26]

The recession of 1937–38 clearly pushed Hansen toward public investment as the basic solution to the economic crisis. In Hansen's analysis the recovery of 1933–37 was a consumption-led rather than a durable investment-led revival. When the public spending stimulus to consumption was partially withdrawn, the severe recession ensued. Durable recoveries in the past, stimulated by exogenous forces, had been based on massive investment, which led in turn to increased consumption and new eras of growth. Consumption followed investment; investment looked forward boldly to new fields of development. In the period 1933–37, by contrast, private investment was narrowly gauged to increased consumption demand rather than stimulated by exogenous forces of a historic kind; it was accordingly timid and calibrated, not bold and massive. It was geared to the short run rather than to the long run. It was not the kind of investment that could or did usher in a new era of sustained expansion. Had such consumption-led investment been the historic norm, Hansen concluded, the country would not have experienced the great spurts of growth of the previous century.[27]

Hansen, in moving toward massive public investment, evidenced an early tentativeness, which was fairly quickly resolved. His initial concern partly reflected the nature of early New Deal pump priming. The point here was that the more government spending became part of the process, the more the withdrawal of such spending could then undermine any recovery in progress; durable recovery would have to await the arrival of new exogenous stimuli to private investment.[28] This concern was resolved with Hansen's conclusion that public spending would now have to be permanent. Hansen was also initially concerned that a larger government spending role might impair private enterprise, and he therefore stressed the need to encourage greater private, along with increased public, investment.[29] His enduring conclusion, however, was that increased public investment did not foreshadow "the doom of private enterprise."[30] Indeed, Hansen was to argue that greater public investment would provide the necessary new environment to ensure the survival and growth of private investment and enterprise.

The promotion of massive public investment and acceptance of a much larger role for public policy were a departure for Hansen, although they were based in part on his longtime acceptance of the Continental school's emphasis on the role of exogenous forces and investment—an emphasis now leading to public investment as viewed through the Keynesian underemployment equilibrium lens and as impacted by the 1937–38 recession. Traditionally, geographic expansion, population growth, and technological advance had been the basic stimuli, but with a weakening of the first two, too much stress was placed on the third, thus requiring the enhanced role of public investment to ensure continued growth and escape from chronic underemployment equilibrium.[31] Such investment would now constitute a needed new exogenous force "injecting a new stimulus to" private investment by way of an "expansionist public program" of "governmental expenditures." In other words, Hansen here added a fourth pillar to the traditional trinity of geography, population, and technology— "public policy of a character which opens up new investment outlets."[32]

According to Hansen, the economy would now likely "need to rely more largely in the future than in the past (1) on public investment as a supplement to private investment; and (2) on community consumption" in addition to private consumption.[33] Hansen often called for a "high consumption" economy, but this did not contradict his consistent emphasis on investment, for by high consumption he meant public investment in what he termed "community consumption," including investment in housing, schools, health, social services, parks, and playgrounds—that is, in consumer goods for the community as a whole in addition to those intended for individual private consumption.[34] Thus Hansen foresaw "community . . . expenditures on an undreamed-of scale" to "take the place of extensive expansion." Expansion would now be "fed from the combined springs of technical progress and a greatly expanded . . . public investment program," including "community consumption."[35]

Community consumption was part of what Hansen presented as a developmental program based on public investment and geared to long-run economic growth. Hansen espoused public investment in human and material resources—education, health, low-cost housing, river valley development, and transportation modernization—to create an expanding and dynamic economy. Those areas, in great need of investment and improvement, were precisely the areas in which public investment could most appropriately be made.[36] Such development involved "a kind of public expenditure not usually thought of as investment," Hansen acknowledged, but could it be denied, he asked, that such investment would "in reality constitute the soundest . . . for the future that our economy can make?"[37]

A developmental program, Hansen argued, would promote growth and provide a climate more conducive to economic stability by lessening cyclical fluctuations. It would invest in areas traditionally not very attractive to private enterprise. Once made, however, public investment would then generate private investments that would not otherwise have been forthcoming.[38] Public investment should not be poured out in any or every direction but should be selective, doing what private enterprise did not undertake or could not adequately accomplish. Public investment could and should make up for what Hansen saw as the grave inadequacies of private investment in this respect. Traditionally, he wrote, the nation allowed private enterprise to determine the nature and direction of demand and distribution. Housing for millions might be wholly inadequate, but if "the automatic functioning of the mechanism did not create an economic demand for housing, houses . . . were simply not built."[39] There was "nothing in a hundred years of experience" to show that "the price system" could rid the nation of slum housing.[40] Public investment, on the other hand, could be consciously directed to meet such needs, a Hansenian dichotomy reminiscent of Veblen's.

Further, Hansen held, even in areas such as scientific research, which historically proceeded in spurts of progress, government should play a more active and positive role by providing support so that such a vital function would not be left to chance.[41] Here and elsewhere Hansen was geared not only to economic necessity but also to social desirability. Adequate housing, as noted, was not likely in Hansen's view to be forthcoming under private enterprise alone. Scientific research might occur automatically, but it was desirable to facilitate it. There is no question that Hansen grounded his public investment developmental program in his economic analysis—it would make up for the deficiency of private investment—but there is also no question that he had come to view public improvements and community consumption as desirable in their own right on social and cultural as well as economic grounds, thus anticipating John Kenneth Galbraith's 1958 *The Affluent Society*.[42] Economists, he was convinced, had been "grossly negligent" in "examining the deficiencies in our society" and the inability of private enterprise alone to resolve them. The "gravest deficiencies" were "exactly in the areas where only public outlays can meet the problem."[43]

Hansen did not ignore the need to enhance private consumption, but he considered it secondary to the focus on public investment and community consumption. The role of consumption was placed by Hansen in a historic context. The decline of "extensive" expansion meant a larger role for consumption in the modern economy, both individual and community, private and public. Promotion of such consumption would stimulate growth and employment.[44] In addition to public investment in community consumption, private consumption could be promoted through such methods as income redistribution, progressive taxation, and social security benefits.[45] Still, Hansen preferred to emphasize the public investment route. First, it was consistent with his basic economic analysis, which stressed the primacy of investment. Second, he considered greater community consumption to be more socially desirable and valuable than greater individual consumption.[46]

Hansen stressed that under modern conditions a larger role for government, with the focus on increased public investment, would provide the needed new economic environment within which private enterprise would now flourish. Hansen, like Keynes, was cognizant of the element of uncertainty in private enterprise, of the factor of "business confidence." Businesspeople, facing uncertainty of particular proportions, were less likely to invest than otherwise.[47] Placing business confidence in historic context, Hansen argued that it was less likely to be inhibited in the buoyant atmosphere of the "extensive" expansion of the nineteenth century than at present.[48] A more positive economic environment fostered by public investment could now replicate in a new way that of the nineteenth century. Public investment, a developmental program, would stimulate private enterprise, increase private investment, assure adequate demand, and create overall a more secure and certain environment in which businesspeople could plan ahead and invest without excessive uncertainty. Public programs geared to the long run would thus shape an optimistic and positive environment for private capital that would be comparable with the extensive expansion of the previous century. Just as businesspeople could once assume that geographic and population expansion would continue for the long run, given a developmental program they could now assume that public investment would provide a long-run positive environment for private enterprise. Just as those in business in the earlier environment were emboldened to invest for the long run, in the new environment they would be emboldened to do likewise. Not lacking in hostility to government innovations and often inclined to blame government for their troubles, businesspeople, Hansen believed, would gradually become more accustomed to new public policies designed to create a more favorable environment. These policies would in time be seen as quite as normal and "natural" as those of the nineteenth century.[49]

As a "hard" secular stagnationist, however, Hansen stressed what he considered to be the underlying economic realities rather than business psychology, confidence, or uncertainty per se. Secular lack of inducement to invest, in Hansen's analysis, was due above all to the exhaustion of sufficient exogenous stimuli—all the confidence in the world could not offset this. Thus Hansen emphasized that statements that government would fill gaps left by private enterprise, in the belief that these statements would generate such confidence that government need not actually do much, would not suffice. Psychology was a factor, but real economic forces were vastly more important. Government's role, accordingly, would have to be substantive and not just declarative. It would be "a great mistake to assume" otherwise, given the decline of "extensive" growth.[50]

With a government-fostered positive environment—with, that is, public investment, stimulation of private investment, assurance of adequate demand, and the buttressing of business confidence—private enterprise could undertake the remainder of the economic task. In particular, private enterprise had historically performed the task of production quite effectively and could continue to do so now in the new context.[51] Hansen did on one occasion evince interest in Swedish publicly owned business, noting that such government ownership facilitated control over investment and thus economic stability.[52] But Hansen and other advocates of public investment basically stressed how this route would avoid the painstaking and difficult intricacies of public structural planning. Government could create an environment in which private enterprise could operate rather than interfere with the structural mechanism itself.

Hansen's stress on exogenous forces also shaped his view of monetary policy. Consistent with the investment emphases of his pre-Keynesian phase, Hansen continued to argue that monetary policy could not effectively offset a secular lack of investment caused by a deficiency of exogenous stimuli. A low interest rate was desirable, but it could not significantly induce investment in an otherwise unfavorable environment; only a renewal of exogenous stimuli, now including public investment, could accomplish that task.[53] Additionally, Hansen disputed the notion that an increase in the money supply per se would assure adequate demand. It depended on distribution, thus requiring linkage to nonmonetary policies.[54] Excessive reliance on economic adjustment through the interest rate, Hansen concluded, flew in the face of the "whole development of modern economic thinking" with its emphasis on "dynamic analysis" versus "static analysis." For example, earlier static analysis assumed that greater savings would mean lower interest rates and hence increased investment. But this ignored the process as it occurred over time.[55] Stressing monetary policy meant toying with the "thermometer" rather than acting to change the "temperature." Investment was "the real problem and mere increase in money" would not adequately ensure it. Faced with Keynesian investment analysis, traditional monetary theory was "an anachronism and quite obsolete." Fiscal policy of the proper kind provided the necessary framework in which monetary policy could function as a secondary tool.[56]

Hansen's secular stagnation theory reached its apogee in the late thirties and early forties, given credence by the shock of the 1937–38 recession.[57] George Terborgh, one of the theory's most vociferous critics, termed it a "contagion," one appearing at the "psychological moment" in the wake of the recession and spreading "like a conquering host," led by its "most distinguished proponent and publicist," Alvin H. Hansen.[58] Stressing, obviously, the secular as distinct from the cyclical, the theory focused attention on the long-run full use of resources as distinct from temporary downturns, fostered the notion of permanent public spending as distinct from pump priming, and provided a historic setting for Keynesian underemployment equilibrium theory as distinct from the idea that large-scale unemployment was merely a "lapse" from the full employment "norm."[59]

Voices like Hansen's, in addition to that of Keynes, were also forthcoming among distinguished British economists such as J. R. Hicks and William Beveridge. Hicks, who was later to be attacked, along with Hansen, for allegedly sabotaging Keynesianism and turning it into a limited, short-run, mechanical formula, speculated "that perhaps the whole Industrial Revolution of the last two hundred years has been nothing else but a vast secular boom, largely induced by the unparalleled rise in population."[60] Beveridge, in his 1945 *Full Employment in a Free Society*, acknowledged, like Hansen, the need for income redistribution, social legislation, and enhanced private consumption, but like Hansen he stressed that this was secondary compared with public investment in social goods. The latter alone could address the "many vital needs which can be met only by collective action." Government, "if it undertakes the responsibility of ensuring sufficient total outlay for full employment, must concern itself also with the direction of outlay."[61] At the end of the 1930s, the battle over New Deal economic theory between the structural emphases of Gardiner Means and the secular Keynesian approach of Alvin Hansen was played out most directly in the New Deal's National Resources Planning Board (NRPB). This battle, with Hansen victorious over Means, led to indignant inquiries as to whether the Harvard economist was the only one now consulted by the NRPB.[62] It also led to new NRPB reports that now emphasized, in accordance with Hansenian perspectives and themes, public investment in human and material resources.[63]

6.
Hansen versus Means, Means versus Keynes

The National Resources Committee, later the National Resources Planning Board, had been Gardiner Means's base of operations since 1935. Under his influence the board, like the Department of Agriculture, was a bastion of New Deal structural planning. That planning was based on an analysis of the structure of the economy which concluded that the malfunctioning of the market required new public mechanisms to coordinate price and production policy. But the impact of the recession of 1937–38, following the failure and demise of earlier and, by the standards of planners such as Means, highly imperfect "planning," such as that of the National Recovery Administration, led to a growing emphasis on fiscal policy, public spending, and Keynesianism. This approach, it was now argued, would stimulate the economy by raising aggregate levels of investment, employment, income, and demand, thereby avoiding the messy intricacies of structural planning. The victory of Keynesians within the New Deal and, more broad and lasting, within heterodox American economic thought was epitomized and symbolized by the triumph of Alvin Hansen over Gardiner Means at the erstwhile NRPB stronghold of structural planning.[1]

The stage was set in 1938 with a National Resources Committee decision to study the "operational" as well as the "structural" aspects of the economy, which reflected the growing impact of Keynesianism.[2] Means himself saw the study of "operational" characteristics as one that should be undertaken in a way that would complement his own "Structure Report" (Means's short title for the forthcoming *Structure of the American Economy*).[3] As he later put it, study of the structure of the economy would serve as a "background for examining its operating characteristics."[4] Means further suggested that an exploratory study be made of fiscal and monetary policies and that Alvin Hansen, already engaged in a related Social Science Research Council project, might appropriately be involved.[5] But the participation of Hansen, among others, led to sharply divergent analyses, disagreement, discord, and Means's ultimate departure from the NRPB.

In late 1939 Means expressed concern over the development of the "divergent analyses" of Hansen and others in relation to his own "Structure Report." In considering "the relation" among the various analyses, Means concluded that the other theories could largely be subsumed under his. Most "theories of business fluctuation," he held, rested "on an inarticulate or semiarticulate major premise of price inflexibility," including wage rates as prices. To be viable, Keynes's analysis, for example, could be seen as relying on wage rate inflexibility. Theories emphasizing factors "extraneous to the market mechanism" nonetheless themselves "involved an implicit assumption of . . . price or wage . . . inflexibility." Institutional inflexibility was the pivot on which extraneous forces acted. It was, accordingly, Means's contention that various theories of business fluctuation could "be given validity . . . only . . . if short-run inflexibility of . . . prices or wage rates . . . is assumed." Theories based on factors "extraneous to the market mechanism" could only be "partial," whereas a theory based "on price inflexibility" offered "the basis for the most comprehensive diagnosis of present difficulties." A theory "making short-run price inflexibility (including . . . wage rates)" its "fundamental basis for rejecting . . . laissez faire" provided "the greatest generality" and "the broadest basis for developing a new system of policies which will insure reasonably full use of resources."[6]

In early 1940 Means warned against confusing analyses based on structure with those based on operating characteristics. In Means's view, Hansen's analysis, for example, rested "primarily on assumptions about the operating characteristics of the economy" and did not deal with structure. But operating characteristics, to Means, had to be understood "in the light of the economic structure."[7] Means's frustration over the growing acceptance of the Keynes-Hansen analysis led to his departure from the NRPB. His projected "operating characteristics" sequel to his "Structure Report" was never undertaken.[8] As Means put it some years later, "Since the Resources Board embraced the Keynesian theory which provided them with an answer to the problems of operating policy, they did not feel it necessary to have a study of the operating characteristics of the economy . . . by a non-Keynesian."[9] Nor was the NRPB any longer interested in pursuing studies of price behavior or consumption trends along the lines he favored.[10] Working for the reform-minded business group the Committee for Economic Development during World War II, Means happily reported that "the C.E.D. has not swallowed the Hansen thesis as did the NRPB."[11]

Much as Means tried to subsume Keynes within a structural framework, the victorious Hansen endeavored to subsume structural factors within his exogenous theoretical framework. Hansen's triumph reflected the ascendancy for the time of his long-run theory over that of Means. Efforts at synthesis or complementariness gave way to subsumption and rivalry. Hansen, for his part, stressed the difficulties involved in trying to effect change through structural as distinct from fiscal means. Efforts to alter wages and prices directly—to deal with the "organization" of the economy—he argued, were less likely to succeed than efforts to use fiscal policy to affect aggregate levels of the economy. Nor did structural solutions, which were geared to the functions of the market mechanism, grapple with the problem of investment.[12]

Hansen placed the question of structure within his own investment emphasis and environmental framework. He held that concentrated business, by amassing excess profits and restricting output, increased savings while further restricting opportunities for investment. In the contemporary environment in which "intensive" investment loomed larger than "extensive" investment, "monopoly" aggravated the problem. The development of business concentration, rigidity, and restrictive practices, however, was due in part to the very decline of "extensive" growth. In a healthy, expanding economy, Hansen argued, competition was invigorated; it was in a more stagnant economy that the restrictive practices of concentrated business held sway, aggravating the problem of investment.[13]

This Hansenian approach applied to Hansen's analysis of Means's specific statements of the importance of relative price inflexibility. Hansen suggested, following the Continental school, that institutions were results, broadly speaking, rather than causes of economic change.[14] Accordingly, Hansen argued that Means's stress on relative price inflexibility was misplaced. Differentiating between the two "main explanations of business cycle fluctuations"—one focusing on price and the other focusing on investment—Hansen, as an adherent of the latter, insisted that what Means considered a basic cause of the intensification of the depression—relative price inflexibility—was in fact an effect of the decline of investment. It was the decline of investment that meant a decline in income and demand, which in turn was reflected in the dispersion between flexible and relatively inflexible prices.[15]

Further, Hansen held, Means's analysis was "static" rather than "dynamic." Means's analysis suggested that what was needed for a healthy, buoyant economy was a properly functioning price system. This Hansen disputed. Such an assumption ignored the dynamic context in which the price system functioned. A properly functioning price system could not of itself provide or guarantee adequate outlets for productive investment. A dynamic and more comprehensive analysis had to "take account of business expectations" and "the manner in which the whole process develops in time" as distinct from a more limited static analysis that related to the price system, with the surrounding context assumed as unchanged.[16]

Hansen was convinced that tinkering with price was not the remedy. Nor were structural alterations, as such. Because the depression was essentially a result of a paucity of investment and price was a significant factor only within this context, the solution would necessarily focus on investment. The primary cure for errant price behavior now lay not within the realm of price itself, Hansen believed, but in the economic expansion made possible by increased investment facilitated by fiscal policy. In an expanding economy made possible by fiscal policy, the dispersion between flexible and rigid prices would close, with flexible prices rising to their former levels. Flexible prices were a destabilizing force. Perfect price flexibility—of which, Hansen acknowledged, following some initial confusion, Means was not an adherent—was no solution, for it would not guarantee the full use of resources, which was made possible only by the expansionary force of greater investment.[17]

Hansen's argument that the disparity between flexible and relatively rigid prices reflected rather than caused the Great Depression in a sense, however limited, dovetailed with Means's own view that price malfunctioning essentially aggravated rather than caused the initial economic decline. Still, Means's point was that the aggravation, not the initial decline, constituted the Great Depression. Hansen himself acknowledged the existence of demand-sensitive and demand-insensitive prices and that "granted a decline in income, price dispersion is bound to follow."[18] Price dispersion was seen here as an effect, but as Gottfried Haberler pointed out, the basic thesis of economists such as Means was precisely that price dispersion aggravated the initial decline; it was in that sense a cause even if initially an effect. John Blair, a disciple of Means, further held that a central point of Means dealt with the correlation between relative price rigidity and declines in production and hence in employment and income. Relatively stable inflexible prices, Blair argued, could not, as Hansen believed, be a positive factor, given their correlation with declining production, employment, and income.[19]

Blair further noted that Means's administered prices thesis "remained more or less outside of the body of modern economic thought" as it was shaped by Keynesians, a factor that Blair attributed in part to Hansen's critique of Means's theory.[20] In the wake of Hansen's triumph over Means and, more broad, the victory of Keynesianism over institutionalist emphases, the focus on structure receded.[21] If Hansen de-emphasized Means's structural focus, Means in turn paid relatively little attention to the exogenous forces that so preoccupied Hansen. With his overwhelming stress on structure and the market mechanism, Means made virtually everything else pivot on this, with little regard for economic phenomena of a noninstitutionalist kind. He merely noted such factors as declining population growth and the ending of geographic expansion, essentially linking the latter to the relative decline of agriculture in comparison with industry.[22] This reflected Means's fundamental belief that the basic problem was institutional, the malfunctioning of the market mechanism, and all else was of importance essentially only in relation to it. As he once put it quite succinctly, "The central problem of unemployment is an equilibrium problem and not a product of dynamic forces."[23]

Thus whereas Hansen downplayed structural factors, incorporating them into what he considered a broader and deeper analysis and framework, Means virtually ignored what Hansen considered vital, basically acknowledging its importance only in relation to his own concern with structure and price. The divisions between Keynesians and institutionalists thereafter may be attributed in part to Hansen and Keynes for what they de-emphasized, but also to Means for what he ignored. There was, in other words, a failure of synthesis on both sides. A visit by Means to Hansen at Harvard apparently served only to clarify differences.[24] Both sides saw a breakdown of traditional theory, one emphasizing structure and the other environment, but instead of thinking largely in terms of complementarity, the dominant emphasis in the end was on rivalry, with each side trying to subsume the other. The result, from the 1940s on, was a Keynesianism without a solid microfoundation based on structure and institutions, and an institutionalist school very much on the sidelines until the problem of inflation flickered in the 1950s and then enveloped the economy in the 1970s. The failure of synthesis and complementariness evident between Hansen and Means was even more evident between Means and Keynes. Keynes had praised the initial development of Means's administered prices thesis, and Means had sought common ground with Keynes. This effort was undermined, however, in the wake of a 1939 visit by Means to Keynes—a visit to which Means frequently alluded during the nearly half century he was yet to live. Henceforth Means considered Keynesianism a rival theory and one he sought to criticize and dislodge from its preeminent place in the 1940s and thereafter.

Means's 1939 visit with Keynes was pivotal in Means's career and in his relation to Keynesianism. He had earlier seen and continued later to see points of similarity between his theory and that of Keynes. Both theories, he acknowledged, rejected laissez-faire. Both called for positive government policy to redress imbalances in the economy that could otherwise lead to underemployment equilibrium.[25] He agreed in 1938 that a gap between savings and investment could be addressed in part by fiscal policy, while expanded consumer purchasing power was stressed as the basic stimulus to increased business investment.[26] Before his 1939 meeting, Means believed that Keynes's theory, as Keynes himself saw it, conceivably rested on a variant of price rigidity—namely, wage rate inflexibility. This would make Keynes's theory and his own similarly characterized by institutional rigidity, each closely paralleling the other.[27] Reflecting on his thoughts before the visit, Means later recalled that because he had developed a theory based on price inflexibility, he had hoped Keynes would confirm that his own theory rested on wage rate inflexibility so that the two theories would "reinforce each other."[28] Although Keynes readily acknowledged and agreed with Means that many prices were relatively inflexible, he consistently responded to Means's queries as to whether Keynes's theory depended on such inflexibility with "not at all." Hence

Means concluded that despite Keynes's agreement as to the fact of inflexibility, Keynes's theory, as the master defined it, did not depend on such inflexibility, that underemployment equilibrium to Keynes could exist apart from inflexibility, and that therefore his own and Keynes's theories were in reality quite different.[29]

Preparatory to his July 1939 meeting with Keynes, Means wrote a memorandum for the British economist; in it he outlined his theory as it possibly related to that of Keynes. One conclusion he reached, Means reported to Keynes, was that given price inflexibility, a lack of balance between savings and investment would be worked out through reductions in production and employment until a lower-level equilibrium was reached. That conclusion and Keynes's were like "blood brothers," yet they seemed "to stem from different assumptions" and were developed along different lines, for Keynes appeared "to assume either perfect competition and flexibility of prices . . . or else . . . inflexibility in wage rates alone. If your analysis rests basically on the assumption of . . . inflexibility of money wage rates," Means wrote for Keynes, "it is in its essential character the same as mine. If, however, it would be equally valid under conditions of perfect competition . . . and perfect flexibility of prices it differs essentially from mine."[30] In a second, later memorandum, Means noted that his theory and Keynes's could be viewed as "independent" but "parallel" theories, each attempting to explain underemployment equilibrium, or his theory could be treated "as a subvariant" of Keynes's. The second possibility, "if justified," seemed to Means "much more desirable," for it would contribute to a unified perspective. But this second possibility in turn depended on a Keynesian reliance on wage rate inflexibility.[31]

In a cover letter for his first memorandum, Means wrote that he had "reached the same conclusion" as Keynes on what appeared "to be quite different grounds" and wanted to "discover . . . whether the grounds are really different."[32] Keynes's response was an unequivocal "yes." In writing, Keynes reaffirmed the conclusions that Means had reached during their personal conversations with each other. Keynes wrote in his letter of response that a distinction had to be made between his "General Theory" and "applications" of it that could be made to particular circumstances. He regarded his "Theory as equally applicable to flexible economies, inflexible economies, and intermediate conditions." Means's theory, he felt, could "be properly treated, not so much as a subvariant of mine, as an application of mine to certain special cases with the appropriate additions which this limitation of purpose makes practicable. Naturally one can arrive at more definite conclusions in a special case than in a general case. You are adding to my general approach by dealing in greater detail with the characteristics of the situation which will arise if certain special assumptions are made."[33]

Thus Means, who had hoped to find Keynes's theory a version of his own, found his theory referred to as an "application" of Keynes's, relevant to a "special case." In his annotations on Means's second memorandum, Keynes again scrawled his objections to Means's hopeful hypothesis that their two theories were "blood brothers." Passages in *The General Theory* applied the theory to inflexible money wage rates, Keynes wrote, but the theory was not dependent on such inflexibility. *The General Theory* itself had to be distinguished from Means's "similar, but less general theory," as the latter constituted "an application . . . to a particular case"; *The General Theory* covered "more than the limiting case because it is applicable to . . . degrees of flexibility and inflexibility of wages and prices."[34] In his letter, Keynes generously allowed that Means had made "some extraordinarily interesting points," including Means's "most interesting analysis of the varying relation between the administered and flexible price levels in the course of the trade cycle," points, Keynes flippantly added, that he found "embedded in . . . a very miscellaneous haystack."[35]

Keynes's recognition of the reality of institutional rigidity, including administered prices, without making such rigidity a basis as such for his general theory, led, Means believed, to a condition whereby rigidity and administered prices could effectively and erroneously be ignored. Because Keynes attributed underemployment equilibrium to noninstitutional factors, the vast institutional changes that formed the core of Means's theory could still, even in a Keynesian framework, be dismissed as "frictions" and "imperfections" that did not basically invalidate traditional theory about the normality of competition and market flexibility. In Means's view, then, Keynes's conclusion in that sense arrested and set back the progress that had been made in understanding institutional and relative price inflexibility in terms of their macroeconomic impact.[36]

Means continued to insist for the remainder of his career that he, rather than Keynes, had made the critical and decisive break with traditional economic theory. The discovery of price inflexibility—the malfunctioning of the market mechanism—explained underemployment equilibrium in a way that Keynes did not. Nothing Keynes postulated, on the other hand, explained underemployment equilibrium given the assumption of market and price flexibility. That is, in Means's view, if the market actually functioned as in traditional theory, if prices were flexible, imbalances that Keynes saw in the economy would be resolved through the market mechanism. It was the mechanism that was at fault and not the factors extraneous to it, as Keynes believed.[37] To be viable, Keynes's theory explaining "an equilibrium at less than full employment as a result of a tendency to oversave" necessarily rested "on an assumption . . . of inflexibility in wage rates." Hence, Means was "convinced that a tendency to oversave or to underinvest is not the initiating or central explanation of unemployment." It was "insensitive prices" that prevented this imbalance from being resolved through the market mechanism. The problem of oversaving or underinvestment arose "as a result of insensitive prices"; it was best understood "as a by-product of price inflexibility and not as an independent problem."[38] Such Keynesian phenomena were of importance essentially only in relation to institutional rigidity.

Means thus considered the central difference between himself and Keynes to be the fact that he made price inflexibility the centerpiece of his theory and Keynes, while recognizing its reality, fashioned a theory that claimed to explain underemployment equilibrium apart from institutional rigidity. Means, in turn, insisted that what Keynes considered crucial— that is, factors centering on investment—would not create underemployment equilibrium, assuming market and price flexibility, and therefore had importance only in Means's own framework of institutional inflexibility. But Means also saw vital differences in monetary theory between himself and Keynes. In other words, in addition to Means's emphasis on institutions, on the functioning of the market, as the crucial distinction between himself and Keynes, Means also focused on money, evincing a view that Keynes had cavalierly dismissed in his 1935 letter of congratulations on Means's statement of the administered prices thesis.

Keynes, Means argued, linked money too totally to the rate of interest, believing that under certain conditions low interest rates would not be effective in inducing enough investment to overcome underemployment equilibrium. According to Means, Keynes ignored and underestimated the "direct effect" of money. Means held that by increasing the money supply, aggregate demand could be increased—that is, monetary policy could help trigger an escape from underemployment equilibrium. In a flexible price economy, prices would fall until the real money supply would be sufficient to achieve full employment. While not applicable to an inflexible price economy, this effect proved the failure of Keynes to explain underemployment equilibrium under conditions of flexibility. In an inflexible price economy, production and employment would fall instead of prices, until a stable underemployment equilibrium was reached, given no increase in the money supply. Expanding the money supply in an inflexible price economy would expand demand in a way comparable with a fall in prices in a flexible price economy.[39] Means made much of this difference between himself and Keynes over the decades, writing in 1978, for example, to the leading American post-Keynesian economist Alfred S. Eichner that he had "always rejected Keynes' explanation of unemployment because he failed to take account of the direct effect of money." Eichner replied, not unlike Keynes over four decades earlier, "that the question of whether money has a direct effect is a minor one."[40]

Following his 1939 visit to Keynes, with Keynes's adamant assertion that *The General Theory*'s approach was valid apart from the question of institutional rigidity, Means came to see Keynes as a rival in the search for an alternative theory to orthodoxy, one who had become more successful than he in establishing his theory as orthodoxy's leading challenger. Means essentially thought in terms of a triad: traditional theory, and the two rival challengers to it, Keynes's and his own. Traditional theory had been outmoded by events; the question was whether it would be replaced by Keynesianism or what Means termed "administrative theory."[41] Means's wife, Caroline F. Ware, has suggested that following the extraordinary success of *The Modern Corporation and Private Property*, Means believed that he was in a position to make great advances, only to see Keynes come and carry away most of his audience.[42] Means had, after all, made a great impression with *The Modern Corporation*, which was followed by *Industrial Prices and Their Relative Inflexibility*. His was hailed as seminal work. Then along came Keynes with a far more influential analysis, as well as Hansen, Keynes's American counterpart and Means's nemesis, dislodging Means at the NRPB. One need not be unduly harsh on Means to see here part of the reason why Means viewed Keynesianism in such adversarial terms.

Keynes's 1939 dismissal of inflexibility, to be sure, undermined Means's efforts at complementariness. But Means may have overreacted. The major adversary of both Means and Keynes (and Hansen), after all, was traditional theory. As Means recognized, of course, his theory and Keynes's were complementary in that both challenged traditional theory and called for a more positive and active role for government. Means's call for planning under public auspices may be seen as the structural analogue of the Keynesian-Hansenian stress on public investment. If Hansen had, in the final analysis, a more broadly based macrotheory, Means may have been more insightful about the nature of power and institutions. Certainly

Means lived long enough, beyond the 1970s, to see inflation ravage a once-dominant Keynesianism. Still, the challenge to traditional theory per se would have been strengthened by a greater effort at synthesis between Means's theory and that of Keynes and Hansen. Each endeavored to fit the other into his own framework. In Means's case the result was a somewhat mechanistic theory that was outcompeted. For Keynes and Hansen it meant a relative de-emphasis on structure, with disastrous results in the 1970s. Keynesians, it is true, have been properly criticized, especially in the wake of the dismal 1970s, for not incorporating into their theory such structural insights as those of Means, but Means's post-1939 distaste for Keynesianism did not contribute to efforts at synthesis either.

Such efforts, of course, were made. J. R. Hicks, an early, influential interpreter of Keynes, for example, also gave serious attention to the role of administered prices in the late 1930s.[43] So did others who had been impacted by both strands of theory.[44] Means, for his part, however, never stopped aiming his shaft at Keynes. In a 1972 letter to the historian Daniel Boorstin, for example, Means challenged the notion that Keynes's work had been seminal. It was the Great Depression, not Keynes, that had discredited traditional theory, Means insisted; had Keynes never produced his *General Theory*, the shift from laissez-faire to a larger governmental role would nonetheless have come. Moreover, lacking Keynes, governmental economic policies would have been more effective.[45] While Means occupied himself from 1939 on with attacks on Keynes, and Keynesians rather ignored Means, debate raged over the form of heterodoxy most influential by the turn of the decade—secular stagnation theory.

7.
Debates over Stagnation
and Structure

The debate over secular stagnation theory developed in the wake of Hansen's full-fledged pronouncements of it, a theory that in 1939 critic Alexander Sachs referred to as "the present idol in academic reformist circles."[1] The American frontier, critics argued, had "closed" in the late nineteenth century and thus could not have led to a depression beginning in 1929. Nor could decline in the population growth rate, unlinked to the income of the existing population, explain the debacle. Similarly, critics insisted, Hansen had overestimated the past importance of "great new industries" such as railroads in propelling historic economic growth; on the other hand, it was alleged that stagnationists too little appreciated the power of technological advance alone to generate future economic growth. And, it was charged, the stagnation of the thirties, if that was what it was, could be attributed to policy factors external to the system, to the suffocating effect on private enterprise of a national administration that undermined business confidence and thereby obstructed normal recovery and growth.[2]

Hansen, for his part, challenged the notion that because the American frontier had "closed" almost four decades before the onset of the Great Depression, this cessation of territorial expansion could not have been an underlying cause of the severity of the economic crisis. He was himself "born and raised on the last American frontier," Hansen noted. In 1890, when critics said the frontier's impact "was all over" and he was three years old, "there were plain-state areas in which economic development hadn't even begun. . . . It took another generation to develop that frontier."[3] Thus to Hansen the critical point was that the last areas opened up to settlement remained in a state of rapid development up to the time of the First World War. That development stimulated economic growth not only in the immediate area but also for the country as a whole, as older areas supplied newer ones with needed investments and products. Did anyone really doubt, Hansen asked, that a sudden availability of new land and resources would give a tremendous boost to investment and consequent economic expansion?[4]

On the impact of population, Hansen similarly responded that the population growth rate did not slow down until after World War I, and even then, in absolute terms, population growth remained high in the 1920s. Thus, to critics who held that the gradual decline in the population growth rate over the course of decades could not have caused the sudden 1929 downturn, Hansen argued that the really dramatic shift had occurred only recently with the decline in the absolute increment in population growth, which impacted, for example, on the fundamentally important housing industry. A growing income for an existing population could not provide the stimulation to investment in housing of a rapidly expanding population. Were not past builders, Hansen asked, greatly encouraged by the prospect of a dynamically growing population, and were not current ones discouraged by its lack?[5] Further, to Hansen, territorial and population expansion historically were deeply intertwined and could not be disentangled. In words that may have haunted him during the postwar baby and economic boom, although these subsequent developments did not wholly refute him, Hansen concluded, "In the absence of new territory, such an increase in population as we had in the 19th century is utterly impossible, . . . and it is no solution of our problem to advocate an increase in population."[6]

Great new industries were, of course, basic to Hansen in explaining eras of economic growth and decline, an emphasis Hansen shared with Joseph Schumpeter. To say that an industry accounted for "only" 20 percent of an aggregate total illustrated its vital importance, not its relative insignificance. New industries of such magnitude could account for the difference between prosperity and stagnation.[7] Further, Hansen felt that he by no means underestimated the importance of technological advance; indeed, it was basic to his whole analysis. But his essential point was that technological advance had historically proceeded along with territorial and population expansion, and great pressure would now have to be placed on technology to stimulate economic growth in the same measure as it had when working in tandem with those "extensive" growth stimuli.[8]

Additionally, what critics saw as governmental fetters on free enterprise that caused the depression to persist, Hansen, of course, saw as new public policies needed to foster enterprise and prosperity, given changed exogenous conditions. Critics, held Hansen, proceeded as if the nation's economic system were an unchanged and unchangeable entity—the same in 1750, 1850, and at present. Actually, Hansen responded, it had changed over time, in terms of both the "natural environment in which it operates" and "the institutional arrangements through which it functions," and it was changing still. Nor was it perfect before 1929, as severe past depressions illustrated, severe depressions less tolerable now in the context of a more urban society. And, in spite of the far-ranging nature of his proposals, Hansen saw precedents in American history for his developmental emphasis. Government in the past had encouraged economic growth through public improvements. Public developmental programs were thus traditional, though "changing conditions" now required "much larger emphasis on a developmental public investment program than . . . in the past."[9]

Given the prosperous nature of the 1920s, many critics held that the depression could be understood in severe cyclical versus Hansen's secular terms.[10] How could the consumption-oriented, booming 1920s collapse into an investment-deficient, depressed 1930s? Consonant with developments of the 1920s, Simon Kuznets, perhaps the country's leading authority on secular economic trends, challenged the investment emphasis of Hansen's stagnation theory. Consumption, he held, was not merely a passive variable of investment, for consumer demand could condition and induce investment; hence consumption had to be given due attention as a dynamic and vital factor in investment and growth.[11] Hansen, of course, agreed that consumption was important, but he also made clear that he based his theory of secular stagnation on the factor of investment. Increased consumption per se did not undermine his theory, which was based on "the problem of investment opportunities." His secular stagnation thesis "related only to investment."[12] This question in the context of analysis of the 1920s, however, proved nettlesome to Hansen. Harold G. Moulton of the Brookings Institution seized on this point, noting that Hansen had acknowledged that 1920s prosperity had in some measure been based on investment induced by enhanced consumer demand, thus, Moulton believed, contradicting Hansen's exogenously based secular investment emphasis.[13]

Hansen's analysis of the 1920s boom was posited, on the one hand, on the idea that distinctly temporary stimuli fueled that decade's prosperity. Hence installment buying and foreign loans to finance American exports were seen as short-term expedients that fended off underlying secular forces tending toward stagnation.[14] Underlying the 1920s boom, trends "were converging . . . to produce the great depression."[15] On the other hand, Hansen agreed that there were also solid and substantive bases of the 1920s boom, including the laying nationwide of hard-surfaced roads, continued urban construction, the further development of electrical products, and above all the emergence of the great new automobile industry. Hansen referred to the emergence of new industries at this time as an "unusually favorable accidental factor" countering the secular trend.[16] Perhaps, with a slight connotative difference, he should have termed them "fortuitous" in that his own analysis had posited a pattern of emerging new industries that reflected technological advance and stimulated economic growth in periods throughout modern history. In any case, Hansen did see the 1920s boom as based in part on "the building up from scratch of a dozen gigantic industries associated with the rise of the automobile" and "the effect on . . . consumers' goods industries" of the large absolute growth of population.[17]

Hansen saw these 1920s developments as consistent with his analysis of underlying secular stagnationist trends in that they did signal a shift toward a more "intensive," consumer-oriented kind of investment, as distinct from the "extensive" investment of the past. But Hansen's whole point, of course, was that this sort of intensive growth would not likely be able to propel economic growth in historic proportions without the concomitant past "extensive" stimuli of geographic and demographic expansion. Thus, wrote Hansen, technological advance as manifested in "revolutionary new industries may turn out to be so important in any given decade that there are ample investment opportunities even though the factor of extensive expansion has become less important. This indeed, to a large extent was what happened in the 20's. . . . This favorable development was, however, fed and sustained in the decade of the 20's by the tremendous growth of urban population and by a vast residential housing boom."[18] As secular forces began to impact negatively and as the stimulus to investment in new industries was exhausted, the depression ensued.[19]

Gardiner Means's theories, too, engendered criticism. Critics questioned whether there was a corporate revolution, whether corporate concentration and administered pricing were so striking and had proceeded so far as to require a new microtheory.[20] Means responded that what was really important was not the precise degree of concentration or administration but the clear trend, as he saw it, toward ever greater concentration and administration. Hence to critics who held that he had overestimated the degree of concentration, Means countered that the vital point was the growth in importance of the large corporation and the way concentration increasingly represented the norm and absence of concentration represented the "special case."[21] To those who held that administered prices were not new, had long existed, and therefore could not be held accountable for the exceptional severity of the Great Depression, Means rejoined that he had never maintained that administered prices were new, only that they had become increasingly dominant as the economy became more industrial and concentrated, and that the severity of the depression corresponded to the impact on the market mechanism of this growth of relative price inflexibility.[22]

As Keynes's and Hansen's perspectives increasingly displaced those of Means and institutionalists, the role of investment per se, apart from the impact of structure or production-consumption imbalance, was increasingly stressed. Means, it was argued, had no real theory of investment. Consumer purchasing power could stimulate investment; malfunction of the market mechanism could hinder it. But this position lacked comprehensiveness and coherence, it was charged. Price relations and consumer buying power treated apart from its sources did not deal directly with what stimulated investment. For example, a 1940 critic, R. H. Whitman, dismissed as "absurd" Means's implication that price adjustment could possibly address deficiencies that arose "out of changes in the level of investment." A balanced price system, a totally flexible price system, could not automatically correct such investment deficiency. Historically, only a volume of investment well above "normal" had ever resulted in an approach to full employment.[23]

Stagnationists typically considered the problem of investment opportunities more basic than structural maladjustments. Structural factors, in their view, essentially reflected deeper currents in the economic environment.[24] Nonetheless, stagnationists also considered corporate concentration and attendant relative price inflexibility important, even if subordinate, problems, and policies relating to structure as useful or needed supplements to the fiscal solution. Fiscal policy alone, they acknowledged, could in some measure be frustrated by large corporations, which could unduly increase prices as government pumped money into the economy.[25]

In *The General Theory*, Keynes only briefly alluded to "administered" prices, although he was well aware of the unreality of "perfect" competition.[26] For Alvin Hansen, however, structure, corporate concentration and power, and administered pricing were subjects he grappled with at some length as important, if from his environmental perspective necessarily secondary, problems. He believed that corporate concentration and administered pricing aggravated problems arising out of secular stagnation, that they hampered fiscal policy by overly high prices, and that structural remedies were needed as supplements to the fiscal solution. A high-wage/low-price/high-production institutional formula would be the structural counterpart of an expansionist fiscal policy.[27] It was thus essential, Hansen agreed, to "break through the frozen structure of administered prices" in the economy.[28]

Hansen thus devoted considerable attention to structural problems and structural solutions. However, despite references to the need for structural policies, he tended to see in fiscal policy the cure to structural problems, even while acknowledging that structural problems could impair fiscal policy's effectiveness. Specifically, Hansen and others argued that in the expansionist environment created by fiscal policy, large corporations would be more likely to practice expansionist policies. Hence administered pricing and other facets of corporate power in such a climate would be geared not to restrictive practices such as lower production and employment but to expansionist modes of administration. Restrictive practices, they argued, were in good measure products of fear and depressed conditions; using fiscal policy to promote an expansionist environment would help remove that fear and those conditions, encouraging corporate managers to increase production and employment. This approach, it was held, would be more fruitful than primary reliance on attacking structural problems directly.[29]

Supporters of fiscal policy also emphasized its general or aggregative character. It was, they contended, the basic remedy that stimulated the overall economy without interfering with the intricacies of the economic mechanism itself. Instead of a structural remedy, such as Gardiner Means's planning, which suggested that price and production policies be given a quasi-public character, fiscal policy could boost the economy externally. It was in this sense exogenous and environmental rather than endogenous and institutional. It could create an external climate to stimulate the economy rather like the exogenous forces of the nineteenth-century era of expansion had. Fiscal policy could promote and stimulate the growth of private enterprise without intervening in or interfering with the mechanisms or structure of private enterprise itself. This made it, according to advocates, the most feasible, available solution to the gross malfunctioning of the economic system.[30]

Those who stressed structural factors as the basic causes of the Great Depression and who correspondingly stressed structural remedies were characteristically critical of the emphasis on fiscal policy. Essentially, the critics argued that fiscal policy did not reach to structural maladjustments in the economy, that it operated on the economy from the outside and therefore was unable to confront or resolve difficulties intrinsic to the system itself. It could give the total economy a boost, but it could not remedy defects in the economy's inner workings, such as maladministered prices. In a sense, it was held, the Keynes-Hansen approach remained too wedded to traditional theory, that is, to the idea that if only exogenous forces—now including public investment—stimulated the economic mechanism, the mechanism itself would work smoothly, despite the failure of fiscal policy to address directly malfunctions of the mechanism itself.[31]

A bevy of economists insisted that Hansen and his fellow stagnationists stressed exogenous at the unjustified expense of institutional factors. Kuznets, for one, believed that Hansen, in accounting for stagnation, gave insufficient attention to such institutional factors as "the restrictive tendencies of the organization of the private business system," as distinct from such factors as geographic and population expansion.[32] Economist Moses Abramowitz similarly argued that if the restrictive practices of concentrated business did not exist, the exogenous factors stressed by Hansen might well seem less vital.[33] Economist Sherwood Fine took Hansen to task for, in Fine's view, Hansen's arbitrary emphasis on exogenous rather than institutional factors in explaining economic distress. In fact, Fine insisted, structural defects were of basic importance and could act as independent factors apart from the exogenous environment; administered prices, for example, could "prolong and intensify" a depression apart from the forces Hansen stressed. Unfortunately, however, Fine concluded, Hansen, despite his attention to structure, in the end based his "conclusions . . . almost exclusively upon . . . external" elements instead of "institutional" ones.[34] It was also held by his critics that Hansen, despite reference to structural remedies, really saw fiscal policy as a virtual cure-all.[35]

Thus while Hansen paid heed to structural concerns, more so than Gardiner Means incorporated exogenous forces into his macrotheory, Hansen's analysis of institutional factors was nonetheless secondary, relatively peripheral, and not truly integrated into his overall exogenous-investment analysis. John D. Black, the veteran Harvard agricultural economist, bemoaning the growing role of Keynesians in his department in 1947, declared that "none . . . considers that he is narrow. In their discussions, to be sure, they draw in all phases of the economy. But they organize it all in terms of a single framework of reference. They pour it all . . . through one narrow funnel, and do some sieving in the process."[36] This description fit Hansen, but not uniquely him or Keynesians; it fit Gardiner Means's institutional emphasis quite as well.

Finally, critics were dubious about the external, aggregate quality of fiscal policy because of its allocative limits. Boosting overall economic growth did not meet the issue of distribution; stimulating economic expansion did not address the nature or quality of that expansion. Hansen, to be sure, was immensely concerned with the nature and quality of growth, greatly emphasizing the need for public investment in social goods and "community consumption." But fiscal policy per se, critics held, operating outside of and impacting on the economy, did not guarantee a socially desirable allocative effect, nor could it deal with the particular problems of sectors or industries apart from the aggregate.[37] Wrote Adolf A. Berle in 1937, "I have sometimes put it to myself that a flexible budget would go a long way towards determining whether there was prosperity or not; but only . . . organization could determine whether the prosperity so achieved was justly enough distributed."[38]

Especially at the end of the 1930s and beginning of the 1940s, there were points of convergence and overlap between the structural emphases of the early New Deal Era and the Keynesian emphases of the later New Deal Era. Keynesians such as Hansen incorporated, however unequally, structural concerns into their analyses; institutionally oriented economists at least grappled with Keynes. Government, which was to play a much enhanced role in the Keynes-Hansen schema via fiscal policy, was, after all, an institution. There was considerable discussion at the time about the way structural defects and stagnationist tendencies aggravated one another and about the need both to combat administered prices and to promote public investment.[39] The factors stressed by Hansen—exogenous forces in relation to investment—were compared at times to fuel, and the structural factors emphasized by Means were compared to an engine. Fuel gave the engine power, but the engine had to be working properly for the fuel to have its desired effect.[40] But each side tried to subsume the other into its own analysis. Gardiner Means, from 1939 on, stubbornly viewed Keynesianism as an adversarial rather than a complementary challenge to traditional theory. Hansen, for all his effort to incorporate structural factors, nonetheless essentially subordinated them in his own Continental Keynesian macrotheory. Thus Keynesianism in the end stood as a rival of institutionalism's claim to be the primary challenger to traditional theory and institutionalism's notion that corporate concentration was the key long-run development in the current state of economic evolution. No genuine or workable synthesis emerged. Instead, the Keynesian tide proved overwhelming vis-à-vis institutionalism, leaving structural emphases as debris in its wake. Given Keynesianism's triumph over institutionalism, its failure to broaden was historically the more important. That triumph was well captured in a 1941 exchange between Mordecai Ezekiel and Alvin Hansen. Over the course of the 1930s, Ezekiel, like Means, had concentrated on structural problems and structural solutions. Now he was trying to grapple with Keynes and add Keynesian analysis to his repertoire. Alvin Hansen was by all accounts a personally modest and unassuming man. But his 1941 commentary in a letter to Ezekiel on the latter's effort to come to grips with Keynes showed how Keynesians by that time, in relation to institutionalist challengers of traditional theory, had indeed arrived like a conquering host. Hansen wrote that "the critical reader will at once conclude from your first page that you have not read your Keynes" and that Ezekiel's effort would only further confuse those "who have not mastered Keynes."[41] Hansen's letter to Ezekiel, like Keynes's 1939 treatment of Means, was symbolic of the ascendancy of Keynesians over institutionalists among the challengers of traditional theory. Both, however, faced a further challenge from an economist who was not a conventional defender of traditional theory. The prolific and profound Joseph Schumpeter, Keynes's great rival, mounted a major assault on both institutionalist and stagnationist theory and posited his own long-run explanation of the nature of depression, growth, and modern economic evolution. Vociferously anti–New Deal, his apotheosis of the capitalist spirit of innovation had resonance in the 1940s era of economic rejuvenation.

PART TWO.
BOOM TIMES TO
TROUBLED TIMES

The vital and durable public policy influence after 1940 was spending or, more broad, fiscal policy. But it was not to be spending in the fashion that its leading American advocate, Alvin Hansen, intended. Victorious over structural planners in the New Deal, Hansen's triumph was undone by events. The National Resources Planning Board was abolished by a hostile Congress in 1943, and the world after 1945 was not the world of the 1930s. The Second World War brought prosperity, and the cold war was associated with a secular economic boom. Even though the wartime boom was linked to public planning and financing, the more general conclusion drawn from the experience was that the private economy, freed from constraints, remained characterized by enormous innovative and productive capacity, and that led by energetic industrialists such as Henry J. Kaiser of shipbuilding fame, it had once again demonstrated to thirties doubters the undiminished dynamism and energy of "free enterprise." There was, however, a vital caveat. Fear of secular stagnation receded, but memories of the Great Depression remained fresh. The stress on security held. Hence while calls for massive public investment faded, a more limited concept of public policy gained center stage. What was needed, it was increasingly held, was a form of public policy that would provide a framework for stability within which the creativity and drive of private enterprise could flourish. This was a cyclically oriented fiscal policy: spending and tax policies designed to buoy the private economy as it slipped and to restrain it if it overheated. This combination of theoretical orthodoxy and Keynesian policy prescription was in time dubbed the neoclassical synthesis. Its legislative analogue was the much toned down Employment Act of 1946, which formally established the Council of Economic Advisers.

The emergent neoclassical synthesis was further aided by the changed postwar global economic environment. The onset of the Great Depression, the impact of the Hawley-Smoot tariff, the failed London Conference, the autarchic policies of Nazi Germany, and the closed economy of the Soviet Union had all contributed to the domestic or nationalist policy emphases of the 1930s. Keynes had stressed combating the depression within essentially domestic contexts during that decade, as did others, with Cordell Hull's effort to stimulate foreign trade via reciprocity treaties something of a sideshow. Now, with victory in war, that changed. With the United States in the lead (playing a role comparable with that of Great Britain before 1914) and Keynes part of the British team that established the framework in negotiations with the Americans, the post-1945 world witnessed a renewal of world trade liberalization and global monetary coordination, minus, to be sure, the Soviet Union and its satellites. Alvin Hansen's 1945 primer on the new international economic organizations, *America's Role in the World Economy*, constituted a paean to global economic cooperation while stressing the fundamental need for the United States to achieve a domestically based stable prosperity. But with international economic coordination, the wartime and postwar boom, and, some added, cold war spending, domestic economic policies, it was widely concluded, need not be as epochal as some of those considered in the depressed and disjointed national and international climate of the 1930s. Or, put differently, the creation of a more open global norm, the ongoing secular economic boom, and the seemingly endless expenditures of the cold war contributed to the sense that domestic economic policies need be focused on only the short run.

The dominant postwar approach reflected this renewed sense of "normalcy," not the pristine normalcy of the 1920s, to be sure, but the belief that a cyclically based fiscal policy, a balance wheel, utilizing such New Deal "cushions" as unemployment compensation, would be sufficient to keep the economy stable in the context of secular growth. With no return of 1930s conditions and in the wake of the exceedingly mild 1949 recession, the notion took hold that society, government, and the economics profession had solved the problem of a really deep depression. The more fundamental solutions of long-run economists of the New Deal Era were dismissed as outdated remnants of an earlier time, and so too was the simple faith in private economic self-correction of the era before 1929 that had failed to stem the tide of the Great Depression. A consensus took hold around the "technical" tools of neoclassical Keynesianism. In the context of postwar prosperity, additionally, the more positive view of corporate business that emanated from wartime continued, although the Antitrust Division remained sporadically active and occasional postwar legislation endeavored to temper the reach of large corporations. *The Modern Corporation*'s Adolf A. Berle served as a 1950s apologist, as some saw it, for modern corporate chieftains, and his intellectual odyssey was not at all unique in this respect. And, indeed, if some businesspeople remained bitterly opposed to the innovations of the 1930s, others made their peace. Those who coalesced in the Committee for Economic Development (CED), for example—styled "corporate liberals" by some historians—essentially accepted New Deal public policies but sought to interpret them in mild and pro-business ways. Hence Keynesianism was acceptable, but not in the form of Hansenian public investment. The CED favored a cyclical version, one geared, moreover, to tax cuts rather than to public spending. The CED thus settled on the common ground of the neoclassical synthesis, essentially differing with others only as to policy details.

In this climate New Deal structural planners found themselves out of vogue and largely out of Washington. Rexford Tugwell, for example, served as governor of Puerto Rico and then at the University of Chicago moved to the study of political science and to the biography and history of Roosevelt and his era. Gardiner Means became an economic consultant and started a zoysia grass business. Mordecai Ezekiel and Isador Lubin turned to work in international agencies. Louis Bean undertook the study of American voting behavior. The planners had been bested by the Keynesians. Secular Keynesians were then bested by the impact of World War II and its aftermath. The Roosevelt administration's open door to Alvin Hansen was gone after 1945. Joseph Schumpeter's 1942 *Capitalism,*

Socialism, and Democracy, reissued in 1947 and 1950, both reflected and contributed, despite its gloomy prophecy of capitalism's ultimate demise, to the more confident capitalist mood of the time. Schumpeter saw capitalism's dynamic as coming from within, as "endogenous," and the wartime economy's "production miracle" seemed to many to support his thesis. But Schumpeter had no depression solution as such other than to give capitalism time and space for self-renewal—not a reassuring thought in the wake of the thirties. The postwar era thus became not one of 1930s heterodoxy or of pre-1929 orthodoxy (consonant with Schumpeter's policy preferences, if not secular theory), but one marked by the dominance of neoclassical synthesis Keynesianism. It was a triumph of short-run technicians over long-run theoreticians.

Although the dissolution of the long postwar boom is usually and properly dated from 1973, there were earlier indications of what was to come. Indeed, far from seeing the 1945–73 era as a restored "norm" in contrast to the aberrant 1930s, some analysts came to view it as exceptional and reflective of a confluence of forces unique to the aftermath of World War II: an unscathed America absorbed in the rebuilding of Western Europe and Japan, a stimulative bunching of technological thrusts coming out of the war, a domestic backlog of goods after fifteen years of depression and war, and a birthrate and population upsurge. But Western Europe and Japan, once rebuilt, emerged as trade rivals as well as partners. World War II technological thrusts gradually lost steam. The domestic backlog was largely filled. The baby boom became the birth dearth. Even in the midst of the secular boom, voices were heard complaining of sluggish growth and of structural "imperfections." In 1960 John F. Kennedy called for getting the country moving again, and the "new economics" of the Kennedy-Johnson era, while still reflective of the neoclassical synthesis and of the sanguine economic expectations of the time, did shift from a cyclically focused fiscal policy to one more stimulative of long-run growth. Similarly, concern over inflation resulted in at least a mildly structural approach in the wage-price guidelines forged in the Kennedy years. More striking, the late 1960s witnessed a cracking of the postwar climate of economic confidence. The war in Vietnam threatened economic overheating and inflation, while President Lyndon Johnson hesitated to increase taxes. The neoclassical Keynesian solution to inflation proved politically less palatable than tax cuts to promote growth. President Richard Nixon, confronted with inflation, resorted to a monetary dampening and then, temporarily, in the face of the 1972 election, to direct wage and price controls.

But the real crunch did indeed date from 1973. As the country was entranced by the Watergate scandal, the bottom began to soften and partially fall out from under the economy. Prices hiked by the oil cartel and an oil embargo emanating from the Middle East fed both inflation and recession. The mild downturns of the postwar era gave way to the major recession of 1974–75. President Gerald Ford, setting out to whip inflation now, saw the economy nose-dive, which forced him to shift to a recession-fighting mode. The dilemma of "stagflation"—the combination of stagnation or recession with inflation—proved to be the intractable economic problem of the decade. The conventional neoclassical Keynesian solution to each only aggravated the other. Policymakers appeared to face a conundrum not explicable in terms of conventional postwar theory or practice, apart from the convenient reliance on the impact of external shocks. The Carter years, with another surge of inflation, combated at the end with a restrictive monetary policy, only reinforced the confusion and frustration, not to mention the economy's contribution to the president's political debacle in the 1980 election. Nor was the wider international economic climate particularly conducive to national economic success. The partial rupture of the international monetary order in 1971, the upsurge of trade competition from Japan, and the challenge to traditionally strong American industries all added to the erosion of confidence and self-assurance.

If the neoclassical Keynesian policies of the postwar era no longer availed, then what would? Calls for a structural planning solution to inflation arose among heterodox economists, but Nixon's temporary controls notwithstanding, no significant hearing from the conservative presidential administrations of the decade was forthcoming. Planning proposals similarly revived to meet stagnation. Western European countries had a measure of "indicative" planning, it was noted, and Japan was never a bastion of laissez-faire capitalism. To compete, the United States would now have to engage in "industrial policy," as it was called in the late seventies, a degree of planning to spur technologically promising industries. This involved government-business cooperation but also a more critical view of corporations than that generally advanced during the long postwar boom. Industrial policy advocates focused on corporate shortsightedness, while echoes of antitrust sentiment, especially expressed in political and publicist circles, were also heard. Although widely discussed and debated in various versions, industrial policy, like structural planning to meet inflation, did not achieve implementation.

If the revived heterodox formulas of the 1970s failed in the effort to claim succession to the dying neoclassical synthesis, there was also ferment on the other side of the analytical and ideological spectrum. The mone-

tarism of Milton Friedman rose in prestige and influence as the neoclassical Keynesian star waned, becoming part of the Nixon policy matrix and
then central to the fight against the rampant inflation of the late Carter
and early Reagan (and in Britain, Thatcher) years. It had the appeal of
simplicity, but its drawback in the political and policy arena lay in its contribution to the severe recession of 1981–82. More widely appealing was
the call for entrepreneurial initiative in an economy freed from government overregulation. The "deregulation" vogue dating back to the Carter
years continued through the Reagan and Bush presidencies. An entrepreneurial emphasis could also be embellished by references to Schumpeter's
legacy and to the long-run effect of Schumpeterian "creative destruction,"
belying any great need for government intervention via industrial policy
or antitrust action. Moreover, supply-side economics, brewed more by
economic journalists than by academic economists and with its own link
to entrepreneurialism, was set forth. Tax cuts, the supply-side argument
went, would fuel initiative and stimulate investment and growth. Further,
a more productive supply side would help douse inflation, and according
to some advocates, lowered tax rates, by stimulating work and increasing
incomes, would still lead to ample government revenues. Inflation did
abate in the wake of the 1981–82 monetary policy–driven recession, with
help from an oil price subsidence and a flood of imports, although an
inflationary bias to the economy remained. But investment did not take
off, and huge federal deficits appeared. It was further argued by critics that
at least some of the Reagan upsurge resulted from increased defense
spending, an application, in effect, of "military" Keynesianism by an
avowedly anti-Keynesian administration.

The recession of the early 1990s brought at least a temporary disillusionment with the formulas of the 1980s. A dose of pre-1929 orthodoxy
might have seemed novel and refreshing a half century after the onset of
the Great Depression. The demise of neoclassical Keynesianism, the revival of orthodoxy in the economics profession, and the Reagan upsurge of
the mid-eighties renewed faith in pre–Great Depression concepts and
policies. The Wall Street crash of 1987, however, suggested that all was not
well, although the late eighties obviously were not 1930–32, as George
Bush's 1988 electoral victory evidenced politically. It was the subsequent
recession that provided the apparent coup de grace. Acting and sounding
like Herbert Hoover, Bush foreswore an activist public policy agenda in
the belief that recovery was just around the corner. It proved a long way to
the corner, and the turning came too late for his 1992 reelection bid.
Meanwhile, the troubles of the late eighties and early nineties led to a call

for increased public investment to stimulate America's productivity and its competitiveness in world markets, a call taken up by Bill Clinton in his successful 1992 campaign and an approach congruent with the secular Keynesianism championed by Alvin Hansen a half century earlier.

The expectation of ever-increasing growth of the post-1945 era, the notion that each generation would do better economically than its predecessor, and the belief in a bright economic future even in the midst of 1960s strife: these all faded after 1973. Post-1973 society was jaded by a distrust of government which dated back to the late sixties and which thereafter was compounded by the stagflationist malaise of the 1970s and by the brevity of Reagan's 1980s promise of "morning again in America." Thus the nation after 1973 neither returned to the economic abyss of the 1930s nor continued the golden economic age, as it now seemed, of the postwar boom. It was betwixt and between, perplexed and unsettled. A society that experienced galloping inflation and severe recession, a society beset by two decades of, at best, slow growth, could be expected to be frustrated, disillusioned, impatient, and fickle.[1]

8.
The
Schumpeterian
Alternative

Joseph Alois Schumpeter, like John Maynard Keynes, was a larger-than-life figure, a legend in his own time. Born like his generational rival in 1883, he grew up in the halcyon days of the Austro-Hungarian Empire. From a prosperous business family, his widowed mother remarried prominently, and young Joseph received the benefits of privileged status, including a first-class education. Because Schumpeter was a spinner of tales, his biographers have only recently separated the fiction from the equally fascinating Schumpeterian facts. Thrice married, once widowed, he was no puritan and no shrinking violet about either personal or professional triumphs. His widely acclaimed *Theory of Economic Development* was published just before World War I, establishing his reputation by the end of his third decade. He served briefly as finance minister of Austria, embarked on a disastrous banking career, and, following an academic stint in Weimar Germany, settled permanently at Harvard in 1932. There, too, his style and personality commanded attention and his scholarly presence was felt, although by the late thirties the Keynesian spell had struck much of the cohort of students around him. Schumpeter has been called the last great polymath, and his range was indeed broad, including not only economics as conventionally defined but also areas usually deemed those of sociology and political science. Whereas Keynes refashioned his thinking under the impact of the Great Depression to produce *The General Theory*, Schumpeter essentially continued to espouse his predepression theories, albeit with important modifications and additions.

Within his encompassing analyses, Schumpeter set forth criticisms of rival theories along with the exposition and development of his own. Interpretations of the depression based on corporate control and institutional rigidity, he held, stressed factors whose importance had been "grossly exaggerated." Further, he insisted, the main effect of concentrated economic power was long-run and developmental rather than short-run and depressive. The degree of security provided by the power of large corporations freed them to take risks by expending funds and energy on long-run research leading to innovations essential to secular economic growth.[1] This, in turn, was related to a central point of Schumpeter's "vision"—that what was key to economic understanding was how a set of institutions or a system evolved and changed over time, not how it functioned at present. What was of prime importance was not the existence of short-run price competition among firms but the long-run competition among firms and industries over techniques and products. The phenomenon of "creative destruction" led to new firms and industries outcompeting and replacing old ones. The key, therefore, was not the "administration" of present structures but how those structures were changed, overcome, and destroyed by far more basic factors. It was the dynamic process rather than the static structure that was of central importance.[2]

Thus while Schumpeter stressed the long-run instability of large corporate structures, he also, especially by the time of his 1942 *Capitalism, Socialism, and Democracy*, saw such structures as permanently encompassing the entrepreneurial function of innovation that earlier in his analysis he had associated with heroic individuals. The traditional entrepreneur, the heroic nineteenth-century figure, was now being displaced by the research laboratories and the trained specialists of large corporations. Progress was becoming routinized.[3] The relationships among entrepreneurialism, creative destruction, and concentrated control—evolving eventually into "socialism" in Schumpeter's famous prophecy—remained somewhat ambiguous or at least subject to varying interpretations.[4] Schumpeter himself suggested that entrepreneurship could function outside its historic context.[5] In 1947, for example, he remarked that "entrepreneurial functions" could now more easily be exercised within existing corporations than in founding new firms. In 1949 he wrote that the Department of Agriculture historically had "acted as an entrepreneur" for American farmers. Earlier he had declared that the "entrepreneurial function," as a manifestation of "economic leadership," was "not confined" to capitalism and could appear "in other forms" as well.[6] The process of creative destruction could also operate in new contexts, Schumpeter believed. Existing manifestations of concentrated power would give way to new manifestations of concentrated power. Creative destruction as a process would remain even as the secular trend toward concentrated control continued.[7]

Thus although Schumpeter dismissed the institutional rigidity theory of the depression's origins, his ultimate acceptance of the reality of permanent concentrated control in some form placed him back with the Berle and Means of *The Modern Corporation*, not to mention, given Schumpeter's intellectual heritage, Karl Marx. That is, along with his emphasis on the continuing processes of entrepreneurialism and creative destruction, Schumpeter also adhered to a notion of secular development moving from the heroic age of nineteenth-century capitalism to a system of concentrated control, whether capitalist or, in time, socialist. Again, creative destruction meant that individual large corporations and industries were not immune to upheaval, but secular evolution suggested that concentrated control as such was not reversible, and to institutionalists the latter was the key point.[8] But institutionalists stressed the structural trend toward concentration, whereas Schumpeter also emphasized the inherent instability of existing concentrated structures because of the recurrence of creative destruction. And although concentration, as well as creative destruction, was central to the mature Schumpeter's overall analysis, it was not central to Schumpeter's depression analysis.

As Nathan Rosenberg has put it, major themes of Schumpeterian analysis included capitalism's "inherent instability," developed in the massive *Business Cycles* of 1939, and the emergence of the large corporation and "industrial concentration," developed in *Capitalism, Socialism, and Democracy*.[9] But the themes remained bifurcated. Allen Oakley, another analyst of Schumpeterian theory, stated that Schumpeter minimized the significance of concentration "as a distorting force in the capitalist system" when dealing with business cycles. The recognition in *Capitalism, Socialism, and*

Democracy of concentrated power left Schumpeter's "theory of . . . business cycles unaffected and he made no endeavor to revise his earlier analyses" of it.[10] This was not unlike the comparable lacuna in Keynes. Or as noted by one of Schumpeter's biographers, Richard Swedberg, Schumpeter believed that "contemporary capitalism was in a stage of institutional transition" toward concentration, but "this whole development . . . of economic institutions" appeared not in the depression analysis of *Business Cycles* but in the more diffuse *Capitalism, Socialism, and Democracy*.[11]

The role of technology also both linked Schumpeter with institutionalists and separated him from them. To institutionalists who emanated from the Veblenian tradition, and particularly to Clarence Ayres, the driving force behind economic growth was technology, not the capitalist market, system, or entrepreneur. To them, Schumpeter assumed technological advance rather than making it an integral and organic part of his analytical system, thus rendering his theory incomplete.[12] To Schumpeter, however, what counted was not technological advance as such but its application to the economy as an innovation—an entrepreneurial function. Inventions, for example, became economically relevant only as commercial innovations, and innovations could take other forms as well, such as new modes of organization and marketing.[13] Further, Schumpeter disputed the institutionalist claim at another level: the nature of the historic evolution of technological advance. Yes, it was based on intellectual freedom and logical rigor, Schumpeter acknowledged. But these, in turn, he insisted, to the incredulity of his critics, were themselves products of capitalist development. It was the nature of capitalism itself—its precision, rigor, and logic—that had given birth to modern patterns of analysis and thought, which in turn underlay technological advance.[14] To his critics, this notion made capitalism a far too overarching, enveloping, and inclusive concept, not unlike that of Schumpeter's fellow analyst of capitalism Karl Marx.[15]

Much as Schumpeter shared certain affinities with institutionalists and yet rejected an institutional rigidity theory of the Great Depression, he shared some affinities with Keynes and especially with Hansen but rejected Keynesianism and secular stagnation theory. The Keynes of *A Treatise on Money* accepted Schumpeter's innovation-based theory of business cycles, and the Continental Hansen, of course, was much influenced by Schumpeter's emphasis on the roles of technology, innovation, and discontinuity in economic evolution.[16] Schumpeter, however, faulted Keynes for excluding from *The General Theory* what Schumpeter considered vital: the changing nature of industry and the impact of innovation on development. *The General Theory*, accordingly, was to Schumpeter anything but general; it was a study of "macrostatics" rather than "macrodynamics." Further, in Schumpeter's evaluation, Keynes was parochial: he overgeneralized from the British experience. In positing the germ of secular stagnation theory, Keynes took certain features of a period of his own country's economic history and extended them too broadly across time and space.[17]

Much of Schumpeter's effort by the late thirties and the forties was devoted to repudiating Hansen's theory of secular stagnation, which made Schumpeter, as one student has put it, Hansen's major American antagonist. Certainly Schumpeter disputed Hansen's emphasis on the core centrality of exogenous stimuli on economic development as distinct from the capitalist process itself, and certainly Schumpeter was convinced that the secular stagnationist conclusion that public spending was now an essential basis of recovery and growth was erroneous, lamenting in 1949 the ruinous effects of public policy "so long as our stagnationist friends rule the roost."[18] That said, Schumpeter continued to see an affinity with Hansen despite their profound differences. As he wrote in 1943, the difference between himself and Hansen in some respects was "not so great as it seems." He, too, after all, "envisaged the possibility of . . . 'prosperityless' cycles," that is, "cycles which would really consist only of slumps interrupted by temporary recoveries." Thus, despite his differences with Hansen over "the diagnosis . . . of the thirties," there were also elements of common ground.[19]

That difference in diagnosis, however, provided a great point of rupture between Hansen and Schumpeter. Whereas Hansen had seen earlier periods of secular stagnation, he believed that the Great Depression of the thirties was different and unprecedented in critical respects. This Schumpeter denied. To him, the thirties did not constitute a "secular break" with the past. The depression of the thirties, really of 1929–32 in Schumpeter's terms, was not unprecedented; severe depressions of this kind had occurred every fifty to sixty years, and there was nothing intrinsically different about this one.[20] Secular investment outlets remained adequate, Schumpeter believed, despite temporary insufficiencies. The driving force in investment was not, to Schumpeter, exogenous, that is, based on such factors as population or geographic expansion, but was engendered from within the system and via entrepreneurial initiative. It was based on the ability to seize technological advances and other opportunities and to make them economically applicable and successful. A dynamic capitalism had in this way continually created new outlets for investment and new industries. Temporary hiatus did not mean secular breakdown.[21]

Here was a basic Schumpeterian point: the driving force in capitalist economic growth was endogenous and not, as Keynes and Hansen would have it, exogenous or environmental. To Schumpeter, this was critical. It was the inner dynamism of the economic process that generated development and growth. Technological advance, new resources, population growth—all these had economic meaning only when transformed via innovation and entrepreneurship. Innovation—including new forms of organization and marketing, as well as the adaptation of invention and technological advance—was the process of turning the raw material of "external" forces into the factors, fabric, and forms of economic growth. All epochs of economic growth were unique in terms of the particular combinations of external ingredients that went into their makeup, but what was continuous was the "capitalist engine" itself. Schumpeter's was thus "a purely economic theory of economic change" based on a "source of energy" emanating from within and transforming that which lay without. External factors, shaped by the capitalist process, were therefore "part and parcel" of the process; the process itself was the "propelling force" of growth and development.[22]

To Schumpeter, the Keynes-Hansen approach, like that of institutional rigidity, took a snapshot and treated it as history. That is, it overgeneralized from the moment. "As a picture of reality," Schumpeter held, Keynes's *General Theory* most nearly made sense "in periods of depression," and thus Keynes's economics could appropriately be called "the economics of depression."[23] But Schumpeter had his own version of an "economics of depression," his own version of "stagnation," believing that a hostile social and political environment could, and in the period from 1933 onward did, thwart business enterprise and recovery. Paradoxically, while Schumpeter's entrepreneur was deemed historically bold, adventuresome, and heroic and Keynes's businessperson was, at least at times, made of more fragile material and easily rattled, 1930s enterprisers were viewed by both as quite susceptible to disturbance from the interventionist policies of a reform government. Keynes wrote in *The General Theory* of how fear of "a New Deal" could depress enterprise as "the mere consequence of upsetting the delicate balance of spontaneous optimism."[24] But followers of Keynes and Hansen saw new public policies as providing the necessary environment for business confidence in the long run, whereas Schumpeter saw those policies as creating an environment that undermined confidence and investment. Government had paralyzed capitalism's "motive forces." It had turned "mere depression" into a "catastrophe," a catastrophe, therefore, that was external to the capitalist process itself.[25] Although Schumpeter had an endogenous theory of economic growth, he here proffered an exogenous theory of the depression's longevity.

Schumpeter remained rather like the Continental Hansen in a sense as contrasted with the Keynesian Hansen. Hansen's analyses were similar in each phase, but his prescriptions sharply diverged. Schumpeter retained continuity of analysis and of prescription. Schumpeter remained convinced that there were recurring cycles in modern economic history, versus discrete periods, a conclusion that flowed from his endogenous theory as opposed to Hansen's exogenous theory. If one views the capitalist process in endogenous terms, each historical epoch was basically shaped by the process itself: historical epochs provided raw material that was then shaped by the process into essentially the same finished products. Although Hansen saw earlier periods of secular stagnation, he essentially thought in terms of discrete periods, because his exogenous theory emphasized external stimuli. For Hansen, therefore, public investment could be seen as a new external stimulus to growth befitting a new and, in some critical respects, unprecedented period of secular stagnation. For Schumpeter, growth would recur despite, not because of, new public policies. In a 1937 letter to a correspondent in England, for example, in which he pointed to elements of economic recovery in that country, Schumpeter lamented that it was "easy to see how all this is liable to misinterpretation in the Keynesian sense." Although future economic historians might "entirely credit" revival to government rearmament spending, such revival, while accentuated by this spending, was "fundamentally independent" of it and "entirely cyclical in nature." Indeed, looking toward a new cyclical boom, Schumpeter predicted that "barring silly policies, an avalanche of consumers goods would pour over England within the next ten years, such as would go far to do away with the phenomenon of poverty."[26]

When Schumpeter referred to severe depressions comparable with that of the thirties occurring every fifty to sixty years, he had in mind a concept he added to his repertoire during the depression decade: the Kondratieff "long wave," after the Russian economist Nikolai Kondratieff, on whose work Hansen had also drawn. No more than others had Schumpeter initially anticipated the extraordinary severity of the depression. Under its impact he hypothesized that its exceptional nature might be linked to the "convergence" of short-run business cycles with the trough of a long-run "Kondratieff cycle."[27] Indeed, it was Schumpeter who facilitated the appearance of Kondratieff's work in English, coined the term "Kondratieff cycle" for the Russian's notion of long waves, and popularized the long wave concept among Western economists.[28]

But Schumpeter did more. What he did was to incorporate Kondratieff's long wave concept into his own theory of economic development. That is, he argued that swarms of innovations, launching new booms, were manifested as long waves or Kondratieff cycles. The original Industrial Revolution had begun in the late eighteenth century. A new industrial revolution came roughly a half century later, propelled by the railroad. This in turn was followed by a third industrial revolution based on developments in chemicals, electricity, and the internal combustion engine. Each wave of innovations ignited cycles of growth. What Schumpeter here provided was Kondratieff via Schumpeter or Schumpeter cum Kondratieff.[29] Long waves, encompassing what Schumpeter termed "the great recurrent industrial revolutions," further included "downgrades . . . of the Kondratieffs . . . characterized by abnormal employment, which . . . each generation" living through one believed to be permanent.[30] The long wave, incorporated into his theory of economic development, illuminated to Schumpeter the whole of modern capitalist evolution: "If one thinks of business cycles as the typical form of capitalistic evolution and if one looks upon those long time movements, . . . called industrial revolutions, as one species of cycles, it is but natural to link up with the cyclical phenomenon practically the whole of the economics . . . of capitalist society."[31]

One can see how Schumpeter could be attracted to the idea of a Kondratieff cycle inherent in the economic process, because Schumpeter's theory was itself endogenous. Still, there remained a tension of sorts between Schumpeter's relation of the Great Depression to a Kondratieff downgrade and his insistence that recovery had been arrested by the exogenous factor of political interference with the economic system.[32] Insofar as the Great Depression was lengthened by noneconomic exogenous forces, Schumpeter's explanation was not wholly endogenous. The one thing it clearly was not was economically exogenous. This was true of Kondratieff himself. The Russian economist disappeared in the Stalin purges and did not have the opportunity to work out to his own satisfaction the full nature of long waves, but he did clearly reject the notion that they were due to exogenous forces. Not unlike Schumpeter, Kondratieff explained the role of exogenous stimuli such as geographic expansion and technological advance in terms of an endogenous economic process. Kondratieff speculated that it was the internal rhythm of the process, as related to the exhaustion of basic capital goods, that led to, stimulated, and caused such developments as geographic expansion and technological advance. It was the rhythm of the economic process that determined whether and how geographic or technological discoveries would become economically applicable, useful, or important.[33]

To many critics of Schumpeter and Kondratieff, however, the notion of long cycles was erroneous. They agreed that there were long periods of economic growth and stagnation, but they rejected what they regarded as the mechanistic notion of an endogenously based long cycle. Long periods of growth or stagnation, they held, were best understood as historical eras that were shaped exogenously and appeared fortuitously rather than cyclically.[34] This was a conclusion that fit Hansen's schema of discrete periods of growth and stagnation. Clearly, the Hansenian exogenous analysis led to the notion of discrete periods, whereas the Schumpeterian endogenous analysis led to the notion of recurring cycles. Put differently, Hansen and Keynes essentially divorced secular from cyclical phenomena, Schumpeter and Kondratieff combined them. Still, lines could blur. David McCord Wright, for example, wondered in the late 1940s whether "adventitious external circumstances" might "somewhat warp the basic movement" of "a fundamental mechanically-recurring process."[35] This was a notion that could perhaps be used to fuse Schumpeter's endogenous Kondratieff and exogenous New Deal intervention explanations of the nature of the Great Depression. William Fellner similarly wondered in 1949 "where the line will have to be drawn in the future between 'the process' and external factors. We may run into a 'Kondratieff' the innovations of which will emanate mainly from the military sector. . . . Will this bring an entirely different pattern or just a different phase?"[36] This question certainly had implications as to the basic nature of the long post–World War II boom, as recognized in its prewar stage by analyst Oscar L. Altman when he observed that rearmament could be viewed "as an innovation" comparable with a "new industry" in its stimulus to investment.[37]

As contrasted with Keynes, Schumpeter failed to develop a school coming out of the 1930s. If Keynes's economics was "depression economics," as Schumpeter alleged, Schumpeter's economics failed to gain a wider following in part because it was not depression economics in that Schumpeter advanced no solution to the great crisis of the decade except to await the morrow. This was long-run economics with a vengeance, the sort of attitude that Keynes castigated in *The General Theory*. Schumpeter's counsel of inaction, as contrasted with Keynes's summons to action, helped to account for the disappointing lack of impact of Schumpeter's 1939 magnum opus *Business Cycles* as contrasted with the extraordinary impact of Keynes's *General Theory*.[38] Further, Schumpeter insisted that new public policies, in part based on Keynesianism, were delaying recovery. Critics held that it was precisely those policies that were providing the climate and basis for revival. Rather than suffer waiting for a "natural" recovery, it was held, recovery could now be stimulated by government. Public policy could provide a sense of security and a level of stability highly conducive to entrepreneurial initiative, innovation, and investment. Indeed, using Schumpeterian concepts and terminology, the new public policy of governmental intervention could be seen as an organizational "innovation" providing a modern basis for a new wave of economic growth. The whole nature of the postwar boom was at issue here. To Schumpeterians, it would be seen as evidence of the regenerative power of the economic process, the "capitalist engine," itself. But to postwar Keynesians, it would be seen in good measure as a product of the new environment created by new public policies. Now the "public sector" had become, in this latter analysis, a vital ingredient in modern economic growth or, in Hansenian terms, a new exogenous source of growth and prosperity.[39]

Looking back on the 1930s from the vantage point of the 1970s, Gerhard Mensch, a leading student of Schumpeterian economics, noted that Schumpeter had rejected Hansenian secular stagnation theory in toto, giving inadequate attention to the theory as "the best explanation" for sectors of the economy that then impacted on the "macrosystem." Hansen's theory was valid, he held, in that simultaneous stagnation in "several branches" of the economy became "visible on the macroeconomic level."[40] This sectoral version of secular stagnation was consistent with Hansen's stress on the role of great industries and with Schumpeter's own argument that innovative new industries led to surges of economic growth and their decline led to depression.[41] In the postwar era, however, short-run Keynesians believed that they had found the formula for stable economic growth in measures affecting aggregate demand levels of the economy. The long postwar boom, stretching over a quarter century after World War II's end, placed long-run economics in eclipse despite elements of persistence. Not until the 1970s would the secular theories of the 1930s be widely revived and adapted to analysis of the nation's reemergent secular economic problems.

9.
Eclipse in the
Postwar Boom

Theories of the Great Depression that were rooted in secular analysis seemed of little relevance or validity once the allegedly secular depression became an apparently secular boom. As the postwar era stretched forward, as the concerns of the 1940s gave way to greater confidence and even complacency in the 1950s and 1960s, there was a strong inclination to dismiss long-run theories of the 1930s as overgeneralizations from an exceedingly narrow and episodic empirical base. What meant administered prices in a time that was simultaneously one of great corporations and great boom? Why focus on chronic stagnation in a period of unprecedented growth? In retrospect, of course, the Great Boom could be seen as fleeting, albeit over a quarter century in duration. As it dissipated during the 1970s, questions were raised as to its genuineness and "normality." But over the course of the 1950s and 1960s, it certainly seemed substantial enough, and critical long-run theories seemed more a rearguard than a vanguard expression. Keynes had died in 1946 and Schumpeter in 1950. Means and Hansen both remained active but in roles less central and influential than those they enjoyed earlier. Nor was either unaffected by the dominant tenor of the boom era.

The boom clearly eclipsed the Means emphasis on the importance of corporate revolution or administered prices. Notions of an epochal corporate revolution or of a vast distortion by administered prices were often dismissed or ignored. Studies appeared purporting to show that concentration was not as great as had been believed or, at any rate, that it was not increasing significantly. New forms of competition, it was held, required even the largest corporations to adjust to market demands. Administered prices, far from requiring a whole new macrotheory, were dismissed as "imperfections," exceptions to the rule of orthodox theory. Finally, Keynesianism, building on its triumph over institutionalist emphases in the late New Deal, provided the coup de grace. Institutionalist analysis, it was believed, was rendered obsolete by Keynesian theory, and corporate price administration was deemed relatively insignificant in a fiscally induced positive macroeconomic environment.[1]

Gardiner Means, associated through most of the 1940s and 1950s with the Committee for Economic Development and then more briefly with the Fund for the Republic, did not during this period change his mind about the nature or secular underpinnings of the Great Depression. The depression had shown that the market mechanism was no longer self-correcting in the face of declining demand. The wartime increase in demand, in Means's analysis, had essentially removed the disparity between market and administered prices that had greatly widened after 1929, leading to depression. Now, during the war, a reversal of the post-1929 pattern occurred and a return to relative balance was achieved. Administered prices remained essentially stable while employment and production in administered price industries increased; market prices, under conditions of increased demand, rose to the levels of administered prices.[2] In 1946 Means, observing a postwar backlog of demand for goods, saw "big differences" between the present and the era that ushered in the Great Depression. A "really bad" depression would not now be forthcoming under conditions of abundant demand.[3]

Means further held that in the wake of the experience of the Great Depression, government had essentially assumed the responsibility for assuring adequate aggregate demand. With demand adequate, there could be no unraveling as a result of market maladjustment as in the disastrous period after 1929; a rough balance between administered and market prices would be maintained. With demand stability, there would be no drastic fall in market prices to generate real buying power in an economy whose administered sector reduced production and employment instead. Government assurance of adequate demand now replaced the flawed market mechanism as the facilitator of economic stability.[4] Rather than rely on the market mechanism, Means declared in 1963, "we now turn to fiscal and monetary policy, and this is the great accomplishment of the last 30 years."[5] Means's conclusion here was not unlike that of postwar Keynesians: government assurance of adequate demand could prevent depression. Where Means differed with postwar Keynesians was in his primary reliance on monetary rather than fiscal policy. Monetary policy could directly increase demand via the money supply. Fiscal policy, although it had its uses—in stimulating construction, for example—was based, in Means's analysis, on Keynes's invalid dismissal of monetary policy's effectiveness and further threatened chronic budget deficits and inflation in a time of strong consumer demand.[6]

Means continued to argue that Keynes's general theory was not based on institutional rigidity, despite hints to the contrary, but was designed to be equally applicable in both demand-sensitive and demand-insensitive price contexts. However, Means also detected changes in Keynesianism as it was interpreted and understood over the course of the 1940s, changes with significant theoretical and policy implications in his view. These changes constituted what he called "neo-Keynesianism." Rather than a theory based on the inefficacy of interest rates, as with Keynes, the premise behind neo-Keynesianism was price or wage insensitivity, of which Keynes, of course, was aware but which he did not make an explicit part of his theory. Neo-Keynesianism's emergence grounded on a form of institutional rigidity, Means believed, vindicated his own judgment that Keynes's theory could not explain the Great Depression without reference to rigid prices. But in Means's view, Keynesian policy conclusions, including the rejection of monetary policy, were based on Keynes's original theory rather than on the implications of neo-Keynesianism, which, if worked out, would suggest the efficacy of monetary policy as a way of increasing aggregate demand so as to offset the effects of institutional rigidity. Neo-Keynesianism thus developed would support not only monetary policy as a way of assuring aggregate demand but also, Means believed, his institutional rigidity theory of depression. What was now needed, Means concluded, was a fully explicit recognition of the role of institutional rigidity that was lacking in Keynes's theory and a readjustment of policy emphases in accordance with the implications of neo-Keynesianism.[7]

In the climate of the wartime and postwar boom, then, Means continued to espouse and defend his theory of the Great Depression and to challenge and refute Keynes's alternative explanation. Here there was continuity with the prewar era, although Means lacked the receptive audience of the earlier period. What Means did not bring into the new period was a concept of structural planning, the centerpiece of his New Deal Era policy advocacy. At that time, Means saw monetary policy as a supplement to structural planning. Now, however, structural planning—the remedial programmatic counterpart of Means's Great Depression structural theory—was abandoned. Means thus maintained his structurally based theory of depression but not his structural planning solution. He still saw his concepts of corporate revolution and administered prices as posing a fundamental challenge to orthodox theory, but he now linked them to nonstructural monetary and fiscal policy solutions rather than to structural planning under public auspices to deal directly with structural maladjustments. The forties decade was not hospitable to structural planning schemes, nor was the fiscal policy–oriented climate of the CED. He was, Means declared in 1943, "interested in . . . avoiding any necessity for . . . Governmental intervention in direct operating policies" such as price and production determination.[8] Although "automatic market mechanisms" could not be relied on to provide full employment, he wrote in 1945, this did "not mean direct governmental control over business." He did not agree that "specific controls" in administered price industries were necessary; assurance of adequate demand would mean maintenance and expansion of production and employment in such industries. Thus Means saw a need for "more governmental responsibility and action than we had in the 20's," not "drastic measures" but essentially "the minimum governmental action . . . needed." He expected "Monetary Policy to play a major role, Fiscal Policy a supporting role, and direct controls only a minor role."[9] Means here found himself in much the same position as his old rival, Alvin Hansen. Hansen had argued that the application of fiscal policy would provide an environment that would limit or negate the exercise of administered pricing with drastic macroeconomic consequences. Means was now saying much the same thing, albeit with an emphasis on monetary rather than fiscal policy. It would take a surge of what Means deemed a new form of inflation to bring him back to a structural remedy.

Means concentrated his energies in the 1940s on an abortive project, a planned though not published book titled "A Monetary Theory of Employment." In the manuscript Means outlined his critique of Keynes from a monetary perspective and called for an increased reliance on monetary policy.[10] "I have in almost complete manuscript," he announced in 1946, a book-length study repudiating Keynesian theory and providing a monetary alternative, but the manuscript was rejected by Macmillan in 1947.[11] A critique of the work took Means to task for concentrating on the monetary question at the expense of his earlier structural emphases. The unnamed critic found "several excursions from the main line which lead the reader to wonder just what the theme or central thread is," in particular "the excursion into insensitive price practices." This excursion suggested that the author "was performing the needed service of demonstrating the implications of insensitive prices for the general theory of employment." Although "wonderfully well done," these excursions were "largely outside his main thesis, and . . . his main thesis is the weaker aspect of the manuscript." This led "to the question whether his emphasis" was not "misplaced. As a book highlighting very important factors given too little attention in Keynesian economics," such as price insensitivity, "it would be more useful than in its present form."[12] It was a telling critique, suggesting that when Means departed from his structural focus for a monetary one, his contribution was significantly less impressive. But Means may not have been thoroughly impressed. He cheerfully announced to Adolf A. Berle in 1962 that his "money book has been simmering on the fire for some years and is just about ready to sugar-off."[13]

Secular theories associated with Keynes, Hansen, and Schumpeter also faded away in the boom. As Hyman Minsky put it in 1975, the economic problems of the "postwar decades were not of the type contemplated by Keynes in *The General Theory*." If over three decades, Minsky continued, there occurred nothing resembling a severe depression, then explanations attributing such depression to policy errors or to "transitory institutional flaws which have since been corrected" could gain credence. "This is what took place as the forties, fifties, and sixties spun their tales of . . . apparent economic success."[14] In this setting concern for the long run gave way to a focus on the short run. Insofar as a long-run focus remained, attention was largely directed to the "economic development" problems of preindustrial societies, and controversy swirled around books such as W. W. Rostow's *Stages of Economic Growth*. For the United States the cyclical or short run once again took center stage with the belief that only minor adjustments were needed to deal with patches of instability in a long-run context that was assumed free of major disruptions. Keynesianism increasingly became a short-run formula designed to avoid cyclical instability. Alvin Hansen, as the nation's leading proponent of secular stagnation theory, was widely considered passé in that respect.

The rejection of secular stagnation theory during the boom was very widespread. "The secular stagnation thesis became not only unfashionable," William Guthrie and Vincent J. Tarascio noted in 1992, "but even a potential source of embarrassment to mainstream Keynesians."[15] To critics, the postwar boom clearly disproved the thesis. Technological advances and industrial innovation propelled economic growth. A birthrate upsurge proved 1930s hypotheses of a stable or declining population erroneous. The stagnationists, it was now held, had been "myopic," overgeneralizing from a limited time frame. Short-run, rather than long-run, factors best explained the sudden crisis of the Great Depression. Short-run policies, accordingly, were vital. A short-run version of Keynesianism geared to aggregate demand took hold in this context, displacing secular stagnation theory's public investment version.[16]

Joseph Schumpeter, as a critic of secular stagnation theory, could feel vindicated by the onset of the postwar boom. In 1945 he declared it "natural" that many would have embraced secular stagnationist theory during the depressed thirties, but he found it hard to understand how that theory could still retain adherents with "prodigious industrial development" now on the horizon.[17] He worried about how fear of collapse might dampen postwar growth, expressing concern in 1949 that "a temporary sharp recession" might result from the belief "that the great flop of capitalist enterprise has . . . arrived or is at least incessantly threatening." Nonetheless, he predicted, "barring political disturbances, a prolonged spell of preponderating prosperities," a "Kondratieff recovery and . . . a Kondratieff prosperity are before us."[18] That prosperity—the boom that stretched into the early 1970s—was at the time, of course, not widely considered a "Kondratieff." The Kondratieff long wave theory and Schumpeter's application of it were also generally rejected or ignored during the boom decades.[19]

The strand of economic thought that emerged triumphant during the postwar boom was short-run Keynesianism, what Joan Robinson was to refer to contemptuously as "bastard Keynesianism," what Paul Samuelson dubbed the "neoclassical synthesis," and what could also perhaps be called demand management Keynesianism. The cyclical emphasis replaced the secular. Government now was to compensate for cyclical fluctuations rather than for secular deficiencies. Automatic "stabilizers" such as unemployment compensation would function in a contracyclical fashion. Government was to provide a "steering wheel," as Abba Lerner put it, to steady the economy, rather than an engine, as the secular stagnationist

Hansen would have it, to help energize and propel it.[20] The assumption was that if government assured sufficient aggregate demand, a satisfactory micro- and macroeconomic performance would follow. Market mechanism rigidity was deemed an "imperfection," a "special case," that need not be significantly disruptive given proper demand management; and the market mechanism itself would effectively handle the task of allocation of resources in a climate of sufficient demand.[21] Accordingly, aggregate growth per se was now emphasized in contrast with Hansen's stress on the public improvements path to growth. Further, what Hansen called consumption-based "induced" investment was emphasized at the expense of "autonomous" investment stimulated by exogenous forces. Government assurance of adequate demand, it was held, would greatly induce investment, providing steady economic growth, even with a diminution of historic exogenous stimuli.[22]

Alvin H. Hansen both developed secular stagnation theory and midwifed American Keynesianism. His secular stagnation thesis was widely rejected after 1945, but a version of American Keynesianism swept the field. To what extent did Hansen deserve the credit or, in the view of later critics, the blame for short-run Keynesianism? There was, some commentators on Hansen's early postwar work suggested, a tendency on his part now to downplay differences and stress similarities between the 1930s and previous periods of secular stagnation.[23] Hansen also focused anew on the short-run cycle and the need for a compensatory program to combat a sharp, immediate downturn in the economy.[24] In a way perhaps comparable with Hansen's, in his 1945 *Full Employment in a Free Society*, William Beveridge, along with a central focus on public investment, devoted much attention to the need for government to assure adequate aggregate demand, citing Hansen's work in the process.[25]

In the postwar period, Hansen did indeed stress the need for government to ensure adequate demand. This was particularly true as postwar prosperity progressed in the 1950s. The Great Depression, he now wrote, had brought forth new policies designed to keep demand afloat in order to arrest a downward movement of the economy. The "consumption base" had been broadened and stabilized, providing a strengthened "intensive" element in the economy in the face of weakened "extensive" factors, which contributed to the "miracle" of postwar prosperity. It offered a positive environment for entrepreneurial initiative and private investment. It helped to stimulate technological advance. It also "stimulated population growth."[26] Clearly, although the earlier Hansen had strongly stressed the investment base of economic growth, this later Hansen gave an increasing role to aggregate demand. Hansen now agreed that aggregate demand could be a primary source of investment—and of technological advance and population expansion, earlier conceived as essentially primary exogenous stimuli to investment and growth. Richard A. Musgrave, in looking back, concluded that "Hansen, the pragmatist"—and Hansen, the synthesizer, one might add—"welcomed the neoclassical synthesis."[27]

Others drew the same conclusion, viewing Hansen as a formulator, along with J. R. Hicks and Paul Samuelson, of neoclassical Keynesianism, often in a vein far more critical than that of Musgrave.[28] John H. Hotson, for example, wrote of the efforts of Hansen, Hicks, and Samuelson "to stuff Keynes back into the neoclassical paradigm," holding that they were "quick to make pieces of Keynes' analysis their own," while "at a deeper level his vision was wholly alien and repugnant to them."[29] They substituted neoclassical synthesis Keynesianism for Keynes's own, and this became the widely accepted version.[30] What was Keynes's own? Hotson's view of true versus bastard Keynesianism could not have been more Hansenian: "As long as there are sufficient profitable investment outlets thrown up by . . . expansion into new lands, . . . rising population and invention—as was the case during much of the 19th century—investment will be sufficient." If such investment outlets dried up, however, the economy could be threatened by "secular depression."[31] How could such a Hansenian version of Keynesianism be the true interpretation from which the neoclassical Hansen allegedly seduced Keynes's progeny?

In his postwar analysis, Hansen alluded to J. R. Hicks's "brilliant" 1937 "Mr. Keynes and the Classics," from which the neoclassical synthesis in part derived. In his 1953 *Guide to Keynes*, Hansen averred that "long-run adjustment processes" were now partly a matter of conscious policy and partly "automatic" and that in this respect "it may be possible, in a measure, to find a reconciliation between Keynesian and neoclassical economics."[32] This, along with his general espousal of the aggregate demand approach of short-run Keynesianism, suggested a degree of conversion on Hansen's part. What had occurred, however, was by no means a sharp shift or reversal. Much of what the secular stagnationist Hansen had argued before 1945, the postwar Hansen continued to argue through the remainder of his long career. Where Hansen shifted somewhat was in the degree of attention he gave before and after the war to the roles of investment and demand. Whereas his prewar analysis, flowing from Continental theory, heavily stressed the primary role of investment, his postwar analysis, while by no means subordinating investment, gave enhanced play to the causal and stimulative impact of increased demand.

In a 1941 letter to Mordecai Ezekiel, Hansen had written: "From your proposition . . . investment is a function of income. But according to Keynes, it is quite the opposite. Income is a function of investment."[33] In this earlier period, Hansen, in keeping with the Continental school, stressed the role of "autonomous" investment—that is, investment stimulated by such exogenous forces as geographic expansion, population growth, and technological advance—as the key to economic growth. Now, in the postwar period, this position was balanced with an increased emphasis on "induced" investment, such as that stimulated by greater aggregate demand, which earlier had been given relatively short shrift, as in Hansen's contemporary analysis of the 1937–38 recession. This emphasis on induced investment was consonant with the thrust of short-run Keynesianism.[34] Hence Hansen could write in 1957 that "investment . . . is a consequence, no less than a cause, of a high and growing national income."[35] Here was a shift of degree and even of kind, but one that was characteristic of Hansen's ability to adapt and to synthesize. The postwar Hansen did not displace the secular Hansen; one was added to the other. Put differently, Hansen did not so much change his Keynesianism after the war as he broadened and diversified it. Secular stagnation theory did not disappear but naturally received less attention in a period of buoyant prosperity. The aggregate demand emphasis of short-run Keynesianism did not appear in place of secular stagnation theory but naturally received more emphasis during a period of consumption-oriented, long-run boom.

Moreover, the secular stagnationist Hansen did not spring wholly from his conversion to Keynesianism; there had been the earlier, immense influence on Hansen of the exogenous-based, investment-oriented Continental school. The post-1937 Hansen was a synthesis of Continental and Keynesian theory, and the Continental element always remained strong and in some ways controlling. That is, Hansen gave increasing attention to Keynesian demand management in the postwar period, but as an early adherent of Continental theory and as a secular as opposed to a short-run Keynesian, the investment element remained consistently strong. Hansen made it clear in 1947, for example, that his secular stagnation theory was related entirely to the deficiency of investment outlets and not to any relationship between savings and consumption.[36] He continued in the postwar era to have his own long-run concerns apart from any espousal of elements of short-run Keynesianism. Hansen's whole original emphasis on investment, coming not from Keynes but from the Continental school, could thus withstand and transcend postwar acceptance of short-run Keynesian aggregate demand policies as part of a larger vision. Finally, one may not be unduly harsh toward Hansen in noting that after 1945, secular stagnationism was largely discredited in the minds of most economists. Hansen in this respect faced severe criticism and even ridicule from among his peers and a diminished reputation. But Keynesianism in its short-run form was increasingly ascendant in economists' minds, and Hansen's identification with American Keynesianism as its pioneer advocate and his role as mentor of many influential young Keynesians in the United States was a counteracting source of prestige. Hence Hansen as a neoclassical synthesizer, expositor, and disseminator of Keynesianism remained a figure of great authority, but at the expense of the bolder and more original secular stagnationist Hansen.

The emphases of short-run Keynesianism reached an apogee during the "fine tuning" of the 1960s. A future of steady economic growth was in hand, it was believed, if only the correct macroeconomic policies were followed. But there remained those who had doubts as to the adequacy of postwar economic policy, the benign nature of corporate concentration and power, and the genuineness of postwar stability and prosperity—doubts which flickered during flurries of inflation and worries over "semi-stagnation" during the late fifties and which then came more fully to the fore as the postwar boom dissipated in the "stagflation" of the 1970s.

10.
Persistence in
the Postwar Boom

n the heady climate of postwar prosperity, one problem through which a perspective more critical of the large corporation could again emerge was that of inflation or, more precise, what some analysts considered a new form of inflation. An inflationary spurt in the latter half of the fifties led to questioning of what had by this time become neoclassical Keynesian orthodoxy. This inflation, occurring even during recession, was not, it seemed, a result of the proverbial too much money chasing too few goods. Attributed by some to the ability of large corporations to administer and hence to raise prices in time of recession, this inflation appeared to account for what in neoclassical Keynesianism terms was an anomaly: simultaneous recession and inflation. The exclusion of administered prices and imperfect competition from Keynes's original theory led to what critics considered the inability of now-orthodox

Keynesianism to explain this aspect of postwar economic behavior. The alternative structural explanation of inflation in turn reopened the door to proposed structural solutions.[1]

The appearance of inflation in the later fifties led to the reemergence of Gardiner Means as an influential voice in economic analysis and public policy advocacy. Relatively quiet for over a decade, given Keynesianism's triumph over his own depression analysis, postwar prosperity, and the loss of interest in structural planning, Means and his concepts of corporate revolution and administered prices reappeared in the context of the controversy over the "new" inflation. Administered price theory was now used to explain the tendency of prices to rise in the face of recession, a condition not accounted for by nonstructural theories or curable by conventional fiscal or monetary policy. The reemergence of Means was facilitated by hearings held by a United States Senate subcommittee chaired by Estes Kefauver with key staff guidance from Means disciple John Blair. Blair persuaded Kefauver to hold hearings on administered prices, the first of which occurred in 1957, and invited Means to testify. So began Means's reinvigorated career, with the use of concepts fashioned in the thirties, as a chief analyst of the impact of the large corporation and administered prices on the inflationary process.[2] As John Blair put it, "Means's concepts regularly have been interred, only to rise, phoenix-like, when prices begin to behave in a manner inexplicable under competitive theory."[3]

As Means suggested from 1957 on, "administrative inflation," as he called it, was a new phenomenon. It could not be found "anywhere in our history of prices." Excess demand provided the traditional context and source of inflation, but the new inflation could occur even under conditions of diminished demand. It reflected the growth of a modern industrial economy with powerful corporations and the ability of those corporations to set, maintain, and raise prices under circumstances heretofore not linked to inflation in either practice or theory.[4] Further, Means held, Keynesianism did not apply. Designed to explain unemployment, Keynesian theory was "ineffective for studying problems of inflation."[5] Keynes had bested Means in the battle for influence over explanations of the Great Depression, but Means was here making a comeback and a counterattack with the emergence of an administrative inflation apparently outside the realm of Keynes's allegedly "general" theory but explainable by Means's own depression-generated analysis.

As a response and solution to administrative inflation, Means rejected as inapplicable both Keynesian fiscal policy and monetary policy. These provided remedies for traditional inflation based on excess demand, but not for the new inflation grounded on administrative power. The use of monetary restraint, for example, to counter this form of inflation led only to recession, because an inflation that "did not arise from excess demand . . . could not be controlled by contracting demand." The solution instead required "nonmonetary measures."[6] By nonmonetary measures Means meant institutional or structural reform—a degree of planning. Just as he reached back to the thirties for concepts to explain administrative inflation, he reached back to the New Deal decade for a structural solution. Administrative inflation, having revived the concept of price administration, also revived Means's interest in structural economic planning. Put more broadly, as short-run orthodox Keynesianism began to be questioned—to a very limited degree when administrative inflation was first observed and then to a far greater degree in the seventies—structural planning, earlier swept aside by Keynesianism, reappeared for consideration and advocacy. Commenting on Means in 1962, Bernard Nossiter noted that for "corporate behavior . . . to reflect . . . desirable goals, . . . new institutional arrangements" were needed.[7]

Means, in the wake of the appearance of administrative inflation, called for legislation placing large corporations in a "new legal category" founded on the concept that the "public interest" required that they be operated not primarily to make "profits but for the purpose of using the available resources of manpower and capital and technology to produce useful goods."[8] Here was a Veblenesque perspective and a harkening back to 1932's *Modern Corporation and Private Property*. To make corporate power "serve the public interest," he added, "an effective system of economic . . . planning," a "mechanism . . . to guide the use of resources," was needed.[9] Such planning would be "advisory" and would bring together "experts" from business, labor, academia, government, and consumers groups to fashion plans to channel corporate power in desirable directions. Again, Means recalled the thirties: "If we had retained the National Resources Planning Board . . . we should today be in a position to discuss . . . devices for bringing performance into conformity with guidelines established by the planning process. . . . But we let the Resources Board die."[10]

Given the splash created by his concept of administrative inflation and the recognition he was again receiving over two decades after *Industrial Prices* appeared, Means took to his pen once more in a way not seen since the productive thirties. The frustrations of the forties had now at least partially passed. In 1962 a collection of essays and papers titled *The Corporate Revolution in America* appeared, as did a comprehensive study of administered steel prices and their inflationary impact on the economy, which was titled *Pricing Power and the Public Interest.* Means was well aware of the continuities in his approach. Of the latter book he wrote, in words that applied to the former as well, that it brought together concepts that he had "introduced into economic theory more than twenty-five years ago." Or as a reviewer of *Pricing Power and the Public Interest* put it, Means here provided "a synthesis of his two favorite themes": the role of the large corporation and the impact of administered prices.[11] A correspondence with his old associate and collaborator Adolf A. Berle highlighted the return of Gardiner C. Means, as the latter energetically headed into the last quarter century of his long and productive life. *Pricing Power and the Public Interest*'s appearance coincided with the dramatic confrontation between President John F. Kennedy and the chairman of the United States Steel Corporation, Roger Blough, over steel price increases. As Means wrote to Berle, "The struggle between Kennedy and Blough—an epic struggle with some truly brilliant scenes," had "certainly made the book timely." He predicted that there would be further "discussion of laissez-faire vs government intervention in . . . concentrated . . . industry" in regard to the "problem of administrative inflation." As a result there was a need to "turn to the problems of economic planning with gusto." The issue, Means concluded, was "fundamental. . . . It was you who laid down the real issue in the *Modern Corporation* when you wrote . . . about the . . . struggle between state and corporation in prospect."[12] Congratulating Means on *Pricing Power and the Public Interest*'s positive reception, Berle noted that their thinking was "back on the old trail again—after having been derailed for awhile." Opponents "could derail the thinking—but not the facts which are now asserting themselves." Berle may have had antitrusters ("the Frankfurter boys") in mind here.[13] But reference could more aptly have been made to the far more importantly influential Keynesians.

The development of administrative inflation gave Means an opportunity once again to apply concepts he had originated during the Great Depression and New Deal Era. As long as postwar prosperity remained buoyant, as long as public policy boosted aggregate demand so that administered prices could not turn a demand deficiency into a severe depression, there was a lack of interest in Means's seemingly dated and depression-bound 1930s concepts. The new inflation was no Great Depression, but it was a worrisome concern amid prosperity, and it gave Means's concepts a new application and renewed life. Means's secular-based analyses were now back into play; the problem was viewed as structural—the power of large corporations to administer prices—and the solution was structural—some form of planning. Moreover, Means's

Keynesian nemesis did not apply. Institutional factors could explain the new inflation in contrast to anything emanating from Keynes or his followers in either theory or public policy. Hence the development of administrative inflation paved the way for a return of an institutionally or structurally based analysis, a reconsideration of structural policy solutions, and a focus on flaws and lacunae in Keynesian theory and practice.

The spurt of the later fifties became a central problem and crisis of the seventies, and Means, still going strong, remained both a great influence on and a major participant in the analysis and proposed treatment of inflation in that decade. In addition to Means, there were other notable intellectual sources on whom 1970s economists drew in this regard and in related areas, most particularly Michal Kalecki, a Pole who had spent some of the more productive years of his life in Great Britain. Relatively unhonored in his own time, Kalecki, in the view of some, independently reached "Keynesian" conclusions in the 1930s and, moreover, went beyond Keynes by incorporating imperfect competition into his analysis. He also linked corporate concentration to investment movements more directly than did Means, which helped explain his later influence. One channel of Kalecki's later impact came by way of a 1952 study that he suggested be undertaken, *Maturity and Stagnation in American Capitalism*, by Josef Steindl, an Austrian living in Great Britain.[14]

Reflecting in part his and Kalecki's Marxist backgrounds, Steindl provided an endogenous, structural rather than exogenous, environmental theory of secular stagnation. His was "an endogenous theory of long-run economic development," he wrote, based on the transition to a larger "oligopolistic pattern in the total economy." The growth of oligopoly had a restrictive impact on investment, he held, thus providing the link between imperfect competition theory and investment theory, going beyond the "familiar characteristic" of "price rigidity." *Maturity and Stagnation* included an assault on Hansen's exogenously based rival theory of stagnation. Steindl viewed stagnation as "inherent in the nature of capitalism" under the impact of oligopoly and hence not due to exogenous factors such as technological or demographic change. Technological advance, for example, he argued, occurred because it was called forth by investment and not vice versa. Technological change accompanied "the process of investment like a shadow"; it did not act on investment "as a propelling force." Reliance on exogenous factors, in Steindl's analysis, meant reliance on "accidental" factors; Hansen's theory did not make clear whether maturity was temporary or permanent. To Steindl maturity was a necessary consequence of the unfolding of internal capitalist development.[15] Steindl's theory had some obvious affinities with others: a common focus on stagnation with Hansen, a stress on corporate power and structure with Means, and an endogenous base with Schumpeter. *Maturity and Stagnation*, appearing as the postwar boom seemingly was on its way to becoming permanent, was largely ignored, given what was seen as its outdated nature.[16] But it developed influence as the postwar boom petered out in the 1970s and thereby provided a source of continuity between 1930s and 1970s concerns over stagnation and structure, as well as a conduit for the Kaleckian influence, which was to emerge with vigor in the development of post-Keynesianism in the 1970s and 1980s.

As atypical of trends in economics as Steindl's work was in 1952, it did fit the pattern of the postwar rejection of Hansenian secular stagnation theory. Others, however, although a distinct minority in terms of overall economic opinion, remained convinced of the essential validity of the theory, holding that postwar prosperity, like that of the 1920s in some respects, was based at least in part on temporary or "accidental" factors—that special conditions of the postwar period had averted a lapse into stagnation. Defense spending, the European recovery program, and the pent-up postwar demand for consumer goods had kept the economy afloat, despite an underlying tendency toward stagnation. Defense spending, in particular, provided a huge governmental impetus to the private economy. This view, it was held, vindicated that of the secular stagnationist Hansen. Hansen, after all, had argued that massive public spending would be the essential remedy for stagnation, and this was precisely what the postwar period had brought. True, it was not the kind of public spending for public improvements that Hansen had envisaged, but it was public spending of a massive kind nonetheless, which was the key point. Also true, population growth rebounded enormously, with the baby boom beginning in the 1940s, which Hansen did not foresee. But this development, too, was seen to vindicate Hansen's thesis. Hansen had conceived of population growth and decline as a basic stimulus or depressant of investment and expansion. For population growth now to be associated with an economic boom was consistent with and supportive of Hansen's position.[17]

Additionally, there were those who argued that the sluggishness of the economy in the latter part of the 1950s, following a slowing down of the thrust of some of the more immediate postwar economic stimuli, also suggested the existence of an underlying stagnationist pull. Here was an economy fortified by enormous public spending, and still there remained a tendency to sputter.[18] In the context of the postwar era, economist Daniel

Hamberg added, stagnation did "not necessarily imply the absence of growth." Fiscal policy now kept downturns mild, but without it, "stagnation would probably take the form of deep and prolonged depressions and upswings that persistently fell short of full capacity and full employment growth."[19] Here was a Hansenian-based idea that decades later was dubbed "contained depression"—the notion that sluggishness did not become stagnation because of new fiscal policies but also the suggestion that the new fiscal policies as undertaken thus far were not enough to ensure a more fully vigorous level of growth.

Alvin Hansen, although not at the peak of the influence and prestige gained at the time when his secular analysis had its greatest impact, remained a significant figure in the postwar era as the pioneer American Keynesian. But he was also more than that, for he still retained much of his advocacy of the long-run economic theories and policies he had developed during the late thirties and the war years. As earlier, Hansen continued to stress the role of exogenous forces in accounting for investment and economic growth, and he continued to view these forces as characteristically proceeding in spurts that gave a correspondingly irregular pattern to modern economic development. Such dynamic factors, he argued, not mere "fluctuations," formed the core of economic analysis. Underemployment equilibrium, flowing from the exhaustion of dynamic exogenous factors, could not be reversed through the functioning of mechanical market phenomena or by monetary policy in the form of lower interest rates. Psychological factors, he agreed, could lead to a prolonged period of inadequate investment, but his overwhelming emphasis remained on "hard" or "real" factors in accounting for economic decline, depression, and stagnation, as learned from the Continental school.[20] As America's senior expositor and interpreter of Keynes, Hansen continued to note Keynes's own lack of rooting in the Continental school. Keynes, he wrote, "had only the foggiest idea of what had been going on for thirty years on the Continent"; as others had related, Hansen went on, "Englishmen read nothing not printed in England and not even that—Perhaps this is why they have proved themselves to be truly creative thinkers."[21] This last comment was perhaps a wistful one for Hansen, steeped as he was in Continental theory and now influential largely as the expositor of Keynes rather than as the originator of his own systematic theory of secular stagnation.

Applying his theoretical concepts to the postwar American economy and to public policy, Hansen fully anticipated the early stages of the postwar boom, given the country's pent-up demand for consumer goods. But he also warned of an eventual collapse unless checked by vigorous fiscal policy, while seeing in cold war defense spending a possible indefinite off-set to stagnation.[22] The ongoing role of that spending, he insisted, belied those who "blandly" assumed that the postwar boom had disproved the secular stagnation thesis.[23] In fact, Hansen saw the postwar boom as combining "spontaneous forces" and conscious policy elements, temporary and more durable supports. He gave greater emphasis to one set of forces or another at different times, not unlike his earlier treatment of the 1920s. Hence in some analyses he stressed "natural" forces and "spontaneous" factors, such as technological advance, an upsurge in population growth, and the development of a mass consumer market. Early postwar prosperity was "natural," having "little to do with . . . Keynesian economics," for "spontaneous forces, not government intervention, held the stage." But here Hansen included Korean War and cold war spending as "spontaneous forces."[24] It was not difficult in other analyses, therefore, for Hansen to warn of insecure foundations for a prosperity reliant in part on defense spending and temporary postwar stimuli, to deny that it was predominantly "natural," and to hold that fiscal policy—the "Keynesian remedy for . . . stagnation"—was essential to prosperity's maintenance and to future sustained growth.[25]

As to more durable factors, Hansen had never posited an exhaustion of technological advance. Indeed, going back to 1942 he saw "great technological developments . . . emerging from the war," of such importance "as to provide the basis for a substantial private investment boom."[26] He was surprised by the population upsurge; still, he saw in it justification rather than refutation of his earlier views, for population growth was "favorable to investment." This, he added, was "the Keynesian view of population growth," though others might have characterized it as even more distinctively Hansenian. Sharply "in contrast with the attitude taken by many economists in the 1930s," he wrote, it was now generally agreed that population growth provided an economic stimulus. But even the baby boom, he emphasized, was "relatively small" compared with the nineteenth-century rate of expansion; a similar increase would have been much larger in absolute terms than the current growth, and a correspondingly equivalent geographic expansion would be several times the size of the North American continent.[27]

Hansen argued that government would have to play a larger role to promote future growth, especially as the "spontaneous forces" that helped boost the first decade of postwar prosperity began in some measure to peter out. The built-in stabilizers or cushions, while undoubtedly valuable, were nonetheless not sufficient in Hansen's view.[28] Beginning in the mid-fifties, Hansen held, a stagnationist drag was evident in the economy. Hansen now characterized sluggish growth as "semistagnation" or "high-level stagnation." Such stagnation, if unattended, would likely continue, he believed, for cyclical stability did not guarantee dynamic growth. Hence government would have to function not merely as the driver at the "cyclical steering wheel" but also as the source of "a growing share of the motive power" to propel the economy.[29] True, Hansen acknowledged, new spontaneous forces might emerge, but to be "masters of our fate we can't sit around waiting for 'prosperity just around the corner.'"[30] Conscious policy was needed to promote secular growth.

Although Hansen gave some ground in the postwar period to short-run Keynesianism's emphasis on aggregate demand and its impact on induced investment, he did not relinquish his Continental-based focus on the necessity of autonomous investment flowing from exogenous stimuli to economic growth.[31] In a 1948 letter to Evsey Domar, for example, Hansen disputed the notion that an assured rise in national income would itself generate sufficient investment to achieve desired growth. This undervalued, he held, the essential role of autonomous investment based on exogenous stimuli such as technological and population expansion.[32] Given this emphasis and his view of the social desirability of public investment, Hansen was by no means fully pleased, whatever contributions or concessions he had made to short-run Keynesianism, with the consumer goods emphasis of the postwar boom or with the policy manifestations of Keynesianism in the early 1960s by way of tax reduction. The proper policy, "in terms of social priorities," he argued, would have been a program of massive public investment to address social needs rather than the "politically popular solution" of tax reduction to promote further "consumer wants." Tax reduction could advance full employment, but it did not advance social priorities. Thus to say that the "'new economics'" had "triumphed" was a trifle "too optimistic." For "the new economics as thus far practiced can appropriately be labeled 'conservative Keynesianism.'"[33]

As distinct from, and in addition to, short-run Keynesianism's demand emphasis, Hansen, continuous with his stress of the late thirties and the forties, forcefully proclaimed the social desirability of public investment—a proclamation that, although always containing both an economic and a social rationale and imperative, shifted in the postwar boom somewhat toward the social side, while by no means jettisoning the economic. If short-run Keynesianism, whatever its economic limits, had succeeded in stabilizing and boosting national income, Hansen believed, it had nonetheless done little to address urgent public social needs. For this, only a

Hansenian-Keynesian solution, massive public investment for public improvements, would do. Further, a long-range policy of public investment would stimulate private investment and promote secular economic growth.[34] What was needed was for government to function "not only as a balance wheel offsetting fluctuations in the private sector, but also as a provider for ever-growing community services and for basic development projects which underlie and support private industry."[35]

Some commentators discerned a dichotomy or at least a tension in Hansen's thought between the social and economic rationales for public investment.[36] The social emphasis could also be seen, however, as a broadening of the scope of economics.[37] To be sure, the economic case did not appear pressing in a postwar boom in contrast to a Great Depression. For this reason alone, a public improvement agenda might take on more of a social desirability than an economic necessity motif. Indeed, Hansen's earlier link of public investment to secular stagnation did not help the former's chances in a boom atmosphere. Hansen himself argued that fiscal policy was concerned with "two types" of goals, one type geared to full employment and the other to allocative social priorities.[38] What was needed, he concluded, was a "grand plan" focused on social priorities that gained public support via its simultaneous stimulus to the "pocket book."[39] Aggregate growth alone was not enough, nor was the market an adequate guide when it came to social desirability. Conscious policy was required so as to transcend market allocation and meet needs in the areas of "human resources" such as education and health. Otherwise America risked becoming a "second-rate country."[40] This theme certainly had future resonance. Raising "the consumption function," Hansen concluded in 1955, took "little or no cognizance of social priorities." It emphasized private consumption at the expense of "urgently needed . . . public investment expenditures."[41] Here was long-run, Hansenian public investment Keynesianism and not short-run, aggregate demand Keynesianism.

In the postwar era, Hansen continued to address problems of economic structure, generally subordinating them to fiscal policy. Any structural interpretation of depression, whether Steindl's emphasis on oligopoly or Means's theory of administered prices, in Hansen's view gave too little attention to the exogenous environmental setting of the system and its institutions. Structures and institutions, Hansen held, must not be treated in a vacuum but in the context in which they operated, a context that itself could be impacted by fiscal policy. Structural alteration, in contrast, would not necessarily correct environmental deficiencies. Structural imbalances were more nearly consequences than causes of depression, Hansen concluded, and judicious use of fiscal policy could shape a setting in which they could be ironed out and administered prices could be administered in nondepressive ways.[42] That said, Hansen also warned against unjustified hikes in administered prices, calling for creation of a federal agency to review them in the hope that publicity would keep them within acceptable bounds.[43]

Hansen has been criticized as one of those Keynesians who downplayed the problem of inflation and did not foresee its growth and eventual negative impact on the influence and reputation of Keynesianism itself. This criticism is not without justification. Hansen did foresee a possible spurt of postwar inflation, but his overwhelming thrust was to de-emphasize the threat of inflation except in a war setting. In normal peacetime, he argued, the threat of inflation was "almost negligible"; price increases in such periods scarcely deserved "the name of inflation." Of far more concern, he believed, were depressive tendencies. Too much emphasis on the menace of inflation, he cautioned, could drag down economic growth and lead to recession. Excessively tight monetary policy designed to curtail inflation could have precisely that negative effect.[44] When inflation did surge in peacetime, however, Hansen found an explanation in Gardiner Means's handbook. Inflation not explainable in traditional supply-and-demand terms was attributed by Hansen to administered prices; indeed, he gave them more of a causal role in accounting for the new inflation than he had in accounting for the depression of the thirties. Public policy to maintain aggregate demand, he wrote in 1960, provided corporate price administrators with a basis for price maintenance and even increases in periods of recession. Here was a "brand-new" economic development, not only the failure of prices to decline but also their tendency even to rise in recession, "a rare occurrence in business-cycle history."[45] Traditional methods to control inflation, Hansen added in 1962, when applied to the administered variety, reduced employment and production rather than prices.[46]

On the issue of inflation, then, Means's analysis made significant inroads in Hansen's thinking, an analysis, moreover, that was to gain even further support during the explosive inflationary surge of the 1970s, a decade during which the still active Means gained greater influence, while the Keynesian star dimmed. Their limited convergence notwithstanding, the visions of Means and Hansen continued in largely separate spheres. Hansen's failure to incorporate Means's price analysis earlier and more fully helped to open the door to the inflationary rout of Keynesianism in the 1970s. On the other hand, Means paid virtually no attention to Hansen's stress on public investment for public improvements as a method of nonmarket resource allocation. Both Means and Hansen were "epochal" in their own ways: Hansen with his vision of public investment in human and material resources and his concept that conscious policy, not just market forces, was needed in the allocation of resources; and Means in his emphasis on the "public" character of modern corporate enterprise and on the need to devise new structures to supplement and augment the market where it had broken down under the impact of administrative power. But neither gave much play to the other's epochal vision. No longer direct rivals as during the late New Deal, Hansen was more far reaching on the question of public versus private allocation of resources, whereas Means was more so on the related but distinct question of the impact of corporate power on the use of those resources.

In critical respects John Kenneth Galbraith was the pivotal figure in both the Meansian institutionalist and Hansenian Keynesian traditions for the generation of economists that came to the fore in the quarter century after World War II. Galbraith was something of an institutionalist in his stress on corporate structure and power; he also continued and amplified Hansen's emphasis on public versus private use of resources. Galbraith agreed with his administrative inflation analysis, Means cheerfully related in 1958.[47] Also in 1958, however, in response to a suggestion for a conference on Galbraith's *Affluent Society*, Means showed little interest in the public as opposed to private consumption question so much a part of Hansen's and Galbraith's concern.[48] Hansen, on the other hand, very much considered this latter Galbraithian emphasis his own. *The Affluent Society*, Hansen wrote to Galbraith late in 1958, contained "brilliant and skillful writing . . . not seen since the great days of Keynes." In 1969 Hansen expressed chagrin that in a new introduction to *The Affluent Society* Galbraith had not given due regard to precursors such as himself and that he had underplayed the social versus the aggregative aspects of Keynesianism.[49] Galbraith, in his reply to Hansen, readily acknowledged that the latter had anticipated arguments of *The Affluent Society*. But on his central point he stood firm. He associated Hansen with a socially minded version of Keynesianism. But in others' hands it had become a mechanistic formula.[50] Although Galbraith continued both the Meansian and the Hansenian traditions—the former most particularly in *The New Industrial State* of 1967 and the latter in *The Affluent Society*—combining them if he did not synthesize them, he was above all the boom economist par excellence, the analyst of the "economics of opulence," a new Veblen satirizing a new, mass conspicuous consumption. He assumed and reflected the Great Boom. He did not carry on the Means and Hansen concern with the Great Depression, departing from it, save for his popular history, *The Great Crash*. Thus in this crucial respect Galbraith could seem somewhat dated by the mid-1970s as the boom dissipated, ushering in the age of "stagflation"—simultaneous inflation and stagnation. Inflation was in the mode of Galbraithian analysis, but stagnation was not. Stagnation suggested Hansen, but given Hansen's association with a declining Keynesianism, it led first and more fully to a Schumpeterian revival. Simultaneous rampant inflation and severe recession meanwhile provided grist for Gardiner Means's analytical mill, going beyond the inflationary blips and mild recessions of the late fifties. Withal, the post–postwar boom era in vital ways had much more in common with the long-run concerns of Means and Hansen going back to the thirties than it did with the prevailing short-run emphases of the fifties and sixties.

II.
The Refocus on Corporate Structure and Power

The dramatic combination of inflation and recession or stagnation in the 1970s—stagflation—constituted a sharp break with the boom decades after 1940. Stagflation, a brief whiff in the late fifties, now posed a new challenge to current orthodoxy. It was for economists of the 1970s what the Great Depression had been to those of the 1930s: a central conundrum forcing reconsideration of heretofore orthodox theories. In this setting a renewed focus on corporate structure and power appeared. There had, of course, been recognition of the important role of large corporations all along, but the tendency in a boom setting was to judge their impact as relatively benign, de-emphasizing negative effects. Now, with stagflation, a more critical thrust reemerged, not unlike that which attributed the severity of the Great Depression in some measure to the exercise of corporate power.[1] Studies appeared positing that corporate power and administered pricing had spread in recent decades, that the small business market sector essentially functioned within an overarching system of private corporate planning, and that new industries featuring small businesses in short order took on an oligopolistic form. Moreover, as in the Great Depression, corporate power, it was argued, had malign macroeconomic effects. Unemployment and inflation resulted as the macroeconomic consequences of the exercise of administered microeconomic power; a basic problem with the economy was thus structural. An economy dominated by corporate power, not by the "free market," was now more nearly the norm, ran the conclusion, precisely that reached by Gardiner Means four decades earlier.[2]

In this setting, Means's 1950s concept of administrative inflation, predicated on his 1930s concept of administered pricing, received a wider hearing and increasing support from fellow economic analysts. Further, if administrative inflation existed as a product of the long-run growth of corporate power, the inflationary explosion of the 1970s could not be wholly attributed to such external jolts to the system as "oil shocks." It had to be seen in part as a result of gradual structural change, as "secular inflation," remediable, short of unacceptably severe recession and unemployment, only by structural change. Based on administrative power and predetermined targets, corporations would, in this analysis, raise prices in the face of falling demand, as in the recession of 1974–75. Instead of inflation or recession, as in conventional theory, including neoclassical Keynesianism, the 1970s thus brought inflation with recession.[3]

The 1970s, a decade of disaster for mainstream Keynesianism, was simultaneously a decade of vindication for Gardiner Means. Short-run Keynesianism proved unable to explain 1970s inflation, and Means undertook to fill the analytical gap. The inflation of the 1970s, like that of the later 1950s, Means held, was in good part administrative in nature, that is, a result of the pricing policies of large corporations. Allowing for the added impact of such immediate events as the oil shocks, Means attributed the new inflation to price administration in the "more concentrated industries." Previously, the economy had remained sufficiently balanced between market and nonmarket forces so that a drop in prices in the former sector would offset a rise in the latter. But in the 1950s, Means held, the economy passed a "great divide," which led to the chronic inflation of the 1970s. At that point, the impact of the administered sector of the economy began to outweigh the offsetting impact of the market sector sufficiently so as to give an inflationary bias to the economy as a whole.

Moreover, now, in recession, a decline in demand led to what Means called "perverse" pricing, the raising, as distinct from the relative inflexibility, of administered prices. This phenomenon, Means insisted, could not be accounted for either by pre-1929 orthodox or by Keynesian theory. Only an explanation based on corporate structure, power, and administration could provide a satisfactory analysis. Administrative inflation appeared to be "endemic" under modern conditions.[4]

Means's solution to administrative inflation rejected both monetary policy and fiscal policy in favor of a structural approach. The Means of the 1970s, like the Means of the 1930s, called for public economic planning to meet the critical problem of the decade. Monetary and fiscal measures, Means held, were proper responses to an inflation due to excess demand; they could reduce demand, thus bringing prices down. But they did not meet the dilemma of administrative inflation. Reduction of demand was no remedy when inflation occurred even under conditions of reduced demand. Driven to extremes, such an approach could undertake to reduce inflation by means of depression. Means held, to the contrary, that just as the Great Depression required new theory and new solutions, so, too, did the inflation of the 1970s. It now had to be recognized that administered power could cause chronic inflation as well as enduring depression, and it now had to be recognized that only external structural intervention could satisfactorily resolve this new crisis.[5]

The Means of the 1930s, devoted to structural planning, became, to be sure, the Means of the 1940s who accepted monetary and to a lesser degree fiscal policy as methods of dealing with depression. But the Means of the 1970s, focused now on administrative inflation and building on his analysis of the late 1950s, returned to a structural planning solution to deal with this new perceived consequence of corporate power. Monetary policy remained preferable to fiscal policy to Means in dealing with the stagnation half of the problem of stagflation. An "easy money" policy could fuel demand so as to overcome recession. But structural change and planning were needed to overcome the inflation half. Large corporations, Means argued, in terms reminiscent of *The Modern Corporation and Private Property* and subsequent 1930s writing, were by their very nature charged with a public obligation. Traditional rights of businesspeople did not include the right to administer beyond market constraints. Hence Means called for legislation proclaiming large corporations subject to public review and possible reversal of their pricing decisions, as well as for new public structures to carry out these functions. The proper coordination, including cooperation between government, business, and labor, could result in stable growth without inflationary excess.[6] The country was now faced, Means concluded, with a need for a "basic change in national policy" because of corporate administrative inflation.[7] Just as the Great Depression had "called for a major revision of macrotheory and of laissez faire policy," administrative inflation now called "for a second major revision of macrotheory" and another "departure from laissez faire." Just as Congress via the Employment Act of 1946 committed government to pursue high employment, legislation should now be enacted to commit government to constrain administrative inflation.[8]

Means's administrative inflation analysis and, more broad, his whole concept of corporate revolution contributed significantly to 1970s and 1980s institutionalist and post-Keynesian economic thought. Means's structural approach grew in influence in the 1970s as that of short-run Keynesianism declined. That said, several caveats must be added. For one thing, some post-Keynesians held that Michal Kalecki provided a fuller theory linking micro- to macroeconomics than did Means. Additionally, there were prominent post-Keynesians who rejected Means's notion of administrative inflation, for example, Sidney Weintraub, to whom it was a "remnant from the Great Depression." Further, as was the case in the 1930s, the concept of administered prices, now in an inflationary context, could be accepted and then relegated to the status of an "exception" or "departure" from the competitive norm, thus obviating Means's central point.[9]

Interestingly enough, and not without irony, one Means convert to the concept of administrative inflation was Alvin Hansen—a conversion that, going back to the late 1950s, was now reinforced by recent events. In his last published piece in 1974, the year before his death, Hansen, accepting Means's administrative inflation analysis, agreed that "fiscal and monetary policy alone" could not provide "price stability" in an economic system with "foundations deeply structured in administered prices," and he called for public strictures on corporate pricing power, indeed seeing "no escape from . . . price controls."[10] Had Hansen departed more fully from neoclassical price theory decades before, had he shifted more fully to Means's position in this regard earlier and taken the body of American Keynesians with him, the story of the 1970s might well have been quite different. Keynesian macroeconomics would then have been fitted with microeconomic foundations better suited to dealing with the problems of the 1970s. It also remains true, however, that Means, in his wholesale rejection of Keynesianism after 1939, held to a traditional concept of monetary policy in combating depression and unemployment, somewhat parallel to Hansen's essential adherence to neoclassical price theory.

Means believed, especially after discarding his 1930s planning schemes, that monetary policy could arrest depression. He did not, of course, believe that it could reverse administrative inflation. He held, for example, that the monetarism of Milton Friedman assumed "a pretty high degree of price-wage flexibility" and came "very close to a reliance on the crude quantity theory of money."[11] But Clark Warburton, commenting on a Means paper titled "Money, Employment, and Inflation," called on Means to recognize his own "theory as a modification and adaptation to present-day reality of pre-1930 traditional theory, meaning by that term the classical equilibrium theory and the monetary theory of business fluctuations taken together, instead of asserting that you are presenting a theory of employment and inflation 'in conflict' with those schools of thought."[12] Means's somewhat mechanical inversion of market theory and his espousal of a monetary alternative to fiscal policy impeded a more unified heterodox challenge to orthodoxy after 1940, as did the neoclassical Keynesian shortchanging of Means. Hansen's subordination of the price problem to fiscal policy—his holding that the former could be eased in the context of the latter—appeared to be largely justified in the postwar boom but then came to ruin in the 1970s. Means's 1930s structural planning, if it had been implemented and institutionalized, could have confronted administrative inflation more directly and effectively than a nonstructural alternative. But instead of synthesis, going back to the late thirties and the forties, Hansen on price and Means on money adhered too fully to traditional theory, thereby hampering a unified micro and macro challenge to orthodoxy that conceivably could have preempted and withstood the disasters of the 1970s.

As it turned out, Keynesianism in the 1970s or, more accurate, short-run, neoclassical synthesis, demand management Keynesianism, came under withering attack and was widely and deeply discredited. Its continuity with orthodox microeconomics left it vulnerable in a period of an inflation of allegedly administrative—that is, microeconomic—origins. Structural factors underlying the new inflation were not reachable by conventional fiscal policy. The orthodox Keynesian remedy for recession—expanding demand—and the orthodox Keynesian remedy for inflation—contracting demand—obviously could not deal with simultaneous recession and inflation. Nor were problems of sectors of the economy effectively met by macroeconomic measures geared to the aggregate.[13]

To some extent the failures of 1970s Keynesianism were laid at Keynes's doorstep. The master had failed to provide an adequate microeconomics for his macrotheory. He himself had opened the door to the neoclassical synthesis: he had not taken corporate power sufficiently seriously, recognizing the reality of price administration without making it an integral part of his general theory. And now it had all come unraveled.[14] John Hicks, whose work had helped lay the basis for neoclassical synthesis Keynesianism and who now used "John" in place of the earlier "J. R." to reflect his disillusionment, lamented in the 1970s that Keynes did not "complete" his "vision" in *The General Theory*, failing to incorporate institutional changes fully into his analysis. He had not entirely "grasped" that it was "a change in market form" that was "at issue," even though he did "draw . . . many of the consequences" that followed from it. "Yet if only it had been possible for Keynes to have set it in this context!"[15] Keynesianism, he now concluded, needed a microeconomics based on administered pricing—or what Hicks called fix price—as an essential complement to its macroeconomics. Often, however, Keynes himself was essentially absolved of blame. The culprit, the bête noire, the villain of the piece, to many 1970s and 1980s critics, was short-run, neoclassical synthesis, bastard Keynesianism. It was short-run Keynesianism, as formulated by Hicks, Samuelson, and Hansen (although not Hansen as secular stagnationist, of course), that had coupled Keynesianism to orthodox price theory, assuming that given adequate aggregate demand the remainder of the economy would function satisfactorily. Keynesianism was thus rendered "simpleminded," vulnerable, and virtually defenseless when confronted with the inflation of the first post–postwar boom decade.[16]

It was this inflation—or, more fully, the simultaneous occurrence of inflation and recession—that provided the coup de grace to neoclassical Keynesianism, which essentially had no answer to stagflation either theoretical or programmatic. With its orthodox microeconomic base, no effective theoretical response could be forthcoming. Meanwhile, its programmatic cures contradicted one another. Short-run Keynesianism's limited repertoire—fiscal and to a lesser extent monetary manipulation—thus fell ingloriously short before the challenge.[17] As the veteran Keynesian Abba P. Lerner acknowledged in 1976, Keynesian theory had been left in a "state of confusion" by the simultaneous emergence of inflation and recession. Two prominent post-Keynesians pressed the point home. To J. A. Kregel the appearance of stagflation was a "crucial event" for it "shattered" short-run Keynesian assumptions. Contributing greatly to the "loss of faith" in Keynesianism, wrote Alfred S. Eichner, was government's "inability . . . to . . . halt . . . the secular rise of prices," and the "culprit" was not "Keynes' own theory but rather the misrepresentation of that theory" by the neoclassical synthesists.[18]

The emergence of "secular inflation" returned to the fore the structuralist and institutionalist criticisms of Keynesianism that were voiced in the late 1930s and the 1940s, namely, that Keynesianism did not adequately confront problems associated with the large corporation, private economic power, and oligopoly. The assumption that the proper macroeconomic policies would dissolve or greatly alleviate those problems was now exploded by inflation. Only an approach focused on structure, on institutions, it was now held, could deal with the forces that had rendered conventional Keynesianism impotent.[19] Linked to the question of structure was that of sector. Aggregative macroeconomic policies did not confront or directly deal with the problems of particular industries or sectors of the economy. In the United States, in the post–postwar boom era, specific older industries were suffering from relatively declining productivity that, it was argued, sector-specific policies could best address. In this respect, as in its inattention to technology as a crucial aspect of economic discontinuity—of economic decline and revival—neoclassical synthesis Keynesianism was faulted for its short-run cyclical focus and its corresponding lack of a long-run perspective.[20]

The ultimate comeuppance for neoclassical synthesis Keynesianism, critics concluded, was that with its discrediting, the Keynesian part of the neoclassical synthesis was dropped, and for many members of a new generation of economists, a species of pre-Keynesian orthodoxy became the accepted alternative. By compromising with traditional theory, short-run Keynesianism had thus signed its own death warrant, although it took several decades for the sentence to be carried out definitively. In this context surviving veterans of the neoclassical synthesis Keynesian cohort offered what amounted to a collective mea culpa or, to use Weintraub's term, "recantation" of their compromise with orthodoxy, of their role in the marriage of convenience between Keynesian macroeconomics and pre-Keynesian microeconomics. John Hicks figured most prominently here.[21] But note also the American duo of Paul Samuelson and James Tobin. To Samuelson, looking back, American Keynesians such as himself did believe that "imperfections of competition" were "an important part of the Keynesian under-employment equilibrium story," and therefore "Keynes-cum-Chamberlin-and-Means would have been better than Keynes alone."[22] Tobin placed some of the blame on Keynes's shoulders, holding that the author of *The General Theory* failed to incorporate a realistic price theory into his overall analysis and had made "tactical mistakes" in trying to best orthodoxy by playing on its "home field," that is, by assuming pure competition, a strategy that "backfired 30 or 40 years later." While Keynesians of his own "generation . . . always had imperfect or monopolistic competition in mind as their micro-foundations," Tobin allowed, they did not in their time undertake "serious theoretical attempts . . . to formalize their vision."[23]

If short-run Keynesians were shortsighted, however, they were not alone. As late as February 1973, for example, when the postwar boom was about to flag, Gardiner Means's disciple John Blair wrote to Walter W. Heller, former chairman of the Council of Economic Advisers and prime exemplar of 1960s "fine-tuning" Keynesianism, and, while noting the emergence of the problem of inflation, congratulated him for his macroeconomic successes. That is, Blair, while very much aware of inflation, did not point to impending stagnation. Wrote Blair to Heller, "Now that you macroeconomists have forged the tools needed to eliminate unemployment and bring about a satisfactory rate of economic growth, inflation has become the unresolved No. 1 economic problem."[24] Therefore it was quite justified for critics of short-run Keynesianism to point out its inadequacies in the face of secular inflation.[25] But the stagnation side of the stagflation phenomenon also had to be addressed. Not only structure but, as other critics observed, problems of sector, productivity, and technology were at issue as well. At this point the legacies of Hansen's secular Keynesianism as well as of Means's quasi institutionalism gained relevance. If the latter could help explain secular inflation, the former might have more explanatory power when it came to the other emergent problems of the post–postwar boom American economy. Keynes's analyses, after all, were rooted in both the depression of the thirties and the British stagnation of the twenties, not without its parallels to the United States a half century and more later. In his analyses, Hansen certainly did not limit himself to the Great Depression per se but endeavored to place that event in a historically grounded context including, among other factors, the role of technology and the rise and decline of great industries over time. Thus although the lack of a Meansian structural element in postwar Keynesianism helped lead to the latter's downfall in the seventies, the displacement of a secular historical Keynesianism by a short-run mechanical Keynesianism similarly contributed to the debacle. For the problem was inattention not only to institutions, structure, and prices but also to history, technology, and sectoral rise and decline. What then was needed—and lacking—in mainstream Keynesianism was both an institutionally grounded microeconomics stemming from Means and a historically and technologically focused perspective stemming from Hansen. In Samuelson's language, Keynes-cum-Means would have been better than Keynes alone, but Keynes-cum-Means-cum–the secular Hansen would have been better than Keynes-cum-Means alone.

The upshot of this discrediting of short-run Keynesianism was the call for a more comprehensive approach than it allowed, one better suited to the rough-and-tumble 1970s and 1980s as distinct from the relatively placid economic climate of the 1950s and 1960s. Short-run cyclical tools would have to be augmented by secularly geared efforts, it was argued. Aggregate emphases would have to be joined by sectoral approaches. Indirect public instruments would have to be supplemented by more direct ones. Macroeconomics would have to be augmented by public intervention in microeconomic decision making that was not in fact left wholly to the "market." Or, put differently, public macroeconomic policy could no longer be seen as external or exogenous in its relation to the private microeconomic—or "real"—economy. One was not external to the other; they were organically joined. Thus it could no longer be considered acceptable to limit public efforts essentially to the macro sphere, leaving the micro largely to itself. The micro impacted macroeconomically as well, thus justifying and necessitating a public role and function. A structurally based microeconomics would fit a Keynesian macroeconomics in theory as well as policy.[26]

Even before the full-fledged failures of short-run Keynesianism became apparent, there was underway, in Great Britain and the United States, the development of a school known in time as post-Keynesianism. In Great Britain, Joan Robinson, her associates, and followers' version of Keynes figured most prominently, and in the United States the structurally based contributions of Means, Galbraith, and others were highly influential. In both countries considerable attention was also paid to Michal Kalecki, whose legacy, some admirers contended, was the most important of all in post-Keynesianism. Trends and developments of the 1970s helped to give post-Keynesianism impetus. The downfall of short-run Keynesianism inspired the effort to rescue a legitimate version of Keynes from the debacle of the "bastard" progeny. The inflation of the decade intensified the search for appropriate Keynesian microfoundations. And the sense of crisis of the era of stagflation contributed, as did the thirties depression, to criticism of the passing orthodoxy and to a search for alternatives with greater explanatory power to illuminate emergent problems.[27]

A central post-Keynesian objective was the decoupling of the neoclassical synthesis of Keynesianism and orthodox price theory, with replacement of the latter with structural microfoundations based on recognition of corporate power and price administration. It was Keynes's error, or at least that of those who followed, to marry orthodox microeconomics to the new macroeconomics. Now was the time for a dissolution. It was microeconomic failure that had wrecked Keynesianism; it would be a more appropriate microeconomics that would salvage and revitalize what was left. Recognition of the preponderance of oligopoly, of corporate power, and of administration, all fused to Keynes's durable legacy, would, it was held, provide the ingredients for a challenge to current orthodoxy. Recognition of the need to extend Keynesianism to encompass long-run institutional and structural change would provide an evolutionary element lacking in the conventional short-run version.[28] Three veterans still active in the 1970s stated the case succinctly. Pre-Keynesian analysis, held Abba Lerner, was essentially microeconomic, and Keynes's analysis was essentially macroeconomic; post-Keynesianism was designed to create a proper synchronization. The competitive market's decline, declared John Kenneth Galbraith, had obliterated the distinction between micro- and macroeconomics, and policy would have to be adjusted accordingly. And the major theoretical element still "to be incorporated into Keynes' theory," concluded Joan Robinson, was "recognition of the prevalence of . . . oligopolistic markets."[29]

If so significant a portion of the problem was institutional or structural, post-Keynesians correspondingly argued, solutions also had to be sought along institutional or structural lines. Some form of planning was in order, planning that would go beyond conventional fiscal and monetary policy. Price, wage, and income relations would also have to be addressed. Macroeconomic policy would now need microeconomic counterparts.[30] To the dean of institutionalists, Allan Gruchy, the post-Keynesians' approach to "national planning" drew them "very close" to institutionalism.[31] Post-Keynesians were also interested in investment—as it related to theory, structure, and policy. As analyst Peter Kenyon put it, they were geared to "selective public sector spending" designed to influence the pattern of investment along lines called for by Keynes in *The General Theory*. And in an emphasis that suggested Hansen or Galbraith even more than Keynes, a leading post-Keynesian, Paul Davidson, called for recognition of the distinction between profitable and socially beneficial investment.[32] Further, it was argued, in a post-Keynesian vein, the boosting of aggregate demand would not solve the problems of secularly declining industries.[33]

The emphasis on structure suggested a Meansian influence on post-Keynesianism, and that on attendant investment, a Kaleckian as well as a Keynesian strain. The whole emphasis on the lack of a structural component in short-run Keynesianism harkened back to the late 1930s dialogues between Means and Keynes as well as to the institutionally based criticisms of Keynes and Keynesianism over the course of the next decade. Hence, wrote Warren J. Samuels and Steven G. Medema in their study of the economist, Means's concept of administrative inflation became "the heart of the post-Keynesian approach" to the subject. In their collection of Means's writings, Frederic S. Lee and Samuels held that given the great interest shown by the 1970s in administered price concepts, "Means was ahead of his time," creating a body of work that "was readily absorbed in post-Keynesian economics."[34]

But there were also limits to Means's influence, ones founded on the notion that his theory was insufficiently comprehensive, especially in regard to investment. Means never significantly followed up on the attention given to investment in his dissertation; his blasts against Keynes were linked essentially to structure—and, above all, market failure—in explaining macroeconomic breakdown. In his critique of Keynes the collapse of investment was attributed to market mechanism failure, as such. Some critics found Means's inattention to a more direct role for investment a lacuna in his effort at an overall macroeconomic theory, just as critics of Keynes stressed his failure to integrate an appropriate microeconomic price theory into his macroeconomic analysis. This opened the door to the legacy of a third figure, Michal Kalecki, as the economist who purportedly bettered Keynes by adding imperfect competition to a Keynesian macroeconomic analysis and bettered Means by adding more of an investment component to administered price theory. The American Marxist Paul Sweezy, for example, much influenced by Kalecki and Josef Steindl, noted that while he had always been "sympathetic" to Means's concepts, he also thought Means's "theoretical framework . . . somewhat simplistic."[35] Proponents of Kalecki's analysis and importance, although they acknowledged the corresponding work of Means, saw the former's theory as more complex, integrated, and inclusive.[36] As critic Peter Wiles put it, the tradition emanating from Means stressed "the administered price as such" apart from consideration of cost "or indeed why it is administered at all."

Means's analysis, compared with parallel efforts in Great Britain, was less complete as to costs, although it "made the contrast with perfect competition more clear."[37] The conclusion of some 1970s and 1980s analysts that Means's treatment was less comprehensive and satisfactory than was Kalecki's somewhat ironically placed Means in a position parallel in that regard to Keynes's.

Some admirers of Kalecki argued that post-Keynesian economics should be called post-Kaleckian given that economist's contributions.[38] No less a figure than Keynes's associate Joan Robinson was an enthusiastic proponent of Kalecki's significance. It was Kalecki, she wrote, "who brought imperfect competition into touch with the theory of employment," thus making "Kalecki's version . . . in some ways more truly a general theory than Keynes'."[39] Compared with Keynes, Kaleckian post-Keynesians held, Kalecki provided his own microeconomics for his macroeconomics—that is, he integrally fused the two, whereas Keynes artificially and in the end disastrously separated them. Basically, Kalecki's micro- and macroeconomics pivoted on imperfect competition, on "degree of monopoly." Further, Kaleckian analysis, with much of the initial impact coming by way of Steindl, related price administration to broader questions concerning costs, profits, and investment. In this way, it was held, Kalecki, to a greater degree than Keynes or Means, provided the essential legacy and ingredients for post-Keynesian economics.[40]

On the other hand, Kalecki enthusiasts sometimes shortchanged Means in regard to his contributions. Kalecki's claim to fame, for example, rested in part on his fusion of micro- and macroeconomics grounded on oligopolistic foundations.[41] The same may be said of Means. Nicholas Kaldor held that it was Kalecki who connected imperfect competition theory with "general equilibrium theory."[42] But, allowing for terminological imprecision, much the same claim could be made for Means—that is, he linked the breakdown of the competitive market mechanism to "general equilibrium theory." Further, Kaldor contended that Keynes and Kalecki "introduced" the "revolutionary new idea" that a new equilibrium could be reached through changes in output rather than, as had previously been assumed, price.[43] But this "revolutionary new idea" was Means's as well. The crux of his administered prices concept dealt with adjustment through reduction of output and employment rather than price in the face of falling demand. It was hardly accurate to say that Keynes and Kalecki, versus Means, introduced the idea. Analyst Malcolm C. Sawyer noted a similarity between Kalecki's "cost-determined and demand-determined prices" and John Hicks's "fix-price/flex-price distinction." Others, including Means, had "usually . . . confined their attention to price formation without drawing out the wider implications for macroeconomics."[44] Means, of course, did draw out wider macroeconomic implications, albeit not in precisely the same fashion as did Kalecki.

The nature of post-Keynesianism and the roles of the legacies of Kalecki and Means can be further understood through the work of Alfred S. Eichner, a leading American member of the school. Eichner's emphasis on oligopoly and corporate power, his acceptance and use of administered prices, and his desire to base macroeconomics on a solid structural microeconomic foundation flowed in part from Means.[45] Eichner wrote to Means that it was the latter's 1959 congressional testimony which had first made him enthused about the study of economics, and it was Means's concept of administered prices that provided "a beacon through the darkness" of his Columbia University graduate training.[46] On the other hand, it was Kalecki who, in Eichner's view, had contributed to some crucial connections. In his major work of 1976, *The Megacorp and Oligopoly: Micro Foundations of Macro Dynamics*, Eichner acknowledged that, along with Steindl's, Kalecki's work provided "one of the important lines of development upon which not only this treatise but all post-Keynesian theory is based." In addition to price administration as such, the line of theory traceable to Kalecki explained pricing in terms of perceived long-run corporate financing needs. As Eichner wrote to Means's wife, Caroline Ware, "a suitable micro analysis" needed "to be synthesized into post-Keynesian theory. . . . That more suitable micro analysis was already to be found in Gardiner's writing," but "this fact was probably not known" among the British progenitors of post-Keynesianism "because the essential link, through investment, had not yet been adequately brought out. . . . As it was, the ideas came in only slowly, largely through Kalecki's influence."[47]

In this respect, Eichner's own intellectual base may be said to be Means on structure plus Kalecki on the link to investment. In building his microeconomics, Eichner founded his concepts in good measure on the idea that oligopoly was of central importance to the economy as a whole, on the reality of corporate administered prices, and on the belief that corporate microdecisions had vast macroeconomic impact.[48] All these were concepts that Means had advanced decades earlier. In building on Kalecki (and Steindl), Eichner further argued that corporate decision making about price, based on costs and targeted profits, was geared to financing needs for long-run investment, expansion, and security. Internally generated, price-based funds financed long-term corporate goals.[49] Recognition of this connection, Eichner held, both illuminated the nature of price administration and served "to regenerate micro with macroeconomic theory." Corporate price and investment decisions were "critical in determining the macrodynamic behavior of the system as a whole."[50] Building on Means and Kalecki, Eichner also linked his work directly to that of Keynes. Keynes had emphasized investment as the key factor in macroeconomics; Eichner was now emphasizing it as the key factor in corporate microeconomics. Hence there was a "common bond" founded on recognition of investment as "the critical factor." But to Eichner, unlike Keynes, the key linkage was institutional and structural—the nature of the modern corporation—rather than exogenous and environmental.[51]

Eichner's basic objective—and a key one in post-Keynesianism generally—was to breach the gap between macroeconomics and microeconomics, to provide Keynesianism with structurally based microfoundations. This would complete "the aborted Keynesian revolution."[52] Eichner, in a sense, and post-Keynesianism generally, attempted to bring together the strands of heterodox thought developed but left unjoined in the 1930s, those pioneered by Means and like-minded analysts and by Keynes. Keynes, however, downplayed structure, and Means after 1939 disdained Keynes. "The result was a job only half done," wrote Eichner, "with Keynesian theory resting on a micro foundation which had not itself been revised to take into account the . . . structural changes which necessitated the writing of *The General Theory*," an institutional rather than environmental fillip in keeping with Eichner's and Means's, if not Keynes's, underlying perspective.[53]

Eichner's work was sufficiently rich and synthesizing so as to reach out in a number of directions. He agreed with Schumpeter's notion of epochal innovations leading to broad upswings and eventual downswings of the Kondratieff cycle, and he argued that innovative industries would become oligopolistic over time.[54] He rejected "Hicks-Hansen" short-run Keynesianism, arguing that its fiscal policies could never effectively deal with the complications of corporate power.[55] Accordingly, he wrote in *The Megacorp and Oligopoly*, his "major policy conclusion" was that "effective social control over the individual megacorp" required regulation of the composition of investment, in essence Keynes's vision of "a somewhat comprehensive socialization of investment."[56] This "major policy conclusion" was also quite like that of the secular Keynesian Hansen. Finally, Eichner completed his synthesis by calling for "national planning" as a sine qua non of "future economic growth," concluding that reliance on "markets alone" would only accentuate American economic decline.[57]

It was the work of Eichner, among others, that led contemporary institutionalists to see common ground between themselves and post-Keynesians. Both groups saw economics in evolutionary terms; both emphasized the role of structure, institutions, and corporate power; and both saw a need for public planning.[58] Dudley Dillard, for example, both an institutionalist and a pioneer student of Keynesianism, wrote hopefully in 1980 that circumstances were "ripening for a new revolution in economic theory," one that would free Keynes, "the revolutionary thinker," from the bonds of the neoclassical synthesis. The result might be to make Keynes's "theory part of a neoinstitutional synthesis," a "macroeconomic theory of institutional economics."[59] Writing three years earlier, Wallace C. Peterson, an institutionalist admirer of Keynes, viewed Keynesianism and institutionalism as akin to "two trains which started out on parallel tracks toward a common destination." The Keynesian train, however, was shunted onto the neoclassical synthesis track, taking it further and further away from institutionalism. Now it was necessary to get the trains back onto "parallel tracks" toward their common "original destination." In 1988 Peterson insisted that "in spite of its limitations" Keynesianism offered "the best theoretical model" available but that a proper microeconomic price theory was "absolutely essential for completing the Keynesian 'revolution.'"[60]

Institutionalist emphases on oligopoly, corporate power, and price administration, flowing in part from Means's work, continued into the 1970s and 1980s.[61] So did institutionalist calls for national planning, going beyond fiscal and monetary manipulation, to coordinate microeconomic policies, a staple of 1930s structural planning such as that of Means.[62] Beyond the ranks of institutionalists per se, planning in the mid-1970s seemed to have awakened from the torpor that had descended on it in the wake of Keynesianism's triumph in the late 1930s and the 1940s. "Planning has resumed the intellectual momentum of the 1930s," wrote historian and planning enthusiast Otis L. Graham Jr. in 1976.[63] The combination of the severe recession of the mid-1970s and inflation—that is, the problem of stagflation—together with the discrediting of short-run Keynesianism, appeared to open the door to the planning alternative. What short-run Keynesianism's fiscal and monetary tools were unable to accomplish, it was argued, structural planning could.[64] Economist Wassily Leontief suggested in 1974 that it was "high time to revive President

Franklin Roosevelt's National Resources Planning Board."[65] Leontief and others formed the Initiative Committee for National Economic Planning to publicize the cause and suggest programmatic applications. The group proposed the Balanced Growth and Economic Planning Act of 1975, which some characterized as "the last product of . . . New Deal thought" as well as the first significant effort to systematize legislatively government's economic role since the Employment Act of 1946 was passed in the New Deal's aftermath. The legislation would have established an economic planning board in the executive branch of government charged, among other things, with analysis of "long-range economic trends and opportunities."[66]

Planning enthusiasts held that there was already considerable planning of the American economy, but much of it was corporate and private and hence geared to corporate and private objectives and goals. Further, such public planning as existed was typically discrete rather than integrative; geared to particulars, not to the whole; ad hoc rather than systematic.[67] Planning, its proponents held, would access a larger array of tools and techniques than the limited repertoire of short-run Keynesians. It would advance a greater measure of public control over the operation and performance of powerful corporations.[68] In 1980 Michael Harrington, for example, in words reminiscent of Gardiner Means's analyses of the 1930s, declared that great corporations controlled more than they responded to the market, and that with corporate power insufficiently checked by the inner "workings of the economy," a public role was now needed to ensure "results which were once supposed to be produced by Adam Smith's invisible hand."[69] Leontief, also quite in keeping with Means's work of the 1930s, wrote that initial steps in developing planning would include "analyzing the operation of the economic system" not just "in terms of a few general indices" of an "aggregative" kind but also "in terms of . . . deeply-lying details" that would, for example, focus on "technological development" and "trends in different industries." In what amounted to a call for a new version of Means's 1939 *Structure of the American Economy*, Leontief proclaimed the need for studies describing relationships "among all the different sectors of the economy, the state of equipment, the structure of the labor force, and prices in very great detail, so that looking at the entire picture, we would see what is happening in each sector, physically as well as financially." A "planning board" would need "a detailed and . . . fully integrated picture, not just disjointed pieces of information."[70]

By the late 1970s the planning debate had taken a new turn and had taken on a new terminology. The debate over planning increasingly focused on the lowered rate of growth in productivity, the problems of particular sectors of the economy, and American competitiveness in world markets. The term "industrial policy," used by Gardiner Means in the 1930s, now came into play. The proper industrial policy, involving a public role in sectoral industrial decision making, its proponents held, unlike the limited formulas of short-run Keynesianism, could deal with the emergent problems of the late 1970s and early 1980s. A balancing wheel role for government was not enough. Business-government coordination and guidance geared to the long run would be necessary to correct the business and government myopia of the 1950s and 1960s. Support for industrial policy continued into the recession of the early 1980s and then gave way as the Reagan upsurge seemingly gave credence to the experiment with pre–New Deal orthodoxy.[71] The dominant policies of the 1980s, instead of planning or industrial policy, consisted of a dose of monetarism to combat inflation, a supply-side emphasis to counter the demand-side economics of short-run Keynesianism, and tax reductions geared to the wealthy so as to promote private investment—à la Andrew Mellon in the 1920s. In addition, the 1980s mix included an entrepreneurial vogue: a focus on the entrepreneur who would restore America's industrial genius, cutting through the bureaucratic maze to fashion whole new industries. The concern over decline, then, in the context of the 1980s, a period that featured a political turn to the right which eclipsed the planning-industrial policy alternative, also made that decade one of Schumpeterian apotheosis. The economist whose grand designs had been swamped by Keynes decades earlier now received renewed attention and acclaim amid the ruins of short-run Keynesianism.

12.
Schumpeterian
Revival and Long
Waves

T he dissonance of the 1970s broke apart the neoclassical Keynesian synthesis of the boom decades and sent economists flying in various directions. It led to the resurgence of interest in planning and subsequent industrial policy and to a period of great influence for monetarism and a vogue of jejune supply-side economics. It also led, climaxing in the 1980s, to the revival of Schumpeter, the great Austro-American economist and rival of Keynes whose influence was overshadowed by that of the Briton in the wake of *The General Theory*. Now, with problems emergent which Keynes had sidestepped in *The General Theory* and which short-run Keynesians generally assumed away as parts of a long run that would take care of itself—problems associated with technological and sectoral discontinuity—the relevance of Schumpeter's work once again became apparent and to some economists imperative. For the very elements of economics on which Schumpeter focused and which Keynes and short-run Keynesians in some measure neglected were now back with a vengeance. In a period of economic slowdown and sectoral decline, the static, mechanical character of short-run Keynesianism seemed hopelessly inadequate.[1] There was talk of a Schumpeterian "renaissance."[2] An "Age of Schumpeter" was replacing the previous "Age of Keynes," and a "Schumpeterian Revolution" was uprooting the "Keynesian Revolution."[3] Now, declared economist Richard Goodwin in 1988, the United States, Britain, and Germany were "committed, for better or worse, to the Schumpeterian path."[4] Schumpeter, of course, was never an orthodox "market" economist; his economics was evolutionary. But his policy solutions fit the emphasis on a more pristine private enterprise of the Reagan-Thatcher 1980s. Still, as with Keynes, Schumpeter's legacy could and did cut in different directions.

A key point made by Schumpeter's admirers was that Keynes as an individual and "Keynesianism"—in essence, short-run Keynesianism, although critics were usually generic and did not distinguish among variations—did not deal with deeply rooted, long-run, sectoral problems. Geared to demand-side management, comfortable in the belief that the assurance of sufficient aggregate demand would bring forth adequate supply, steady economic growth, and progress, "Keynesians" neglected such factors as technology and developments in particular industrial sectors. They ignored what Schumpeter could have taught them about entrepreneurship, innovation, and industrial rise and decline.[5] Analyst Bruce Williams noted that Schumpeter's stress on the "introduction of new technologies" explained strong "wave-like supply-side forces which Keynesian demand management policies were not powerful enough to offset." Peter Drucker, a great admirer of Schumpeter, announced flatly that "within the Keynesian system" there was "no room for productivity, no way to stimulate or spur it . . . to make an economy more productive."[6] But the criticism of "Keynesianism" was really of short-run Keynesians and to a degree of Keynes himself; it did not apply to a secular version such as that of Alvin Hansen.

Neoclassical synthesis Keynesianism was so conventionally assumed to be Keynesianism in the 1960s and was so vulnerable to attack in the 1970s that other varieties of Keynesianism tended to get lost in the shuffle. Gerhard Mensch, for example, whose *Stalemate in Technology* provided a powerful impetus to the Schumpeterian revival, held that Keynesian macroeconomics did "not differentiate between exceptional developments in individual sectors" and that "the answer" lay in "Schumpeterian economics," with its "strong emphasis on innovative investment," the "attribute" that set "it apart from Keynesian economics."[7] Mensch, who was critical of Schumpeter for failing to adopt a sectoral version of Alvin Hansen's secular stagnation theory, was here basically indicting short-run Keynesianism, flaying it for lacking attributes characteristic of Schumpeterianism, which were, however, also characteristic of secular Hansenian Keynesianism. Similarly, Christopher Freeman, a Schumpeterian who, like Mensch, employed a wide-ranging focus, including, in his case, a publicly oriented version of the creed, held that "neither Keynes nor the Keynesians" focused on "the crucial role of technical innovation."[8] Again, this certainly could not be said of Hansen's technologically focused secular version of Keynesianism. To the contrary, as one writer accurately observed in 1986, while "Schumpeter's Creative Destruction" sharply contrasted with neoclassical Keynesianism's "demand-side" concept of "continuous and manageable change," Hansen, like Schumpeter, thought in terms of the discontinuities of technological thrusts and exhaustion, of the rise and decline of whole industries.[9]

Schumpeterians largely blamed Keynesianism for the economy's loss of dynamism in the 1970s. What Keynesians, including in this case Hansen, had argued would be the sense of security among businesspeople that proper fiscal policy would foster, thus inducing private investment, Schumpeterians viewed as the creator of sloth, inefficiency, and decline. Events, one analyst put it, had proved "erroneous" the Keynesian idea that aggregate demand management provided the best environment for entrepreneurial initiative.[10] Government supports and guarantees, wrote another, produced a "dependence effect," negating pressures needed to stimulate the innovations required for adaptation and adjustment.[11] Contrary to Keynesian assurances, declared economist Tibor Scitovsky, government assumption of risks did "more to ossify the corporate structure than to raise . . . animal spirits," leaving "the Schumpeterian entrepreneur, the imaginative newcomer, . . . out in the cold."[12] The Schumpeterian Christian Seidl put it most forcefully in a piece aptly titled "Schumpeter versus Keynes." The "failures of the capitalist engine," he held, had been "caused by Keynesian economic policy," which over the course of three decades had lessened pressure to adapt to changing circumstances. Instead of following market signals to redirect resources, Keynesianism extended an "invitation to lobbyism." Keynesianism thus made "life far easier," but it undermined "the efficiency of the economy."[13] In this version of state intervention in the economy, somewhat at variance with Schumpeter's own, the result was not "capitalism in an oxygen tent," as Schumpeter once put it, but capitalism in a luxury resort, fattened up, bloated, comforted, content, complacent, and therefore unable to galvanize, redynamize, and reenergize itself in the face of competition from newer, younger, leaner, and hungrier national capitalisms.

Such Schumpeterian criticism was also related to the debate over the nature of the postwar secular boom. Schumpeter's admirers disputed the Keynesian claim to credit. Neoclassical Keynesians might have thought that they were guiding the economy toward growth, but in reality they were riding the crest of a Schumpeterian wave. Fiscal policy did not create the boom; rather, it was propelled by the powerful thrust of innovative technologies and industries.[14] No less a figure than Robert Heilbroner declared that it was Schumpeter who "most fully anticipated and cogently explained the economic élan" of the boom decades, who "would surely have seen" the secular boom as "a vindication of his expectations," and whose concept of growth appeared to be "borne out" by it.[15] Heilbroner, to be sure, qualified his words carefully, but to full-fledged Schumpeterians, the boom of 1945–70 was unqualifiedly Schumpeterian in its causal essence. Further, allowing for differences between historical eras, it could be replicated by a Schumpeterian revival, by implementation of the principles of "Schumpeterian economics" as they had developed over time. These principles included a longer-run perspective so as to allow "regenerative forces" to engender and develop new industries, and "Schumpeterian competition," that is, competition between and among industries over research and development, innovations, and products, as distinct from sterile price competition. They also called for an economics geared to "movement" rather than stasis, to sectors as opposed to the aggregate, and to "pathbreaking entrepreneurs," not corporate bureaucrats.[16]

Schumpeter himself was not exempt from criticism in this context by latter-day Schumpeterians. These Schumpeterians, and others, criticized Schumpeter for his later emphasis on the large corporation's innovative economic role, versus his earlier focus on the individual entrepreneur. That is, the early Schumpeter stressed the innovative importance of the new, pioneering, small-scale entrepreneur. The later Schumpeter, especially the Schumpeter of *Capitalism, Socialism, and Democracy*, geared to what he saw as the secular trend, believed that the heroic age of the pioneer entrepreneur was now over and that innovation and progress would henceforth be "routinized" in the laboratories and via the teamwork of large organizations. Events, his erstwhile supporters and others argued, had proven the later Schumpeter wrong. Large corporations were not the prime innovators; new firms were. Entrepreneurial capitalism was not going or gone but revived and renewed. The later Schumpeter, it was argued, was dated; the earlier Schumpeter was far more relevant to the entrepreneurial spirit and drive of the eighties.[17] There was a "tremendous resurgence of entrepreneurship" in that decade, declared enthusiast Chaitram J. Talele, who characterized the later Schumpeter "a victim of myopic vision," a charge normally reserved for the Keynesian foe.[18]

In other respects as well, in a period of economic flux, Schumpeter's legacy could be interpreted in different ways and be linked to differing alternatives. As John D. Sterman put it, in a Schumpeterian context, a "measure of . . . flux today is the frenzied search for . . . new management techniques, entrepreneurship, an industrial policy."[19] The very mention of "industrial policy" in such a context illustrated the range and array of the discussion and perceived possibilities. One linkage drawn was to Keynes, by implication to Hansen, and to a secular rather than short-run version. Gerhard Mensch deemed Keynes's dictum that "the weakness of the inducement to invest" was "at all times the key to the economic problem" as "probably correct in general" but lacking penetration "down to . . . sectoral differences in this weakness at a given time, or to changes over time."[20] Here Hansen's secular version of Keynesianism seemed particularly relevant. This in turn led to a public sector version of Schumpeterianism, a version that the vociferously anti–New Deal Schumpeter certainly did not develop but one loosely consistent with a notion that he occasionally and elliptically alluded to in obiter dicta fashion with references to the entrepreneurial functions of such public agencies as the United States Department of Agriculture. Thus while Schumpeter by no means foresaw a Schumpeterian–public sector synthesis, others, arguing that such a synthesis had played a crucial role in the postwar boom, championed it, calling for an enlarged role for government in promoting research and development and technological innovation.[21] Here was a Schumpeter-Keynes or, perhaps more accurate, a Schumpeter-Hansen synthesis.

To Mensch, for example, conventional Keynesian aggregate spending could not deal with the problem of sectoral decline or inefficiency or provide the high "rate of innovative investment" geared to "research and technology" needed to do so. But "public investment programs" oriented toward "innovative projects" could provide "an expansionary policy" applicable to the problem of "overcoming stagnation."[22] Schumpeterian analyst François Chesnais declared that a basic failure of most believers in the creed, including Schumpeter himself, lay in their lack of under-

standing of the importance of a positive public role in innovative development. To fail to acknowledge "government-funded R&D and procure-
ment as . . . an almost sure requisite . . . of Schumpeterian recovery"
amounted "to an attempt 'to play Hamlet without the Danish prince.'"
Like-minded Schumpeterian Alfred Kleinknecht called for an "active
government innovation policy" to stimulate a "Schumpeter boom," a
"public technology policy" eschewing sole reliance on market processes
and geared to sectors, "an active sector-specific industrial policy." And
Christopher Freeman called for new Schumpeterian organizational innovations comparable with those of the Keynesian revolution, thus synthesizing the legacies of the two great rivals.[23] To overcome the contemporary
economic crisis, Freeman held, reliance could not be placed solely on "a
process of spontaneous recovery." Also needed was a "viable strategy," one
combining the strengths of Keynes and Schumpeter. Freeman added
Kondratieff, and, given what he proposed, he might also have added
Hansen. Renewed economic growth, he held, required "public policies,"
including a public investment strategy geared to Schumpeterian targets for
the "introduction of new technologies," to public investment of "an infra-
structural type," withal to "neo-Keynesian public investment."[24]

The revival of Schumpeter also meant a revival of Schumpeter's version
of the Kondratieff long wave. Schumpeter's long wave concept was
eclipsed during the postwar boom, as were all others. In boom periods
prosperity and growth were deemed normal, and stagnation or depression was deemed abnormal. But in the 1970s as in the 1930s, lengthy
bouts of stagnation or depression stimulated doubts about continuous
economic progress, leading to renewed interest in the concept of long
waves. Thus in the context of long wave theory, the 1940–70 boom could
be seen as a Schumpeter-Kondratieff upswing, and the subsequent period,
a Schumpeter-Kondratieff downswing awaiting a new upsurge. It was a
Schumpeterian version of a Kondratieff insofar as it was based on the belief that the long wave process was shaped by the pattern of technological-
innovative progress. Schumpeter's concept of innovation and its exhaustion explained the propelling force behind each Kondratieff upswing or
downswing; upswings founded on new processes and industries gave way
to downswings upon their exhaustion and decline.[25]

The revival of the Schumpeter version of the long wave brought with it
renewed discussion as to whether it was properly deemed cyclical or
episodic, deterministic or random, endogenously or exogenously based—
all interrelated questions, with a cyclical explanation, for example, linked
to an endogenous one.[26] But these latter-day Schumpeterians, anxious to

proceed to policy implications, characteristically did not dwell on such questions. As Freeman put it, appreciation of Schumpeter's concepts did not require acceptance of the "idea of cycles as such and certainly not the notion of fixed periodicity." F. M. Scherer preferred even looser phrasing, noting that his argument did not require acceptance of the idea of "regular cycles." What counted was "merely this: that from the 1940s into the late 1960s there was a distinct surge of economic activity very much like a Kondratieff-Schumpeter upswing," followed by a period with "all the earmarks of a Kondratieff-Schumpeter downswing."[27] This looseness helped to explain how the concept gained support among economists not thought of as Schumpeterians; so, too, did the tendency to seek alternatives as an era of economic decline eroded assumed orthodoxies.[28] Some post-Keynesians thus spoke in Schumpeterian terms of shifting sources of economic growth over time. Joan Robinson, for one, declared her support of "Schumpeter's theory" of the economic impact of "major technical discoveries," applying the concept to the postwar boom and to its eventual exhaustion.[29]

Beyond Schumpeter, although often in tandem with him, the revival of interest in long waves also brought a vogue of Kondratieff, whose name dramatically reappeared in economic discourse from the 1970s on. The slow growth of the 1970s, beyond what could be attributed to a mere cyclical downturn, led to the search for explanatory long-run analyses.[30] Mensch called them theories geared to "discontinuity" rather than to "continuity." Thus, to W. W. Rostow, a leading Kondratieff enthusiast, the economy in the early 1970s "experienced a turning point. . . , a break as sharp as those of the 1790's, 1840's, 1890's, and 1930's." The 1970s could not be explained by traditional business cycle theory any more than the 1930s could, held Jay Forrester, another Kondratieff analyst; it was the long wave concept that could illuminate the "present economic turbulence."[31] The Kondratieff long wave was applied to the whole period since 1940, viewed as a Kondratieff upswing from the 1940s through the 1960s, based on backlogged needs and new technologies, whose exhaustion was reflected in a Kondratieff downswing from the early 1970s on. Hence, there was a "secular boom" followed by a "secular slump."[32]

Supporters of the Kondratieff long wave concept aimed their shafts at Keynes or, more accurate, the version of Keynes articulated by the neoclassical synthesizers of the 1940s, 1950s, and 1960s. Short-run Keynesians of the 1960s attributed the postwar boom to Keynesian macroeconomic management, to fiscal policy's assurance of adequate aggregate demand. The Kondratieff critics thought otherwise. Macroeconomic management helped, but it was essentially peripheral; deep-lying forces fed the boom, including technological thrusts, new industries, and military spending. Short-run Keynesians erroneously claimed more than that to which they were entitled; the long wave sustained them, not vice versa. They "nurtured" but did not create it. When the underlying causes of the boom in some measure approached exhaustion, the inadequacies of short-run Keynesianism became apparent.[33] As Rostow put it, Keynesian "macroeconomists . . . were dealing with economies driven forward by powerful . . . engines they did not fully understand, and they tended to mistake their marginal guidance of the economy for the basic motive forces at work." Nor, Rostow noted, did mainstream Keynesianism provide "a framework that illuminated the growth problems of the 1970s and 1980s."[34]

Rostow evidenced the divide between the Keynesian era and the rediscovery of the Kondratieff long wave. He allowed that Keynesian aggregate demand management helped to foster the postwar boom and to keep 1970s stagnation from plunging into a 1930s-style depression. But he insisted that the mainstream Keynesians' "vision of growth" failed "to grip and generate understanding of the great boom of the 1950s and 1960s."[35] Neoclassical Keynesians were out of their element when it came to technological spurts, innovation processes, and sectoral developments—that is, the ingredients of long-run economic growth and decline.[36] They did not "know how to deal with the generation and diffusion of technologies as an integral part of mainstream economics." They thought about investment in aggregate terms and became "distinctly uneasy" over suggestions involving "the need to change the directions of investment."[37] Rostow's strictures against short-run Keynesianism—and to some degree Keynes himself—did not apply to Alvin Hansen's secular version, which, with its Schumpeterian overlap, encompassed essential ingredients that Rostow felt neoclassical Keynesianism and, in some measure, Keynes lacked.

This was quite evident when it came to policy implications and prescriptions. Rostow and others agreed that the demand-oriented, short-run Keynesianism of the boom decades would clearly not suffice for a new era in which priorities were quite different—an era focused on stimulating new sources of economic growth rather than operating within those already under way and one geared to technology and investment as distinct from aggregate demand and consumption.[38] These objectives, Rostow further argued in what could be deemed quasi-Hansenian terms, required "an expansion of investment in certain sectors," which was obtainable only through "public policy." In language reminiscent of that of the Continental-based Hansen, Rostow proclaimed a return to "the pre-1914 world where growth was driven forward in the first instance by investment . . . in railroads, steamships, new technologies in metals and chemicals, the opening up of new areas." Research and development would now "be the equivalent . . . to the great open frontiers" brought "into the world economy, to restore its balance, in the three pre-1914 Kondratieff upswings."[39]

Questions as to the underlying nature of the Kondratieff long wave came with its revival. Was it a truly cyclical, self-repeating, causally interrelated phenomenon, or was it a product of a series of similar but discrete historical developments? Was it endogenously based on an inner rhythm of the system per se, or did it flow from the impact of exogenous external forces?[40] An endogenous explanation, Kleinknecht noted, was consistent with a concept of "true cycles," whereas an exogenously based explanation was consistent with a concept grounded on "historically unique events."[41] Klas Eklund, in his exhaustive survey and analysis of long wave theories, concluded that "secular wave-like fluctuations" were "quite compatible with explanations based exclusively on exogenous factors" as distinct from the concept of "a self-generating cyclical pattern." And while "no cyclical pattern" had been proven, "the existence of . . . turning-points and successive trend periods" was "an indisputable fact." Long waves were thus not cycles per se but manifestations of particular historical periods.[42] This was a conclusion very much in keeping with the Hansenian concept.

Schumpeter, together with Kondratieff, had a field day in the eighties, traveling on the up escalator as Keynes went down. But as divisions among his own supporters and enthusiasts evidenced, the Schumpeterian revivalists were not altogether uncritical of their progenitor. The old Schumpeter was discarded by some in favor of the young, whereas others favored a public sector reincarnation to the original. Nor was secular reaction to economic slackening limited to the Schumpeter-Kondratieff long wave; echoes of stagnation theory were also heard.

13.
The Specter of
Secular Stagnation

n addition to Schumpeter's and others' versions of Kondratieff long wave theory, long-run explanations appeared in the 1970s, stemming in part from Steindl and more broadly from Marx. Paul Sweezy, who had studied under Schumpeter, had been initially persuaded by Hansen's secular stagnation theory, and had later embraced Steindl's analysis in *Maturity and Stagnation in American Capitalism*, saw in the new era of stagnation further evidence of "mature" capitalism's inherent tendency to stagnate, offset only by adventitious external forces such as those of the postwar boom. If Kondratieff enthusiasts saw capitalism as a history of long up- and downswings and orthodox defenders of the system saw growth as the norm, and depression as a deviation, Sweezy saw stagnation as "late" capitalism's norm, with collapse of the system avoided only through exogenous fortuities.[1] In his 1980 *Long Waves of*

Capitalist Development: The Marxist Interpretation, Ernest Mandel tried to tie together exogenous and endogenous explanations. On the one hand, booms were triggered by exogenous forces, but on the other, the capacity to exploit those forces depended on the system's rate of profitability. Thus, like Sweezy, Mandel denied that recovery from long waves came from the inner workings of the system and so insisted that such recovery required exogenous stimuli. But, like Steindl in *Maturity and Stagnation*, he held that only when the system engendered sufficient capital could those exogenous stimuli be exploited commercially.[2]

The end of the postwar boom also brought renewed interest in Alvin Hansen's secular stagnation theory. The 1970s did not see a Great Depression, but the decade did witness a slowdown, a sluggishness, which suggested problems going beyond the short run with connections to a long run that, lacking government supports now in place, could conceivably lead to another abysmal collapse.[3] Hence 1970s analysts, as W. W. Rostow put it, again raised "the specter of secular stagnation."[4] In 1976 Leonard Silk, for example, noted that economists were now speculating as to whether emergent problems were "not cyclical but secular—that is, due to long-term changes," akin to those discussed by Alvin Hansen decades earlier. The population growth rate was down, impacting demand for housing and other products and services. The technological thrusts underlying the postwar boom were winding down and "may now be largely exhausted."[5] In 1986 R. D. Norton wrote that Hansen's secular stagnationist concern included a focus on sectors and the causes of industrial rise and decline, with strong relevance to post–postwar boom America, and thus was "a far cry" from the version of stagnation theory found in "textbook footnotes." As "an industry-specific vision of economic decline," it foreshadowed "the industrial upheaval of the 1970s" and "contemporary references to 'old-line' . . . or 'smokestack' industries."[6]

There were other efforts to suggest the relevance or to test the validity of Hansen's secular stagnation concept. The new industries of the boom decades were seen as supportive of Hansen's views as to the relation between and among technological advance, rising sectors, and economic growth.[7] The birth dearth underway by the late 1960s renewed interest in the Keynes-Hansen notion of the economic impact of demographic change.[8] In 1978 Clarence L. Barber revisited the role of population change in the Great Depression, linking a decline in the rate of population growth to a decline in residential construction, a decline that in turn "may well have been the most important single factor in turning the 1929 downturn into a major depression." Beyond that, Barber speculated, awareness of population growth rate decline may have led businesspeople to scale back investment expenditures generally in expectation of ultimately contracting markets, just as the later boom encouraged them to expand in expectation of growing markets. Barber capped his discussion, however, by citing not Hansen but John Hicks on the relation between population trends and secular economic growth.[9]

Hansen received explicit attention in some analyses of stagnation that appeared during and after the 1970s, but not the degree of attention given to the contributions of Schumpeter or Kondratieff. Seemingly Hansenian accounts sometimes failed to allude to him, whereas others misconstrued his thesis. Charles Kindleberger, citing Hansen's stagnation thesis, wrote in 1986 that events since the Great Depression indicated that investment could "be stimulated by fiscal policy" and thus was "not as intractable as . . . implied by the stagnation theories."[10] There are fiscal policies and then there are fiscal policies, of course, but in Hansen's own theory, a proper fiscal policy to unleash investment was precisely the cure for stagnation. Nor was the cavalier dismissal of stagnation theory evidenced during the postwar boom altogether in abeyance. George Stigler, of the University of Chicago, long a thorn in Gardiner Means's side, also as late as 1985 pronounced that as a result of the receding of the stagnationist "fad," Alvin Hansen's name would "never regain its onetime prominence."[11]

In accounting for the greater attention afforded the Schumpeter and Kondratieff legacies of long-run theory compared with Hansen's in the 1970s and beyond, chronological origins and associations came into play. Although there were pre-1929 Continental roots of Hansen's secular stagnation theory, his theory as a systematic whole was conceived, presented, and discussed during and in the close aftermath of the Great Depression. It was indelibly associated with and linked to the Great Depression. When the Great Depression ended and fears of recurrence had receded, interest in, support for, and even respect for the stagnation thesis receded as well. The 1970s slowdown was a slowdown, not a 1930s collapse. It brought a renewed interest in secular forces, but the strong linkage of Hansen's stagnation analysis to the Great Depression militated against a more widespread revival now. Hansenian secular stagnation theory could be too easily seen as a one-shot Great Depression analysis that was not transferable chronologically. Despite Hansen's efforts to use his analysis to illuminate American economic history more generally, the history could be viewed as a mere backdrop to the 1930s. The Schumpeter-Kondratieff tradition, on the other hand, had pre−Great Depression origins. Schumpeter's *Theory of Economic Development* had appeared on the eve of the First World War; Kondratieff's work had appeared in the 1920s. They were synthesized by Schumpeter in his 1939 *Business Cycles*, but given the Schumpeter-Kondratieff long wave theory's origins and nature, it could be seen as less Great Depression–bound than Hansen's concept. Hansen, despite his forays into economic history, was above all determined to understand the Great Depression. Schumpeter, despite his reference to the Great Depression, was above all determined to understand the nature of the capitalist process per se as it evolved through time. In this sense Schumpeter via Kondratieff could well seem more relevant and applicable to the post–postwar boom era than was Hansen.

Further, the cyclical, endogenous nature of the Schumpeter-Kondratieff concept could also make it appear more relevant and applicable across time periods than was Hansen's, even lacking formal theoretical acceptance of such a concept. A cyclical and endogenous concept postulated repetition and recurrence of the same underlying inner causes and of the same oscillating pattern. If it foretold the 1970s slump, it also foretold the great preceding boom. If the basic motive forces emanated from within the system, they could continue into new time frames. If the pattern was one of decline and revival, revival and decline, then in later as in earlier periods the pattern could be expected to repeat itself. That is, the Schumpeter-Kondratieff endogenously based concept had a simplicity, harmony, and predictability that may have enhanced its appeal in a new time of troubles: a boom will follow the slump given the very nature of long waves. Hansen's exogenously based concept offered no clear crystal ball. It could be seen as more complex, less easily predictable, and less easily transferable to a new time of troubles. Hansen, after all, postulated that the exogenous sources of economic growth changed somewhat over time. To be sure, technology was a constant in modern economic expansion, but geographic and population expansion were becoming less potent stimuli in Hansen's analysis by the time of the Great Depression. Hence greater reliance would now have to be placed on technological advance and, of course, public investment as a newly decisive, though not unprecedented, economic stimulus. There was no concept of an inner force unleashing recovery, nor any guarantee that revival would be forthcoming through exogenous stimuli. It was neither precluded nor assured. It all depended. One would have to sort out the stimulative forces involved to see what remained dynamic and then calculate what addition would now be conducive to renewed growth—for example, public investment coming out of the thirties. Applied to the new era of stagnation, aging industries and population growth rate decline had reappeared, but Hansenian analysis involved a messier, less clear-cut process than the broad certainties of the Schumpeter-Kondratieff long wave. New analysts could not just take up where an earlier generation had left off by simply applying an endogenous cyclical process to the new period. Hansen's exogenously based concept was less easily latched onto across time. It offered a way of looking at phenomena rather than a set conclusion, a list of questions rather than a survey result. Or, put differently, Hansen provided a historical perspective, whereas Schumpeter and Kondratieff tried to marshal evidence for generalizations across time, each approach appropriately fitting an exogenous or endogenous theory.

Additionally, there was the matter of time frame and public policy. Kondratieff could be seen as essentially policy neutral. His work remained unfinished, and a Rostow no less than a Schumpeter could apply his own substantive content and his own policy twists to Kondratieff long wave theory. But Schumpeter was hostile to public economic intervention, whatever use later public sector Schumpeterians might try to make of his legacy. In that sense a Schumpeter long wave or stagnation concept suited the mood of the late 1970s and certainly the 1980s far better than anything the Hansen legacy had to offer. Schumpeter fit the ethos of the Reagan-Thatcher era and fit it very well. Suffocating government had led to stagnation. Free the spirit of entrepreneurial initiative, and prosperity will blossom. Indeed, Reagan-Thatcherism could even be seen as a primitive form of Schumpeterianism, and Schumpeter's long wave concept could be appropriated and popularized to serve the current policy prescription. Quite the opposite was true of Hansen at this point. The theory of secular stagnation was associated with Keynesianism and public spending, both now under attack. How much of a revival could a secular analysis make in this period, given the competition and alternatives, when it was associated with the devil Keynes and with a fiscal policy that was widely blamed for budgetary excess and inflationary disaster? Add to this that the Hansen who was best known and remembered in the 1970s and 1980s was not the secular Keynesian of the late 1930s into the 1940s but, despite his crosscutting secular concerns, the short-run, neoclassical synthesis, Samuelson-Hicks-Hansen Keynesian of the boom decades. How much of a chance did the secular Keynesian Hansen have to emerge when the short-run Keynesian Hansen was among those being lambasted for the economic failures of the time, as well as for, among post-Keynesians, the disgrace that neoclassical synthesizers had made of Keynes's name and legacy? Beyond this, heterodoxy was increasingly shifting in the 1970s from fiscal to structural solutions via planning and industrial policy, although some of the latter could and did overlap with Hansenian prescriptions, as did public sector Schumpeterianism.

Finally, there was no Hansen "classic" or single book that had withstood the test of time to be forever cited, if also forever unread, as constituting the essence of the economist's contribution. Keynes had *The General Theory*; Means had his coauthored *Modern Corporation*; and Schumpeter had especially perhaps *Capitalism, Socialism, and Democracy*, not to gainsay his *Theory of Economic Development* or *Business Cycles*. But Hansen's books, while highly learned and lucid, were also partly pastiches of previously published articles, geared to contemporary problems, typically well-received and often highly influential in their time but without a high degree of permanence in and of themselves. The strains of Hansen's thought were in that sense diffused rather than concentrated. Thus there was for Hansen no flagship volume to which a later generation of economists could at least refer, no single work they could latch onto as the classic exposition of a thesis. Lacking a magnum opus, Hansen's legacy tended to fade from sight, only to reemerge in analyses and proposals not always recognized as characteristically Hansenian. An influence may be diffused and then reappear often without explicit reference to or even awareness of its original source: such was Alvin Hansen's fate.

The policy implications of a revival based on Hansenian secular stagnation theory at least suggested or implied an emphasis on innovative public investment.[12] In his 1976 analysis of new interest in secular stagnation theory, Leonard Silk, discussing economic policies designed to "overcome long-term stagnation," held that "new sources to spur investment" would likely involve government stimuli to research and development.[13] This recommendation would be heard again, but not in volume until the vogue of Schumpeter and the experiment with Reaganism gave way to a renewed interest in public investment. Meanwhile, Hansenian prescriptions were mixed in with post-Keynesian concepts, industrial policy proposals, and public sector Schumpeterianism.

Hansen's legacy in the context of the post–postwar boom era was replete with irony. Skeptically viewing Schumpeter's cyclical long-wave concept, economic analyst J. J. van Duijn questioned why it should be "a self-repeating process, in which every phase is necessarily followed by the next one," rather than a long wave ending "in secular stagnation, as some of Schumpeter's contemporaries thought."[14] Secular stagnation here amounted, as Hansen agreed, to Keynesian underemployment equilibrium, that is, an indefinite low level of activity, lacking an external jolt. Hansen's analysis also well fit the conclusion of Christopher Freeman in 1982: "Almost all . . . now prefer to speak of long waves rather than long cycles," that is, a less deterministic model.[15] Further, 1970s and 1980s rejections of short-run Keynesianism in favor of calls for a lost long-run Keynesianism fit Hansen. Note, for example, Gordon Fletcher's lament for "Keynes's . . . thesis of secular stagnation," lack of attention to which ultimately contributed to the downfall of the "Keynesian system."[16] Richard Chase rued the loss of secular Keynesianism even as the crisis of Keynesian economics was underway in 1975. Keynes, Chase was certain, felt that the short-run analysis of *The General Theory* took its "meaning" in a "fundamental sense" from a "relationship to longer-term historical . . . processes." But short-run Keynesianism, alas, was largely understood "in an unhistoric context." American Keynesians, "for example, Alvin Hansen in his influential *Guide to Keynes*," considered Keynes's "long-term views" as "not to be regarded seriously." This rupture of "Keynes's short-run . . . system" from its "longer-term historical moorings" altered in a fundamental way "the very nature of the theory," making the consequent "demand management" Keynesianism unable to cope with newer problems that could be "analyzed only under the mantle of a long-run" perspective.[17]

The irony in such accounts, of course, was that Hansen, here faulted as a neoclassical synthesis Keynesian, was typically unrecognized as the secular Keynesian whose long-run analysis provided much of what was lacking in short-run Keynesianism and called for in a lost secular Keynesianism. First, of course, Hansenian Keynesianism, unlike neoclassical Keynesianism, was long-run in outlook. Further, Hansenian Keynesianism was very much focused on the historic role of technology, in contrast with the technological lacuna of the short-run version. Hansenian Keynesianism had a sectoral component—a concern for rising and declining industries—that was lacking in the aggregate emphases of neoclassical Keynesianism. And Hansenian Keynesianism was oriented to and driven by investment, incorporating but subordinating consumption in its analysis, setting it apart from the demand management approach and consumption-oriented approach of mainstream Keynesianism. Thus while the lack of a structural Meansian component unquestionably hampered Keynesianism in dealing with the problems of the 1970s and beyond, the lack of a Hansenian long-run perspective had a similar effect. The first lack rendered neoclassical

Keynesianism seemingly simpleminded in dealing with inflation. The second lack rendered it seemingly irrelevant in dealing with stagnation. More attention to both long runs—the Meansian and the Hansenian, the structural and the environmental—would have provided Keynesianism with the perspectives and tools to understand, withstand, and combat more effectively the economic challenges and problems of the post–postwar boom era.

14.
Public Policies
for the Long Run

The troubles of the 1970s economy and the failure of neoclassical Keynesian formulas to resolve them led to renewed dissonance in economic theory and to competing public policy alternatives. On the one side came heterodox responses; on the other came challenges from a revived pre-1929, pre–Great Depression, pre–*General Theory* orthodoxy. For a new cohort of orthodox economists, the unraveling of the neoclassical synthesis consensus of the boom years also constituted an unraveling of the hitherto established wisdom of the older generation, an unraveling of Keynesian theory, and an unraveling of decades of Keynesian and interventionist public policies as such. The memory of 1929 was a half century past by 1979, thus setting the stage for a "new" approach that seemed novel largely because it had been relegated to intellectual byways for so long. To be sure, the Reagan administration, the political home of the refurbished orthodoxy, had diverse elements in its intellectual and policy makeup, including a strong early dose of monetarism, but its most distinctive and attention-grabbing element was 1920s-style tax reduction, now rechristened "supply-side" economics. The perception, once again, was that the private economy, freed from government intervention and harassment, would be self-propulsive and self-sustaining.[1]

Supply-siders believed in the basic efficacy and efficiency of the market, in the long run as well as the short. Great corporations were not immortal. Regulation, antitrust, and public policy, generally, they held, could not compare with the competitive rigor of long-run Schumpeterian "creative destruction." Hence, the young Schumpeter was right, they believed, and the old Schumpeter, Berle, Means, and Galbraith were wrong. Neoclassical Keynesian policies were also wrong. Demand management, whether fiscal or monetary, did not reach to such basic questions of supply as productivity and innovation. The answer, held supply-siders, lay in freeing private economic dynamism from the dead hand of government, above all through tax reduction. This would unloose entrepreneurial initiative, leading to innovation and investment, productivity and growth. Moreover, while the economy's basic problem according to supply-siders lay in laggard productivity, the solution would also reach to the problem of inflation: enhanced productivity would combat inflation without government-induced recession and without government controls. Not only was government responsible for current problems, claimed supply-siders, it also caused the Great Depression—through passage of the 1930 Hawley-Smoot tariff. Government intervention then as now was the problem, and public policy was of use essentially to free the economy from previous public policies, all in keeping with pre-1929 orthodox theory and policy.[2]

Paul Craig Roberts, a leading architect of supply-side economics, quite explicitly pointed to the 1920s precedent. There was "strong evidence," he wrote, that supply-side economics worked: "The Mellon tax cuts of the 1920s . . . produced a noninflationary economic boom."[3] The Great Depression was not here noted as a denouement. But critics were quick to attack Reagan economic policies in general and the supply-side component in particular. America's main competitors in world markets, they held, were hardly exemplars of a new laissez-faire economics, driven as they were by deeply involved public policy agencies.[4] Moreover, supply-side economics did not work, it was argued. Productivity rates were not up. Long-run growth was not renewed. Inflation's relative decline could be attributed to external forces and to monetary restriction. Further, recovery from the 1981–82 recession was basically demand- and not investment-driven. Tax cuts had triggered a consumption spree. In this, supply-side economics in practice had much in common with the neoclassical Keynesianism it abhorred. Finally, critics pointed to the stimulative effects of Reagan's increased defense spending, coupled with ballooning federal deficits. Thus supply-side economics was characterized as a failure by its critics and was viewed at best as demand-driven, neoclassical-cum-military Keynesianism in supply-side clothing.[5] To economist Wolfgang Stolper, for example, styling himself "a Schumpeterian and a real supply-sider," the mid-eighties upsurge combined "a real . . . Schumpeterian boom" with "the most primitive Keynesian policy, calling itself with unequaled gall supply-side economics."[6]

The course and critique of supply-side economics contributed to a renewal and refurbishing of heterodoxy, particularly in the form of secular Keynesianism. In terms of both policy and theory, neoclassical Keynesianism had proved defenseless against the onslaught of events and the resurgence of orthodoxy. Nor did the association of supply-side economics and the mid-eighties recovery with demand-oriented Keynesianism give a fillip to the latter: a consumption-based upsurge provided no answer to long-run stagnation, slow growth, or sluggish productivity increases. But the supply-side failure did help to trigger a reassertion of investment-oriented Keynesianism. Supply-siders, the argument ran, assumed that tax cuts would increase savings and hence investment. But Keynes had taught that it worked the other way around. Investment expanded growth, incomes, and savings. And although private investment depended on expectations, public investment could proceed as a matter of public policy.[7] This, combined with the concern over chronic sluggishness, provided the basis for an effort at long-run Keynesian rejuvenation. Ever since the mid-seventies, alarm had developed that sharp recessions followed by ephemeral upturns reflected an underlying stagnationist pull.[8] The recession of 1974–75, linked to inflation, triggered the sense that a new era was at hand. The painful recession of 1981–82 was assuaged by the glow of the Reagan upsurge. But the downturn of the early nineties seemingly discredited Reaganism, facilitating the attempted reversal of public policy in 1993.

The recession of the early nineties was not provoked as part of a fight against inflation.[9] It compared most aptly, some analysts held, not with previous recessions but with the 1930s depression.[10] Its basic significance was not cyclical but secular as a manifestation of underlying stagnation, a cyclical recession combined with a secular undertow.[11] John Kenneth Galbraith speculated that the economy had entered "an underemployment equilibrium of small or negligible growth." To James Tobin the recession belied the notion of "well-behaved cycles" of easy predictability and smooth adjustment. The downturn was further placed in long-run context as part of an interim between technologically driven epochs of expansion.[12] It was viewed as an economic consequence of population growth rate decline as evidenced by the slow growth in housing construction. It was judged a result of the diminution of the military spending prop to the economy in the wake of the end of the cold war.[13] And it was seen as a reaction to 1980s overbuilding, especially in the area of commercial office expansion.[14] The result was "a secular weakening of . . . investment."[15]

Perceived policy implications called for an enhanced public role. The concept of "contained depression" was advanced, the idea that the recession of the early 1990s might have repeated the experience of the early 1930s had it not been for safety nets dating back to the New Deal Era, hence giving government policy credit for the prevention of a disastrous debacle.[16] Further, interest rate reductions were deemed relatively ineffective in this setting. Lower rates did not attract investment in an economy lacking attractive outlets. Again, parallels were drawn to the 1930s.[17] A Schumpeterian revival might come, it was acknowledged—a burst of economic energy fueled by dynamic technological innovation.[18] But the downside was time: How long could a society sit by and wait for spontaneous forces to end stagnation? Analyst Allen Sinai held that the American economy had "never 'self-combusted' out of . . . stagnation. External stimulus" had "always been necessary," only then leading to self-generating expansion. To a growing number of economists in the early nineties, that external stimulus would have to be fiscal policy—specifically public investment—not only to spur the economy in the short run but also to galvanize the economy for the long run.[19]

The downturn of the early nineties was thus intertwined with longer-term analyses of stagnation, and prescriptions for recovery were intertwined as well. The short run was again seen as part of and inseparable from the long run. The long run, in turn, was now increasingly linked to the role of the American economy in a global setting. Global competition, some economists argued, institutionalists prominent among them, was eroding the familiar two-tiered oligopolistic/competitive view of the American economy, associated especially with the work of Galbraith but dating back to Means. Perhaps a more relevant view, it was suggested, was an "old" and "new" two-tiered version: old industries facing stiff competition from abroad undermining their domestic oligopolistic practices, including their ability to administer prices in the face of large-scale imports, and technologically advanced and globally more competitive new industries.[20] Galbraith himself now suggested that a "bureaucratic sclerosis" afflicted older oligopolistic industries faced with vigorous challenges from abroad.[21] If America's role in the world economy was now of growing importance, if corporate power was eroding domestically even as it spread globally, the implications for public policy were profound. Focus would have to be placed on improving what remained in America as it competed abroad: people and infrastructure.

Stretching back into the 1980s and accelerating as the Reagan boom faded in the early nineties recession, calls arose for greater public investment in infrastructure, in "human capital"—education, training, health—as well as in research and development to reverse America's perceived relative economic decline and to stimulate American competitiveness in world markets. In a sense such advocacy involved a recapture of the concept of government as playing a vital role in providing for economic growth, but a concept that had now shifted from short-run demand management via postwar Keynesianism to long-run public investment via a retrieved secular version.[22] Supporters of increased public investment in infrastructure, human capital, and technological development further linked its relative lack in the 1970s and 1980s to the country's declining rate of productivity growth. Declines in public investment in such areas correlated with and conceivably in some measure caused the productivity growth rate declines and lessened national competitiveness that had occurred over two decades.[23]

Hence, to deal not only with the short run but also, more significant, with the long run, the early 1990s witnessed a revival of public investment advocacy. Public investment in infrastructure, in education, and in technology, it was held, would help reverse two decades of relative stagnation, restoring economic vigor, growth, and global competitiveness.[24] David Alan Aschauer, for example, a leading analyst of the relation between public infrastructure investment and productivity growth rate decline, contended that "public infrastructure capital" was vital given the "myriad ways" it raised "productivity . . . across industries," making it perhaps several times "as potent in affecting the macroeconomy as private investment."[25] The "pay off," as Aschauer put it, for such public investment would be the curative impact on economic problems decades in the making.[26] The agenda for public investment included an emphasis on the long run over the short, public needs over private wants, and investment—

"public consumption"—over individual consumption.[27] In essence it was an agenda calling for Hansenian over neoclassical Keynesianism.

In 1988 economist Alan Blinder saw a "Keynesian counter-revolution" under way. In 1992 he pronounced a "Keynesian restoration" in place.[28] But it was a secular Keynesianism that had reemerged, not the short-run variety. Indeed, the vogue of the latter during the boom decades impeded the retrieval of the former thereafter. During the postwar boom, short-run Keynesianism was generally deemed to be Keynesianism, despite the protestations of Joan Robinson and others. When the events of the 1970s discredited short-run Keynesianism, it was widely assumed that Keynesianism as such had been discredited, and a search for alternatives was undertaken, which led to the abortive planning movement and early versions of industrial policy, as well as to the politically more successful Schumpeterian revival and other formulas of the Reagan-Thatcher era. It was not until these formulas had apparently been exhausted that the way was opened to a secular Keynesian revival. Put differently, short-run Keynesianism seemed to have won the race among economic theories in the 1960s, and its collapse affected anything deemed Keynesian, in effect making long-run Keynesianism the last out of the gate thereafter. Thus the emergence of long-run problems in the 1970s overthrew short-run Keynesian hegemony, but only later did analysis of long-run problems lead to a secular Keynesian revival. The public investment movement of the late eighties and early nineties marked the reemergence of a secular, investment-oriented Keynesianism.

The late eighties and early nineties provided fertile ground for a secular or Hansenian Keynesian revival. The Reagan boomlet had faded into a lengthy recession, which apparently discredited the policy prescriptions of the 1980s. Additionally, the recessionary downturn of the early nineties took place against the backdrop of two decades of relative stagnation—in contrast to the gloried boom decades of the postwar era. Public investment during the early 1990s was not propounded so much in terms of social desirability, as with Hansen and Galbraith in the 1950s, as in terms of economic imperatives, which made it more akin to Hansen's analyses and proposals of the late thirties and early forties. In policy terms, if the 1970s concern with inflation contributed to a Meansian influence and a faltered grasp at structural planning and if the 1980s brought a Schumpeterian revival and Reaganite strictures against government, then the early 1990s reactions pointed to a more activist public economic agenda in the spirit of Alvin Hansen and the secular Keynes. It took the 1990s and the Clinton administration to provide a political home, whatever its limits, to Hansenian Keynesian public policy advocacy.

But may one speak of a Hansenian revival without much explicit touting of Hansen? Yes. First, Hansen came to the fore under the Keynesian umbrella as Keynes's pioneer advocate in America. He was thought of as a Keynesian, albeit with his own secular stagnationist version. To talk of a Keynesian renewal focused on long-run public investment is to mean a secular Keynesian or Hansenian Keynesian revival. If the content, thrust, and emphases are Hansenian Keynesian, then the revival may be deemed Hansenian Keynesian. Explicit or direct links are less important than the common nature of analyses and prescriptions. Further, as noted, Hansen wrote no work to which later analysts could make routine reference as representative or symbolic of the oeuvre. Galbraith, by contrast, as a more recent figure and as author of *The Affluent Society*, could be pointed to as a lodestar for a reform-minded administration.[29] This, even though the ideas involved were Hansenian before they were Galbraithian. And even when Hansen was explicitly mentioned, there was a risk of misunderstanding and unintentional misrepresentation. Alan Blinder, for example, on his way to posts in the Clinton administration beginning in 1993, declared a year earlier that for two decades the country had suffered "from secular stagnation" and called for "building human capital to address the long-run secular problem." He then proceeded to announce that Hansen's secular stagnationism was geared to alleged problems with consumer buying power rather than investment—an exact reversal of Hansen's own argument. Hence Blinder could provide a Hansenian analysis and prescription at the same time as he dismissed Hansen's misstated and erroneously understood theory as "nonsense."[30] The revival of interest in public investment could perhaps best be described under these circumstances as a manifestation of subterranean Hansenianism.

The "track of slow growth" stretching back to the 1970s, declared economic analyst and incoming Clinton administration secretary of labor Robert Reich in late 1992, required long-term initiatives to restore "long-term growth."[31] Accordingly, efforts were undertaken beginning in 1993 to increase public investment in infrastructure, education, research, and technology.[32] In addition to the Clinton administration's interest in public investment, there were forays into, if not full-fledged "industrial policy," at least a degree of public-private planning or public sector Schumpeterianism, combined with public investment. These drew on state experiments of the 1980s. Although the Reagan boom of the mid-eighties put a halt to national debate over industrial policy, versions of the concept were discussed and in some measure implemented at the state level in economically hard-hit regions where they were billed as "economic development," "competitiveness strategy," and state "entrepreneurship." They involved state government investment in education, training, technology, and research and development, as well as attempts to foster technologically advanced competitive "sunrise" industries. The emphasis was long-run, geared not only to recovery from the 1981–82 recession but also to a future in which the old bedrock manufacturing industries would never regain their former importance. Here the states were endeavoring to facilitate the transfer of technology from laboratories to commercial enterprise, an entrepreneurial role, in Schumpeterian terms, such as the United States Department of Agriculture's Extension Service had historically provided.[33]

These state efforts provided a further basis for the policy debates of the late eighties and early nineties, along with the push to develop a national competitiveness strategy in a global context.[34] In 1992 economic analyst Robert Kuttner proclaimed the "re-emergence of industrial policy"; after fading from national view for a decade, the notion that the country needed "a strategic industrial policy" had "evidently come of age."[35] But there were different concepts of industrial policy. The historian Otis L. Graham Jr., in his 1992 book *Losing Time: The Industrial Policy Debate*, differentiated between "industrial policy" as "a form of planning" and "industrial strategy." Industrial policy, he wrote, involved an element of structural, targeted microplanning, whereas industrial strategy distanced government from microplanning decisions. Rather than arranging "a particular industrial portfolio"—that is, attempting to target certain industries for development—government would endeavor to strengthen education, infrastructure, and public services across the boards.[36] The sojourns of Robert Reich illustrated shifts from industrial policy, involving efforts to target specific industries for public support, to industrial strategy, geared via public investment to upgrade the economic vigor of the nation as a whole.[37] A lawyer rather than an economist by training, a friend of Bill Clinton going back to their Rhodes Scholar days, Reich in the early and mid-1980s was a vigorous, prolific, and peripatetic proponent of industrial policy, while also advocating increased public investment. In his 1989 *The Resurgent Liberal*, however, Reich stressed the latter as the key to "long-term economic health." Most Americans, he held, supported public investment in infrastructure, education, training, health, and research and development, and they wanted these "economic-development policies" to be made "more 'strategic.'" On the other hand, Reich concluded, Americans disliked "complicated plans" and would not support "industrial policy" conceived of as an "elaborate plan."[38]

The strong Clinton administration interest in greater public investment appeared to fit this concept of industrial strategy as it undertook initiatives enhancing federal support for research and development to spur technological advance and stressed the need to nurture human capital by way of education and training. These initiatives were designed to spur the health and vigor of the economy as a whole. But along with this macro and aggregate emphasis came micro or sectoral initiatives too, including government interaction with particular industries to focus research on promising technologies.[39] An emphasis on public-private cooperation and coordination recalled the planning schemes of the 1930s, as distinct from an antitrust approach. "We're trying to replace lawyers with engineers," one government official declared.[40] The Clinton administration's long-run stress on public investment, therefore, could also be seen as industrial strategy, to which was added at least a soupçon of industrial policy, all of which in turn cohered with public sector Schumpeterianism. Or, tracing these strains back to the New Deal Era, there was a public investment emphasis drawn from Hansenian Keynesianism, an interest in public-private coordination and planning pioneered by Means and others, and a sectoral technological focus stemming especially from Schumpeter. These legacies were now especially geared to the enhancement of American competitive vigor in a global setting.

Epilogue

John Maynard Keynes, like his contemporary Franklin Delano Roosevelt, has been rewarded with an "Age": Arthur Schlesinger Jr.'s "Age of Roosevelt" is also Robert Lekachman's "Age of Keynes." Keynes's death in 1946, like Roosevelt's in 1945, was followed by the beginnings of what became a huge outpouring of literature over the next half century. Already in 1951 there appeared Roy Harrod's hefty biography, and in recent times there have been the massive works of Robert Skidelsky and Donald Moggridge, chronicling and detailing Keynes's life in both the long run and the short. A steady stream of exegetical and analytical publications has also continued to flow, detailing nooks and crannies of Keynes's intellectual development and contributions. He did indeed cut a wide swath through not only economic and intellectual but also political and cultural history. In the wake of *The General Theory*, he dominated his profession, and his impact remained powerful through the 1960s. With the dissolution of the "Age of Keynes" in the 1970s, however, he was taken to task and blamed—or those who misinterpreted and misapplied his ideas were blamed—for the disasters of that decade. Nonetheless, whether viewed positively or negatively, there remained no question as to his continuing "consequences." A key question on which students of Keynes have focused is the connection between his general theory and the traditional economics in which he was reared, including his failure to incorporate imperfectly competitive microfoundations and his role in the original Hicksian formulation of the neoclassical synthesis.[1] Keynes's public policy proposals, however altered and truncated, were widely accepted, but not in the end on the basis of orthodoxy's incorporation into the general theory. Rather, the general theory was incorporated as a "special case" into the neoclassical synthesis.

Gardiner C. Means, a major figure as of the mid-1930s, was thereafter overwhelmed by the Keynesian avalanche. Eclipsed by Alvin Hansen as a New Deal public policy influence at decade's end, he somewhat retreated from the scene in the early postwar period, returning with the economic developments of the later 1950s and then commanding greater attention and renewed respect with the inflationary surge of the 1970s. Means has fared well since, having been adopted by the hardy band of institutionalists in the economics profession and now considered a valued precursor among post-Keynesians. Although he felt he lacked a "flair for writing" and although the stylistic verve of *The Modern Corporation* was Adolf Berle's, Means did have a gift for language when it came to brief encapsulations of economic concepts, as even his most severe detractors have acknowledged, however left-handedly.[2] Hence the lasting impress of his "administered prices" and "administrative inflation," as well as his use of "corporate revolution" and "industrial policy." Further, corporate downsizing and lagging real wages during the post-1992 recovery suggested the continued relevance of Means's focus on the lack of a necessary coherence between the micro- and macrofunctioning of a modern economy. For all his substantive contributions, however, notably his analysis of the macroeconomic impact of corporate microdecision making, Means's stubborn adherence to a version of monetary orthodoxy contradicted his otherwise heterodox economics and constituted a flashpoint between his economics and Keynes's. Means's structural heterodoxy did not reach into the monetary realm, nor was it complemented by a fully developed investment theory such as Keynes and Hansen produced.

Alvin Hansen, in contrast to Means, has been relatively eclipsed in recent historical memory and scholarship. A figure of considerable magnitude in the late 1930s and first half of the 1940s, advising major political and policy leaders, dividing his time between Harvard and Washington, and hailed as the "American Keynes," Hansen found the postwar world inhospitable to his prewar secular theories, even while it embraced Keynesian tools and techniques with which he was also associated. More honored in his own time than Means, he has been less recognized since. Unlike Means, Hansen was linked to neoclassical synthesis Keynesianism and was, it seemed, among its formulators, and so despite secular credentials, he appeared beyond the realm of resuscitation and revival with its demise. And while Means's reputation was enhanced by that demise and could be sustained by the kinship felt for him among institutionalists and post-Keynesians, those who felt the greatest kinship with Hansen—who were in some cases his students—had themselves been discredited by the debacle of neoclassical synthesis Keynesianism. Further, with the return of chronic economic sluggishness after 1973, Hansen's concept of discrete periods of secular stagnation was less revived than the Schumpeter-Kondratieff long wave. Still, despite Hansen's limitations from a heterodox perspective, notably his relative de-emphasis on structure and his role in the neoclassical synthesis, there remained much of value from that perspective in Hansen's oeuvre. Those analyzing trend-based secular stagnation and calling for an investment-oriented version of Keynesianism or industrial policy qua strategy need only look to Hansen for inspiration.[3] Further, it was Hansen's public policy advocacy, although not often recognized as such, that resonated with the late 1980s and early 1990s resurgence of interest in public investment.

Joseph Schumpeter's lifelong goal to be the greatest economist of his generation was dashed by Keynes; still, his standing remained prominent and his place in the history of economic analysis remains secure. Very much in the shadow of Keynes during the postwar boom, although by no means neglected, Schumpeter as an economic influence and historical figure began his comeback as the "Age of Keynes" unraveled. Like Keynes, he cut a wide swath: not only economists but also historians, sociologists, and political scientists have drawn on his work. He has been the subject of recent biographies by Robert Loring Allen and Richard Swedberg, books that have illuminated his personal and intellectual development, including his private musings and hitherto unpublished views of contemporary events. Additionally, a flow of more specialized studies continues, and for

Schumpeter, as for Keynes, one focus has been on links to orthodoxy. Schumpeter, to a greater extent than Keynes, and despite his evolutionary theory, never broke free from key pre–Great Depression assumptions, including the notion that in the long run the depression would give way to a boom through processes of self-adjustment.[4] Keynes concluded that this long run was too long under the devastating circumstances and produced his general theory; Hansen, long influenced by Schumpeter, was here persuaded by Keynes and opted for new public policies; but Schumpeter did not so conclude and was not so persuaded, resorting instead to an exogenous political explanation of depression longevity. Conceivably, had Schumpeter broken free to the degree that Keynes did, had he developed a public sector Schumpeterianism in his own time—that is, had he championed new public policy as a seminal, growth-producing "innovation"— he might have joined Keynes atop the pantheon.

Keynes, Means, and Hansen all contributed to New Deal thinking and policy discussion, with Schumpeter in adamant opposition. But the fissures between Hansen and Means and between Means and Keynes—in each case partially due to continuing links to orthodoxy—divided the challenge to orthodoxy into heterodox rivalries, with the Keynesians overwhelming the institutionally oriented planners. Keynesians, then, with the end of the depression and the continuance of the boom, jettisoned their secular motif in favor of the neoclassical synthesis. This in turn was largely identified as the economic legacy of the New Deal, obscuring connections to earlier long-run themes. But these other elements of the New Deal legacy, although neglected during the boom decades, regained resiliency and relevance as the boom dissipated and the neoclassical synthesis turned to ashes. The idea of structural planning was revived in the 1970s to combat inflation. Certainly a Gardiner Means could argue that the disastrous inflation of that decade could have been largely prevented or alleviated by the structural planning that neoclassical Keynesianism disdained. The revival of secular public investment Keynesianism toward the end of the 1980s and into the 1990s achieved a political standing via the advocacy of Bill Clinton in the 1992 campaign. Certainly an Alvin Hansen would have argued that the decline of American economic dynamism could have been largely prevented or alleviated by massive public investment geared to technological research, infrastructure, and human capital.

Evolutionary economics has been resurgent since the early 1970s, yet it has faced a reassertive orthodoxy also emboldened by the collapse of neoclassical synthesis Keynesianism. If heterodox economists saw that collapse as a basis for a revival of evolutionary theories, a new generation of orthodox economists saw the collapse as a basis for rejection of Keynesian policy prescriptions as well as theory. In the 1970s, public policy seemed poised to go in either one of two alternative directions. Calls for structural planning and industrial policy, however, were swept aside in the late 1970s and the 1980s by a monetarist, supply-side, primitive Schumpeterian amalgam. During the postwar boom, an activist public economic policy had been associated with short-run Keynesianism, and when the boom ended and short-run Keynesianism proved unable to deal with the vicissitudes of the 1970s and was discredited and repudiated, other activist public economic policy proposals, including structural planning and industrial policy, were subject to dismissal as parts of the same failed interventionist package. If the presumed legacy of the 1930s had faltered in the 1970s, the reaction was to disinter the legacy of the 1920s. Further, structural planning promised an attack on inflation, and with industrial policy, it also reached to stagnation. But lacking a secular Keynesian dimension, heterodoxy fell short of a fully comprehensive macroeconomic alternative to the intellectually and politically facile Reagan promise both to end inflation and to restore economic growth without pain and without an expanded governmental role. That secular Keynesian dimension was retrieved via the upsurge of interest in public investment of the late eighties and early nineties, but even then, given the long dominance of neoclassical synthesis Keynesianism, connections between the Roosevelt and Keynes era and the time of Clinton were obscured. The Clinton administration, for example, was accused by one economist critic of adhering to "a pure form of supply-side economics," offering no "demand management . . . policy," and stressing instead an increase in "the supply of infrastructure" and education and training to advance knowledge and skills. The approach was, ran the final rapier thrust, "pre-Keynes."[5] But whose Keynes? Clinton's approach was certainly not that of a neoclassical synthesis Keynesian. But it was fully consonant with that of a secular Hansenian Keynesian.

Bill Clinton often referred to public investments as "the things I got elected for."[6] His administration, however, included those who gave priority to deficit reduction and those, including the president himself, who tried to balance or synthesize public investments and deficit reduction.[7] Similarly, Roosevelt's administration included, along with New Deal reformers, the likes of Jesse Jones and Lewis Douglas, and despite his work relief spending, the New Deal president long remained a budget balancer at heart. If Clinton's concern over sluggish productivity and relative American economic decline brought a focus on the long run, necessary short-run foci included low interest rates to sustain recovery from recession.

Roosevelt's long-run reform goals were also interspersed or intertwined with "emergency" programs to meet the immediate crisis of 1933. If the Clinton administration's more conventional policies can be viewed as will-o'-the-wisps that draw attention away from more fundamental emphases such as public investments, much the same could be said about the Roosevelt administration's monetary manipulation or antitrustism in relation to structural planning or long-term public spending. Clinton's great early legislative triumph was passage of the North American Free Trade Agreement (NAFTA), with the specter of the 1930 Hawley-Smoot tariff set forth in debate as a disaster never to be repeated. Roosevelt lambasted Hawley-Smoot in the 1932 campaign, and although the New Deal's emphasis was overwhelmingly domestic in the international context of the 1930s, victory in World War II facilitated efforts to weave anew the depression- and war-torn fabric of global economic cooperation. Clinton, while continuing global trade liberalization, nonetheless, like Roosevelt, viewed domestic programs as essential prerequisites. (While NAFTA was inherited from the preceding Republican administration, Bush-Reaganites did not share Clinton's belief in public investments and industrial strategy as keys to the reinvigoration of American productivity and global competitiveness.)

Clinton entered office as recovery from recession was under way. Roosevelt entered at the depth of the deepening depression. Clinton faced a difficult political context, whereas Roosevelt confronted by far the greater immediate economic challenge. It took the recession of the early nineties for a more activist public policy agenda to become again a political possibility, and the Clinton administration in 1993 undertook to reverse policy prescriptions of the 1980s. Clinton's popular vote plurality of 1992, however, was no match for Roosevelt's landslide majority of 1932, and the recovery from recession apparent during the interregnum of 1992–93 stood in sharp contrast to the spur to action and change provided by the crisis of 1932–33. Thus Clinton's 1992 campaign was geared to an activist public investment agenda, and Clinton initially "focused the whole thrust of his economic program on the long-term."[8] But political difficulties intervened. "Clinton saw himself as a descendant of FDR," wrote the journalist Elizabeth Drew in 1994, "but he . . . lacked a perceived emergency."[9] Clinton's use of public policy to generate economic renewal in the long run was not easily demonstrable in the short. Roosevelt's charge in 1933 to put the country quickly on the road to recovery from unprecedented collapse was clear-cut and more easily measured. Clinton inherited Reagan's ballooning federal debt. It was hard to make the distinction, as one administration official put it, between productive public "investments" and possibly wasteful government "spending" to an audience awash in a sea of red ink.[10] Roosevelt inherited the "Hoover depression" and in succeeding the repudiated and exhausted Hoover in 1933 could be envisaged as reparting the Red Sea.

For all their similarities as times of economic difficulty and dissonance, the 1930s and the post-1973 era also evidenced major differences. The essential "story of the U.S. economy since the early 1970s," wrote economist Paul Krugman in 1990, was one of basic "stability without progress," avoidance of "depression without . . . sustained economic growth."[11] Gradual and relative weakening, added Robert Kuttner in 1991, "never . . . shows up as a highly visible cataclysm that would spur remedial action."[12] The Clinton administration, then, for all its focus on public investment and concomitant interest in industrial strategy and public sector Schumpeterianism, faced major hurdles and obstacles. Long-run programs were not an easy political sell, all the more apparent in the wake of the 1994 election reversals, which stood in sharp contrast to the pickup in congressional seats enjoyed by Roosevelt in 1934. Whatever the political vicissitudes, however, the ideas forged in the late seventies that intellectually fueled the Reagan era were no longer fresh and novel in the nineties and could be dismissed by foes as "tired . . . supply-side economics that failed in the last decade."[13] Further, reformist alternatives, building on legacies of the New Deal Era, were now in place for those who believed that the complexities of the late-twentieth-century economy required an activist public agenda.[14] The questions remained poised. Did orthodox or heterodox theory provide greater explanatory power for understanding economic upheaval and transformation? Did unimpeded corporate power best serve the general interest, or were public constraints and coordination required? Would economic renewal flow automatically from within, or would vigorous public policy be needed? Questions and issues central to the 1930s remained central to the 1990s.

Notes

INTRODUCTION

1. Gary Gerstle and Steve Fraser, introduction to Steve Fraser and Gary Gerstle, eds., *The Rise and Fall of the New Deal Order, 1930–1980* (Princeton, N.J., 1989), xxiv.
2. Otis L. Graham Jr., "Franklin D. Roosevelt and the Intended New Deal," in M. R. Beschloss and Thomas E. Cronin, eds., *Essays in Honor of James MacGregor Burns* (Englewood Cliffs, N.J., 1989).
3. Ulrich Witt, "Evolutionary Concepts in Economics," *Eastern Economic Journal* 18 (Fall 1992): 405; Richard W. England, "Time and Economics: An Introductory Perspective," in Richard W. England, ed., *Evolutionary Concepts in Contemporary Economics* (Ann Arbor, 1994), 5; Geoffrey M. Hodgson, *Economics and Evolution: Bringing Life Back into Economics* (Ann Arbor, 1993), 284.
4. Quoted in Hodgson, *Economics and Evolution*, 130.

PART I

1. Books useful for understanding the 1930s in relation to economic developments include Anthony Badger, *The New Deal: The Depression Years, 1933–1940* (New York, 1989); Michael A. Bernstein, *The Great Depression: Delayed Recovery and Economic Change in America, 1929–1939* (New York, 1987); Alan Brinkley, *The End of Reform: New Deal Liberalism in Recession and War* (New York, 1995); Ellis W. Hawley, *The New Deal and the Problem of Monopoly: A Study in Economic Ambivalence* (Princeton, N.J., 1966); Barry D. Karl, *The Uneasy State: The United States from 1915 to 1945* (Chicago, 1983); Charles P. Kindleberger, *The World in Depression, 1929–1939*, rev. ed. (Berkeley, 1986); Dean L. May, *From New Deal to New Economics: The American Liberal Response to the Recession of 1937* (New York, 1981); Jordan A. Schwarz, *The New Dealers: Power Politics in the Age of Roosevelt* (New York, 1993); and Herbert Stein, *The Fiscal Revolution in America* (Chicago, 1969).

CHAPTER ONE

1. Allan G. Gruchy, *Modern Economic Thought: The American Contribution* (New York, 1947), 622–23; Bernard Sternsher, *Rexford Tugwell and the New Deal* (New Brunswick, N.J., 1964), viii–ix.
2. Quoted in H. H. Liebhafsky, "An Institutionalist Evaluation of the Recent Apparently, but Only Apparently, Fatal Attack on Institutionalism," *Journal of Economic Issues* 22 (Sept. 1988): 846.
3. "Institutional Economics" (symposium), *American Economic Review: Papers and Proceedings* 22 (Mar. 1932): 105.
4. George Soule, *A Planned Society* (1932; Gloucester, Mass., 1965), 147–48.
5. Gruchy, *Modern Economic Thought*, 3; Allan G. Gruchy, *Contemporary Economic Thought: The Contribution of Neo-Institutional Economics* (Clifton, N.J., 1972), 24, 70; Stephen W. Baskerville, "Cutting Loose from Prejudice: Economists and the Great Depression," in Stephen W. Baskerville and Ralph Willet, eds., *Nothing Else to Fear: New Perspectives on America in the Thirties* (Manchester, England, 1985), 269.

6. Joseph Dorfman, *The Economic Mind in American Civilization, 1918–1933*, vol. 5 (New York, 1959), 743–44.

7. Sternsher, *Rexford Tugwell and the New Deal*, 17–18, 20–22, 25, 99–100; Ellis W. Hawley, *The New Deal and the Problem of Monopoly: A Study in Economic Ambivalence* (Princeton, N.J., 1966), 171–77, 179; Allan G. Gruchy, "The Economics of the National Resources Committee," *American Economic Review* 29 (March 1939): 60–65, 67–68; "Prices—Discussion," *American Economic Review: Papers and Proceedings* 37 (May 1947): 262–64.

8. Adolf A. Berle to George W. Anderson, Dec. 16, 1931, box 4, Adolf A. Berle Papers, Franklin D. Roosevelt Library (hereafter FDRL), Hyde Park, N.Y.

9. "Speech of Mr. A. A. Berle, Jr., before the National Industrial Conference Board on January 23, 1936," 8, 11–13, box 140, Berle Papers.

10. Isador Lubin to H. S. Gilbertson, Aug. 10, 1932, 1, box 7, Isador Lubin Papers, FDRL.

11. Mordecai Ezekiel, "Neither Socialism nor Fascism," ca. 1934–35, pt. 2, 10–11, box 30, Mordecai Ezekiel Papers, FDRL.

12. Louis H. Bean, "The Need for an Industrial Production Program as a Basis for Sound Price and Employment Policies," Jan. 31, 1935, 1, 10, box 42, Louis H. Bean Papers, FDRL.

13. Adolf A. Berle and Gardiner C. Means, *The Modern Corporation and Private Property* (1932; New York, 1967), xli, 42–43, 46, 116, 306–8, 310, 312–13.

14. Jordan A. Schwarz, *Liberal: Adolf A. Berle and the Vision of an American Era* (New York, 1987), viii; Frederic S. Lee, "*The Modern Corporation* and Gardiner Means's Critique of Neoclassical Economics," *Journal of Economic Issues* 24 (Sept. 1990): 679–81.

15. Gardiner C. Means, "Hessen's 'Reappraisal,'" *Journal of Law and Economics* 26 (June 1983): 297, 300; Gardiner C. Means, "Corporate Power in the Marketplace," *Journal of Law and Economics* 26 (June 1983): 469.

16. Jerome Frank, review of *The Modern Corporation and Private Property*, by Adolf A. Berle and Gardiner C. Means, *Yale Law Journal* 42 (April 1933): 989.

17. Joseph V. Kline, review of *The Modern Corporation and Private Property*, by Adolf A. Berle and Gardiner C. Means, *Columbia Law Review* 33 (Mar. 1933): 557.

18. Gardiner C. Means to Beatrice A. Rogers, Aug. 19, 1933, box 86, Gardiner C. Means Papers, FDRL.

19. George B. Galloway to Lewis L. Lorwin, May 7, 1934, box 1, Central Office Records of the National Resources Planning Board, RG 187, Personal Desk File of Dr. Lewis Lorwin, entry 36, National Archives II, College Park, Md.

20. William E. Stoneman, *A History of the Economic Analysis of the Great Depression in America* (New York, 1979), 63–64, 96; Charles A. Beard and Mary R. Beard, *America in Midpassage*, vol. 2 (New York, 1939), 873.

21. Paul A. Samuelson, "Alvin H. Hansen, 1887–1975," *Newsweek*, June 16, 1975, 72.

22. Rexford G. Tugwell, *The Battle for Democracy* (1935; New York, 1969), 20; Rexford G. Tugwell, *To the Lesser Heights of Morningside: A Memoir* (Philadelphia, 1982), 227.

23. Mordecai Ezekiel, "After the New Deal," *New Republic*, Aug. 23, 1939, 64–66.

24. Arthur Smithies, "Schumpeter and Keynes," in Seymour E. Harris, ed., *Schumpeter: Social Scientist* (Cambridge, Mass., 1951), 140; Charles K. Wilber and Kenneth P. Jameson, *An Inquiry into the Poverty of Economics* (Notre Dame, Ind., 1983), 198.

25. Douglas Dowd, *Thorstein Veblen* (New York, 1964), 45–47.

26. Peter Temin, "The Impact of the Depression on Economic Thought," in Charles P. Kindleberger and Guido di Tella, eds., *Economics in the Long View: Essays in Honour of W. W. Rostow*, vol. 1, *Methods and Methodology* (London, 1982), 70–72.

27. Theodore Rosenof, *Patterns of Political Economy in America: The Failure to Develop a Democratic Left Synthesis, 1933–1950* (New York, 1983), 85–87.

CHAPTER TWO

1. Richard F. Kahn, *The Making of Keynes' General Theory* (Cambridge, England, 1984), 120–21; Charles H. Hession, *John Maynard Keynes: A Personal Biography of the Man Who Revolutionized Capitalism and the Way We Live* (New York, 1984), 271; Geoffrey C. Harcourt, "Theoretical Methods and Unfinished Business," in David A. Reese, ed., *The Legacy of Keynes* (San Francisco, 1987), 3.
2. Allen M. Sievers, *Revolution, Evolution, and the Economic Order* (Englewood Cliffs, N.J., 1962), 8, 11–13, 17; James R. Crotty, "Keynes on the Stages of Development of the Capitalist Economy," *Journal of Economic Issues* 24 (Sept. 1990): 762; Robert Skidelsky, *John Maynard Keynes*, vol. 2, *The Economist as Saviour, 1920–1937* (New York, 1994), 501.
3. R. F. Harrod, *The Life of John Maynard Keynes* (1951; New York, 1971), 332; Joseph A. Schumpeter, *Ten Great Economists: From Marx to Keynes* (New York, 1951), 267–68; Robert Skidelsky, *John Maynard Keynes*, vol. 1, *Hopes Betrayed, 1883–1920* (New York, 1986), 400–401; Skidelsky, *Economist as Saviour*, 130–31, 220.
4. James R. Schlesinger, "After Twenty Years," in Bernard S. Katz and Ronald E. Robbins, eds., *Modern Economic Classics: Evaluations through Time* (New York, 1988), 127, 135; John H. Williams, "An Appraisal of Keynesian Economics," *American Economic Review* 36 (May 1948): 275–76; Mark Blaug, "Second Thoughts on the Keynesian Revolution," *History of Political Economy* 23 (Summer 1991): 179; William Guthrie and Vincent J. Tarascio, "Keynes on Economic Growth, Stagnation, and Structural Change: New Light on a 55-Year Controversy," *History of Political Economy* 24 (Summer 1992): 381, 395–96.
5. Sievers, *Revolution, Evolution, and the Economic Order*, 23–24; Gottfried Haberler, "The *General Theory* (4)," in Seymour E. Harris, ed., *The New Economics: Keynes' Influence on Theory and Public Policy* (New York, 1947), 163; Benjamin Higgins, "Concepts and Criteria of Secular Stagnation," in Lloyd A. Metzler et al., *Income, Employment, and Public Policy: Essays in Honor of Alvin H. Hansen* (New York, 1948), 87.
6. Schumpeter, *Ten Great Economists*, 268.
7. Robert Skidelsky, "The Reception of the Keynesian Revolution," in Milo Keynes, ed., *Essays on John Maynard Keynes* (Cambridge, England, 1975), 92–93.
8. John Maynard Keynes, *The General Theory of Employment, Interest, and Money* (New York, 1936), 307.
9. Ibid., 161–62, 249–50; Kurt W. Rothschild, "Capitalists and Entrepreneurs: Prototypes and Roles," in H.-J. Wagener and J. W. Drukker, eds., *The Economic Law of Motion of Modern Society: A Marx-Keynes-Schumpeter Centennial* (New York, 1986), 193–95; Skidelsky, *Economist as Saviour*, 271; Richard Kahn to A. H. Hansen, Dec. 28, 1951, HUG (FP) 3.10, box 1, Alvin H. Hansen Papers, Harvard University Archives, Cambridge, Mass.
10. John Maynard Keynes, *General Theory*, 347–48.
11. Ibid., 317, 320.
12. Ibid., 249–50.
13. Clarence L. Barber, "Keynes' View of Investment," in Omar F. Hamouda and John N. Smithin, eds., *Keynes and Public Policy after Fifty Years*, vol. 2, *Theories and Methods*

(New York, 1988), 37; Vincent J. Tarascio, "Keynes on the Sources of Economic Growth," *Journal of Economic History* 31 (June 1971): 429; Vincent J. Tarascio, "Keynes, Population, and Equity Prices," *Journal of Post Keynesian Economics* 7 (Spring 1985): 303–4; Donald E. Moggridge, *Maynard Keynes: An Economist's Biography* (New York, 1992), 597.

14. "Some Economic Consequences of a Declining Population," in Donald Moggridge, ed., *The Collected Writings of John Maynard Keynes*, vol. 14, *The General Theory and After*, pt. 2, *Defence and Development* (London, 1973), 125–26.

15. Quoted in John Hicks, *Economic Perspectives: Further Essays on Money and Growth* (New York, 1977), 22. John Hicks had previously signed his writings as "J. R. Hicks."

16. William E. Stoneman, *A History of the Economic Analysis of the Great Depression in America* (New York, 1979), 99–100; Roger Opie, "The Political Consequences of Lord Keynes," in Donald E. Moggridge, ed., *Keynes: Aspects of the Man and His Work* (New York, 1974), 78; Peter Clarke, *The Keynesian Revolution in the Making, 1924–1936* (New York, 1988), 281.

17. Farhad Mahloudji, "Hicks and the Keynesian Revolution," *History of Political Economy* 17 (Summer 1985): 292; D. G. Franzsen, "The Secular Stagnation-Thesis and the Problem of Economic Stability," *South African Journal of Economics* 10 (1942), 282; Hicks, *Economic Perspectives*, 141 n. 6.

18. R. F. Harrod, *Towards a Dynamic Economics: Some Recent Developments of Economic Theory and Their Application to Policy* (London, 1948), 73; Clarke, *Keynesian Revolution*, 230; David McCord Wright, *The Keynesian System* (New York, 1962), 40; Joan Robinson, "What Has Become of the Keynesian Revolution?" in Milo Keynes, *Essays on John Maynard Keynes*, 125–26.

19. John Maynard Keynes, *General Theory*, 33, 324–25, 368, 372–73, 378; Keynes to W. H. Beveridge, July 28, 1936, in Moggridge, *Defence and Development*, 58; Stoneman, *Economic Analysis of the Great Depression*, 119–20.

20. John Maynard Keynes, *General Theory*, 325, 347–48, 367–68, 370; Piero Ferri and Hyman P. Minsky, "The Breakdown of the IS-LM Synthesis: Implications for Post-Keynesian Economic Theory," *Review of Political Economy* 1 (July 1989): 134; Skidelsky, *Economist as Saviour*, 535, 542–43, 558.

21. John Maynard Keynes, *General Theory*, 317, 320, 378; D. E. Moggridge, *John Maynard Keynes* (New York, 1976), 103; Robert W. Dimand, *The Origins of the Keynesian Revolution: The Development of Keynes' Theory of Employment and Output* (Stanford, 1988), 88; Clarke, *Keynesian Revolution*, 196, 230, 278–80, 292, 296; J. R. Hicks, *Value and Capital: An Inquiry into Some Fundamental Principles of Economic Theory*, 2d ed. (London, 1946), 259; J. M. Keynes to Mordecai Ezekiel, June 6, 1941, 3–4, box 6, Mordecai Ezekiel Papers, Franklin D. Roosevelt Library (hereafter FDRL), Hyde Park, N.Y.

22. J. Ronnie Davis, *The New Economics and the Old Economists* (Ames, Iowa, 1971), 145, 150; Victoria Chick, *Macroeconomics after Keynes: A Reconsideration of the "General Theory"* (Cambridge, Mass., 1983), 325; Dudley Dillard, *The Economics of John Maynard Keynes: The Theory of a Monetary Economy* (New York, 1948), 106.

23. Steven Pressman, "The Policy Relevance of *The General Theory*," *Journal of Economic Studies* 14, no. 4 (1987): 17; James Love, "The Orthodox Keynesian School," in Douglas Mair and Anne G. Miller, eds., *A Modern Guide to Economic Thought: An Introduction to Comparative Schools of Thought in Economics* (Brookfield, Vt., 1991), 162–63; Harold G. Vatter, "The Atrophy of Net Investment and Some Consequences for the U.S. Mixed Economy," *Journal of Economic Issues* 16 (Mar. 1982): 243; Clarke, *Keynesian Revolution*, 288.

24. John Maynard Keynes, *General Theory*, 320, 378.

25. Ibid., 379.
26. Ibid., 378.
27. Ibid., 380–81.
28. Alvin H. Hansen, "The *General Theory* (2)," in Harris, *The New Economics*, 138.
29. Allan G. Gruchy, "Uncertainty, Indicative Planning, and Industrial Policy," *Journal of Economic Issues* 18 (Mar. 1984): 161.
30. Alan Coddington, *Keynesian Economics: The Search for First Principles* (London, 1983), 98–99; T. W. Hutchison, *On Revolutions and Progress in Economic Knowledge* (New York, 1978), 238; Elizabeth Durbin, "Keynes, the British Labour Party, and the Economics of Democratic Socialism," in Omar F. Hamouda and John N. Smithin, eds., *Keynes and Public Policy after Fifty Years*, vol. 1, *Economics and Policy* (New York, 1988), 40–41.
31. John Maynard Keynes, *General Theory*, 378–79.
32. Elizabeth S. Johnson and Harry G. Johnson, "The Social and Intellectual Origins of *The General Theory*," *History of Political Economy* 6 (Fall 1974): 269; Allan G. Gruchy, "Keynes and the Institutionalists: Important Contrasts," in C. Lawrence Christenson, ed., *Economic Theory in Review* (Bloomington, Ind., 1949), 117; Robert L. Heilbroner, "Economics and Political Economy: Marx, Keynes, and Schumpeter," in Suzanne W. Helburn and David F. Bramhall, eds., *Marx, Schumpeter, Keynes: A Centenary Celebration of Dissent* (Armonk, N.Y., 1986), 19.
33. Alfred S. Eichner to Gardiner C. Means, July 31, 1978, box 68, Gardiner C. Means Papers, FDRL.
34. Guy Routh, *The Origin of Economic Ideas* (White Plains, N.Y., 1975), 274–75; Hession, *Keynes*, 287; Harcourt, "Theoretical Methods and Unfinished Business," 19; Marjorie S. Turner, *Joan Robinson and the Americans* (Armonk, N.Y., 1989), 47–48.
35. R. F. Harrod to Alvin H. Hansen, Jan. 2, 1952, HUG (FP) 3.10, box 1, Hansen Papers.
36. Harcourt, "Theoretical Methods and Unfinished Business," 12–13; G. C. Harcourt, *Controversies in Political Economy: Selected Essays of G. C. Harcourt* (New York, 1986), 260; James Tobin, "Keynesian Economics and Its Renaissance," in Reese, *Legacy of Keynes*, 117; David McQueen, "The Hidden Microeconomics of John Maynard Keynes," in Hamouda and Smithin, *Economics and Policy*, 117; Chaitram J. Talele, *Keynes and Schumpeter: New Perspectives* (Brookfield, Vt., 1991), 51.
37. J. A. Kregel, "Marx, Keynes, and Social Change: Is Post-Keynesian Theory Neo-Marxist?" in Edward J. Nell, ed., *Growth, Profits, and Prosperity: Essays in the Revival of Political Economy* (New York, 1980), 267–68; Clarke, *Keynesian Revolution*, 279–82, 296, 324; Claudio Sardoni, "Market Forms and Effective Demand: Keynesian Results with Perfect Competition," *Review of Political Economy* 4, no. 4 (1992): 378; Skidelsky, *Economist as Saviour*, 440.
38. John Brothwell, "*The General Theory* after Fifty Years—Why Are We Not All Keynesians Now?" in John Hillard, ed., *J. M. Keynes in Retrospect: The Legacy of the Keynesian Revolution* (Brookfield, Vt., 1988), 47, 55; George R. Feiwell, "The Legacies of Kalecki and Keynes," in Mario Sebastiani, ed., *Kalecki's Relevance Today* (New York, 1989), 56.

CHAPTER THREE

1. Alfred S. Eichner, "Gardiner C. Means," *Challenge* 22 (Jan./Feb. 1980): 56–57; Frederic S. Lee and Warren J. Samuels, "Introduction: Gardiner C. Means, 1896–1988," in Lee and Samuels, eds., *The Heterodox Economics of Gardiner C. Means: A Collection* (Armonk, N.Y., 1992), xv; Glenn Fowler, "Gardiner C. Means, 91, Is Dead; Pricing The-

ory Aided U.S. Policy," *New York Times*, Feb. 18, 1988, B 10; Unofficial Observer [John Franklin Carter], *The New Dealers* (New York, 1934), 93–95.

2. Lee and Samuels, "Introduction," xviii–xix; Frederic S. Lee, "*The Modern Corporation* and Gardiner Means's Critique of Neoclassical Economics," *Journal of Economic Issues* 24 (Sept. 1990): 675–76; Caroline F. Ware et al., "Consumer Participation at the Federal Level," in Erma Angevine, ed., *Consumer Activists: They Made a Difference* (Washington, 1980), 304; Gardiner C. Means to Carliss Y. Baldwin, Feb. 4, 1983, 1–2, box 67, Gardiner C. Means Papers, Franklin D. Roosevelt Library (hereafter FDRL), Hyde Park, N.Y.

3. Lee, "*Modern Corporation* and Gardiner Means's Critique," 674; Gardiner C. Means, "The Veblen-Commons Award," *Journal of Economic Issues* 9 (June 1975): 153.

4. Eichner, "Gardiner C. Means," 57; Unofficial Observer, *New Dealers*, 95.

5. Eli Ginzberg, "Economics at Columbia: Recollections of the Early 1930s," *American Economist* 34, no. 2 (1990): 17–18.

6. Gardiner C. Means, "The Corporate Revolution," Jan. 1, 1933, 134, 173, 175–76, box 2, Means Papers; Gardiner C. Means, "The Growth of the Relative Importance of the Large Corporation in American Economic Life," *American Economic Review* 21 (Mar. 1931): 36–37; Gardiner C. Means, "The Separation of Ownership and Control in American Industry," *Quarterly Journal of Economics* 46 (Nov. 1931): 97; Gardiner C. Means, review of *The Masquerade of Monopoly*, by Frank A. Fetter, *Columbia Law Review* 32 (Feb. 1932): 391–92.

7. Quoted in Ware et al., "Consumer Participation," 303.

8. Lee, "*Modern Corporation* and Gardiner Means's Critique," 684–85, 689; Means, "Corporate Revolution," 134–35.

9. Warren J. Samuels and Steven G. Medema, "Gardiner C. Means's Institutional and Post-Keynesian Economics," *Review of Political Economy* 1 (July 1989): 180, 182–84; Lee, "*Modern Corporation* and Gardiner Means's Critique," 681–82, 691; Means, "Corporate Revolution," 152–59.

10. Means, "Veblen-Commons Award," 151–52; Gardiner C. Means to W. H. Ferry, Dec. 3, 1957, 4, box 59, Means Papers; Gardiner C. Means, interview by Norman Silber for the Center for the Study of the Consumer Movement, Feb. 23–25, 1978, 5, box 68, Means Papers; Gardiner C. Means to Willard F. Mueller, Dec. 11, 1974, box 70, Means Papers; Warren J. Samuels and Steven G. Medema, *Gardiner C. Means: Institutionalist and Post Keynesian* (Armonk, N.Y., 1990), 148–50, 172.

11. Gardiner C. Means to Rexford G. Tugwell, Mar. 17, 1953, 1–2, box 22, Means Papers.

12. Caroline F. Ware and Gardiner C. Means, *The Modern Economy in Action* (New York, 1936), 11, 231; Gardiner C. Means, "The Major Causes of the Depression," Oct. 15, 1935, 22, box 3, Means Papers; Gardiner C. Means to Henry A. Wallace, July 25, 1934, 3, box 5, Means Papers.

13. United States National Resources Committee, *The Structure of the American Economy*, pt. 1, *Basic Characteristics: A Report Prepared by the Industrial Section under the Direction of Gardiner C. Means* (1939; New York, 1966), 106, 145; Gardiner C. Means, "Big Business, Administered Prices, and the Problem of Full Employment," *Journal of Marketing* 55 (Apr. 1940): 373.

14. Means, "Major Causes of the Depression," 10, 14, 22; Gardiner C. Means to Willford I. King, May 10, 1935, 4, box 4, Means Papers.

15. Gardiner C. Means, "A Reply by Gardiner C. Means," *American Economic Review* 24 (Mar. 1934): 85; *Structure of the American Economy*, 155; Gardiner C. Means, "Competition Called Far from Ordinary," *New York Times*, Nov. 4, 1934, sec. 4, p. 5; Gardiner C.

Means, "The Location of Economic Control of American Industry," *American Economic Review: Papers and Proceedings* 29 (Mar. 1939): 112–13.

16. Means to Wallace, July 25, 1934, 1.

17. *Structure of the American Economy*, 106 n. 21.

18. Means, "Major Causes of the Depression," 10, 14, 22–23; Gardiner C. Means, "The Distribution of Control and Responsibility in a Modern Economy," *Political Science Quarterly* 50 (Mar. 1935): 62.

19. Means, "Major Causes of the Depression," 15; Means to Wallace, July 25, 1934, 1; Means, "Major Causes of the Depression," 22.

20. Ware et al., "Consumer Participation," 305–6; Frederic S. Lee, "A New Dealer in Agriculture: G. C. Means and the Writing of *Industrial Prices*," *Review of Social Economy* 46 (Oct. 1988): 199; Gardiner C. Means to Richard Heflebower, Dec. 10, 1952, box 21, Means Papers.

21. Means to Tugwell, Mar. 17, 1953, 1.

22. Means, "Major Causes of the Depression," 10, 18, 22–23.

23. Means, "Big Business, Administered Prices, and the Problem of Full Employment," 373–74; Gardiner C. Means to Paul T. Homan, Oct. 27, 1934, 1, box 2, Means Papers.

24. *Structure of the American Economy*, 120.

25. Gardiner C. Means, "Notes on Inflexible Prices," *American Economic Review: Papers and Proceedings* 26 (Mar. 1936): 32–33; Ware and Means, *Modern Economy*, 32, 36; Means, "Major Causes of the Depression," 15; Means to Wallace, July 25, 1934, 1.

26. Means, "Major Causes of the Depression," 22.

27. Gardiner C. Means, "Inflexible Prices," 1935, 15, box 89, Means Papers.

28. Means, "Distribution of Control and Responsibility in a Modern Economy," 62; Gardiner C. Means, "Price Inflexibility and the Requirements of a Stabilizing Monetary Policy," *Journal of the American Statistical Association* 30 (June 1935): 405; Means, "Major Causes of the Depression," 2, 10–11; Means, "Notes on Inflexible Prices," 33, 35.

29. Ware and Means, *Modern Economy*, 32, 36; Means, "Price Inflexibility," 405; Means, "Major Causes of the Depression," 11–12, 16.

30. Gardiner C. Means to Jerry Cohen, Mar. 20, 1964, 1–2, box 89, Means Papers; Gardiner C. Means to John Blair, Aug. 10, 1971, 8–9, box 107, Means Papers; Gardiner C. Means, "Administered Prices," in Douglas Greenwald, ed., *Encyclopedia of Economics* (New York, 1982), 11.

31. Means to Wallace, July 25, 1934, 1.

32. Gardiner C. Means, *Industrial Prices and Their Relative Inflexibility*, 74th Cong., 1st sess., 1935, S. D. 13, 8; Means, "Administered Prices," 12.

33. Means, "Price Inflexibility," 405; Gardiner C. Means, "An Administrative Theory of Employment and Inflation," mid-1970s, V-V-1-12, box 92, Means Papers.

34. Means, "Big Business, Administered Prices, and the Problem of Full Employment," 373; Means to King, May 10, 1935, 4; Gardiner C. Means to George Stigler, Feb. 5, 1960, 1, box 126, Means Papers; Gardiner C. Means, "The Controversy over the Problem of Full Employment," in United States National Resources Committee, *The Structure of the American Economy*, pt. 2. *Toward Full Use of Resources: A Symposium* (Washington, D.C., 1940), 15.

35. Means, "Major Causes of the Depression," 2; Means, "Price Inflexibility and the Requirements of a Stabilizing Monetary Policy," 404; Means, "Major Causes of the Depression," 23; Gardiner C. Means, "The Consumer and the New Deal," *Annals of the American Academy of Political and Social Science* 173 (May 1934): 13.

36. Means, "Price Inflexibility," 407; Means, "Major Causes of the Depression," 11, 15, 22;

Means to King, May 10, 1935, 4; Gardiner C. Means to Yakov Amihud, July 17, 1980, box 67, Means Papers; Gardiner C. Means, "Business Combinations and Agriculture," *Journal of Farm Economics* 20 (Feb. 1938): 55.

37. Gardiner C. Means to Richard A. Lester, Nov. 14, 1952, box 21, Means Papers; Means to Cohen, Mar. 20, 1964, 3.

38. U.S. Congress, Senate, "Statement of Gardiner C. Means," in *Administered Prices: Hearings before the Subcommittee on Antitrust and Monopoly of the Committee on the Judiciary*, 85th Cong., 1st sess., 1957, pt. 1, 93–94, 108; Means to King, May 10, 1935, 4; Gardiner C. Means to William Benton, Jan. 21, 1944, 3, box 20, Means Papers; Means to Stigler, Feb. 5, 1960, 2.

39. Means to Homan, Oct. 27, 1934, 2.

40. Gardiner C. Means to J. M. Keynes, July 16, 1935, box 4, Means Papers.

41. Gardiner C. Means, *The Corporate Revolution in America: Economic Reality vs. Economic Theory* (New York, 1962), 161–62; Means to Benton, Jan. 21, 1944, 1–2; Gardiner C. Means to Raymond Rubicam, May 12, 1945, 1, box 22, Means Papers; Means to Amihud, July 17, 1980.

42. Gardiner C. Means, "Conglomerates and Concentration," *University of Miami Law Review* 25 (Fall 1970): 17, 21; Gardiner C. Means, "The Economics of Administered Prices," Jan. 29, 1940, 4, box 8, Means Papers; Gardiner C. Means, "Implications of Price Administration for Economic Investigation," Jan. 3, 1951, 1, box 38, Means Papers; Gardiner C. Means, "Pricing Power and the Public Interest," in U.S. Congress, Senate, *Administered Prices: A Compendium on Public Policy, Subcommittee on Antitrust and Monopoly of the Committee on the Judiciary*, 88th Cong., 1st sess., 1963, 220.

43. Means to Blair, Aug. 10, 1971, 5.

44. Ellis W. Hawley, *The New Deal and the Problem of Monopoly: A Study in Economic Ambivalence* (Princeton, N.J., 1966), 293–94; Richard S. Kirkendall, *Social Scientists and Farm Politics in the Age of Roosevelt* (Columbia, Mo., 1966), 90; Rexford G. Tugwell, "Addendum to Diary for the Hundred Days," 6, box 15, Rexford G. Tugwell Papers, FDRL; Lee, "New Dealer in Agriculture," 188, 198; Mordecai Ezekiel to George Leighton, Jan. 27, 1934, 2, box 6, Mordecai Ezekiel Papers, FDRL.

45. Charles A. Beard to Gardiner C. Means, Feb. 11, 1935, box 5, Means Papers; Stuart Chase to Gardiner C. Means, Feb. 14, 1935, box 5, Means Papers; J. M. Keynes to Gardiner C. Means, Mar. 18, 1935, box 4, Means Papers.

46. Gardiner C. Means to Charles A. Beard, Feb. 25, 1935, box 5, Means Papers.

47. Ware and Means, *Modern Economy*, 141–43, 197–99, 209–10; Means, "Distribution of Control and Responsibility in a Modern Economy," 67–68.

48. *Structure of the American Economy*, 145–46; Gardiner C. Means to H. I. Harriman, Oct. 27, 1934, box 2, Means Papers; Means to Homan, Oct. 27, 1934, 2; Gardiner C. Means, "NRA and AAA and the Reorganization of Industrial Policy Making," Aug. 29, 1934, 1, box 89, Means Papers.

49. Means, *Industrial Prices*, 13–14; Ware and Means, *Modern Economy*, 147–49; Means, "Distribution of Control and Responsibility in a Modern Economy," 59, 63–64, 67, 69.

50. Ware and Means, *Modern Economy*, 142–43.

51. *Structure of the American Economy*, v; "Statement Submitted by Gardiner C. Means, Industrial Committee, National Resources Committee," Nov. 22, 1935, box 7, Means Papers; Gardiner C. Means to Charles E. Merriam, Jan. 23, 1937, 1, 3, box 11, Means Papers.

52. *Structure of the American Economy*, 4–5; Gardiner C. Means et al., *Patterns of Resource Use* (Washington, D.C., 1938), 1; Gardiner C. Means to Frederic A. Delano, June 3, 1938, 1, box 6, Central Office Records of the National Resources Planning Board, RG

187, Papers of Thomas Blaisdell Jr., National Archives II, College Park, Md.

53. Means, "Price Inflexibility," 409; Means to Delano, June 3, 1938, 1.

54. Means, *Industrial Prices*, 13–14; Ware and Means, *Modern Economy*, 150, 198–99, 225; Gardiner C. Means to Raymond L. Buell, Apr. 16, 1935, box 5, Means Papers; Gardiner C. Means, "The Industrial Section of the National Resources Committee," Jan. 13, 1936, 1, box 6, Blaisdell Papers.

55. Ware and Means, *Modern Economy*, 150–51, 160; Means, "Consumer and the New Deal," 13–14, 16–17; Means, "Distribution of Control and Responsibility in a Modern Economy," 69; Gardiner C. Means to Henry A. Wallace, Aug. 10, 1934, 1–2, box 5, Means Papers.

56. Means to Wallace, July 25, 1934, 3–4.

57. Means, *Industrial Prices*, 12–13; Means, "Distribution of Control and Responsibility in a Modern Economy," 63, 68; Means to Harriman, Oct. 27, 1934.

58. Gardiner C. Means to Walter Lippmann, Feb. 7, 1935, box 2, Means Papers; Means, "Location of Economic Control of American Industry," 113.

59. Means, "Distribution of Control and Responsibility in a Modern Economy," 68; Gardiner C. Means, "Proposals for Bringing the Technical Phases of National Planning to a National Focus," Nov. 28, 1936, in Lee and Samuels, eds., *Heterodox Economics of Gardiner C. Means*, 97; Means, "Notes on Inflexible Prices," 35; Mordecai Ezekiel to Dudley Windel, Apr. 16, 1936, box 19, Ezekiel Papers; Marion Clawson, *New Deal Planning: The National Resources Planning Board* (Baltimore, 1981), 92–93; Otis L. Graham Jr., *Toward a Planned Society: From Roosevelt to Nixon* (New York, 1976), 53–54.

60. Ware and Means, *Modern Economy*, 208.

61. Means to Wallace, July 25, 1934, 4; Means, "Industrial Section of the National Resources Committee," 1.

62. Gardiner C. Means to Alfred S. Eichner, Sept. 22, 1978, 7, box 68, Means Papers; Allan G. Gruchy, *Modern Economic Thought: The American Contribution* (New York, 1947), 478.

63. Means, "Problem of Full Employment," 10; Means, "Major Causes of the Depression," 19–20, 23; Lee, "New Dealer in Agriculture," 186.

64. Gardiner C. Means, "Background Memorandum for the Cremona Conference," July 20, 1971, 71, 73, box 48, Means Papers; Means, "Administrative Theory of Employment and Inflation," V-III-I, 10; "Statement of Gardiner C. Means," 86, 109.

65. Gardiner C. Means to R. G. Tugwell, Sept. 8, 1934, 3–5, box 2, Means Papers; Means, "Major Causes of the Depression," 17–18; Gruchy, *Modern Economic Thought*, 495–97.

66. Means, "Major Causes of the Depression," 18.

67. Gardiner C. Means to Henry A. Wallace, Dec. 18, 1934, box 2, Means Papers.

68. Keynes to Means, Mar. 18, 1935.

69. Means, "Big Business, Administered Prices, and the Problem of Full Employment," 378; Means, "Major Causes of the Depression," 20; Frederic S. Lee, "The Marginalist Controversy and the Demise of Full Cost Pricing," *Journal of Economic Issues* 18 (Dec. 1984): 1109; Gruchy, *Modern Economic Thought*, 499, 501; Means, "Problem of Full Employment," 15; Samuels and Medema, *Gardiner C. Means*, 85–86.

CHAPTER FOUR

1. William J. Barber, "The Career of Alvin H. Hansen in the 1920s and 1930s: A Study in Intellectual Transformation," *History of Political Economy* 19 (Summer 1987): 192; Anna Rothe, ed., *Current Biography, 1945* (New York, 1945), 264–65, 267; Richard A. Mus-

grave, "Hansen, Alvin," in John Eatwell et al., eds., *The New Palgrave: A Dictionary of Economics*, vol. 2 (New York, 1987), 591; Richard A. Musgrave, "Caring for the Real Problems," *Quarterly Journal of Economics* 90 (Feb. 1976): 1–2.

2. Musgrave, "Caring for the Real Problems," 3–4, 6; Gottfried Haberler, "Some Reminiscences," *Quarterly Journal of Economics* 90 (Feb. 1976): 9–10; Paul A. Samuelson, "Alvin H. Hansen as a Creative Economic Theorist," *Quarterly Journal of Economics* 90 (Feb. 1976): 24–25; James Tobin, "Hansen and Public Policy," *Quarterly Journal of Economics* 90 (Feb. 1976): 32–33.

3. Alvin Harvey Hansen, *Business-Cycle Theory: Its Development and Present Status* (Boston, 1927), iii; Musgrave, "Caring for the Real Problems," 2; Alvin H. Hansen, "Thrift and Labor," *Annals* 87 (Jan. 1920): 47.

4. Alvin H. Hansen, "The Sequence in War Prosperity and Inflation," *Annals of the American Academy of Political and Social Science* 89 (May 1920): 234.

5. Wesley C. Mitchell to Alvin H. Hansen, Mar. 19, 1924, HUG (FP) 3.10, box 2, Alvin H. Hansen Papers, Harvard University Archives, Cambridge, Mass.

6. Hansen, *Business-Cycle Theory*, iii, 67–69, 77, 79–81, 182, 189, 203–4.

7. Alvin Harvey Hansen, *Economic Stabilization in an Unbalanced World* (New York, 1932), 94, 99, 112; "The Business Depression of Nineteen Hundred Thirty—Discussion," *American Economic Review: Papers and Proceedings* 21 (Mar. 1931): 199–201; Alvin H. Hansen, "The Business Cycle and Its Relation to Agriculture," *Journal of Farm Economics* 14 (Feb. 1932): 60, 66; Nikolai Kondratieff to Alvin H. Hansen, Feb. 1928, HUG (FP) 3.10, box 1, Hansen Papers.

8. Hansen, *Economic Stabilization*, vii, 320; Alvin H. Hansen, "The Theory of Technological Progress and the Dislocation of Employment," *American Economic Review: Papers and Proceedings* 22 (Mar. 1932): 31.

9. "Business Depression of Nineteen Hundred Thirty," 201; Hansen, "Business Cycle and Its Relation to Agriculture," 66.

10. Alvin H. Hansen, "The Flow of Purchasing Power," in Robert M. MacIver et al., *Economic Reconstruction: Report of the Columbia University Commission* (New York, 1934), 214–15, 218; Alvin H. Hansen, "Capital Goods and the Restoration of Purchasing Power," *Academy of Political Science Proceedings* 16 (Apr. 1934): 11–12, 17.

11. Alvin H. Hansen and Herbert Tout, "Investment and Saving in Business Cycle Theory," *Econometica* 1 (Apr. 1933): 119–20.

12. Hansen, "Capital Goods and the Restoration of Purchasing Power," 11–12; Alvin H. Hansen et al., *A Program for Unemployment Insurance and Relief in the United States* (Minneapolis, 1934), 168–70.

13. Hansen and Tout, "Investment and Saving in Business Cycle Theory," 130–33, 143–44.

14. Arthur Schweitzer, "Spiethoff's Theory of the Business Cycle," *University of Wyoming Publications* 8 (Apr. 1, 1941): 4, 15–16; Robert Aaron Gordon, *Business Fluctuations*, 2d ed. (New York, 1961), 356–57, 360–65; Donald Winch, *Economics and Policy: A Historical Study* (London, 1969), 159; Alvin H. Hansen, *Business Cycles and National Income* (New York, 1964), 281–82, 287–88, 290–95.

15. Samuelson, "Hansen as a Creative Economic Theorist," 27–28; Dennis Robertson to Alvin H. Hansen, Sept. 1953, HUG (FP) 3.10, box 2, Hansen Papers.

16. Alvin H. Hansen et al., "Recent Trends in Business-Cycle Literature," *Review of Economic Statistics* 18 (May 1936): 56–57; Alvin H. Hansen, "Schumpeter's Contribution to Business Cycle Theory," in Seymour E. Harris, ed., *Schumpeter: Social Scientist* (Cambridge, Mass., 1951), 79.

17. Hansen, "Business Cycle and Its Relation to Agriculture," 60; Alvin H. Hansen, *Mon-*

etary Theory and Fiscal Policy (New York, 1949), v; Hansen, "Schumpeter's Contribution to Business Cycle Theory," 79.

18. Hansen, "Business Cycle and Its Relation to Agriculture," 60.

19. Alvin H. Hansen, review of *Prices and Production*, by Friedrich A. Hayek, *American Economic Review* 23 (June 1933): 334.

20. Samuelson, "Hansen as a Creative Economic Theorist," 29; Paul H. Douglas to Rexford G. Tugwell, Nov. 8, 1933, 2, box 7, Rexford G. Tugwell Papers, Franklin D. Roosevelt Library, Hyde Park, N.Y.

21. Tobin, "Hansen and Public Policy," 32; William E. Stoneman, *A History of the Economic Analysis of the Great Depression in America* (New York, 1979), 108, 123.

22. Alvin H. Hansen to J. M. Clark, Aug. 8, 1934, 1–2, 4–6, HUG (FP) 3.10, box 1, Hansen Papers.

23. Alvin H. Hansen, "Monetary Policy in the Upswing," in A. D. Gayer, *The Lessons of Monetary Experience: Essays in Honor of Irving Fisher* (New York, 1937), 97–99; Hansen et al., "Trends in Business-Cycle Literature," 56, 59; J. Ronnie Davis, *The New Economics and the Old Economists* (Ames, Iowa, 1971), 149; Seymour E. Harris, "The Appraisal of the General Theory, 1936–37," in Harris, ed., *The New Economics: Keynes' Influence on Theory and Public Policy* (New York, 1947), 35–36.

24. Hansen, "Monetary Policy in the Upswing," 96; Alvin H. Hansen, "Harrod on the Trade Cycle," *Quarterly Journal of Economics* 51 (May 1937): 523–24; Alvin H. Hansen, "The Situation of Gold Today in Relation to World Currencies," *American Economic Review: Papers and Proceedings* 27 (Mar. 1937): 130–31.

25. Hansen, "Harrod on the Trade Cycle," 531.

26. Hansen, "Monetary Policy in the Upswing," 89.

27. Barber, "Career of Alvin H. Hansen in the 1920s and 1930s," 200, 202, 205; Haberler, "Some Reminiscences," 11; Walter S. Salant, "Alvin Hansen and the Fiscal Policy Seminar," *Quarterly Journal of Economics* 90 (Feb. 1976): 15–16.

28. Alvin H. Hansen, *A Guide to Keynes* (New York, 1953), 5–7, 11; Barber, "Career of Alvin H. Hansen in the 1920s and 1930s," 203, 205; Alvin H. Hansen, "Keynes and the General Theory," *Review of Economic Statistics* 28 (Nov. 1946): 182, 187; Walter S. Salant, "The Spread of Keynesian Doctrines and Practices in the United States," in Omar F. Hamouda and John N. Smithin, eds., *Keynes and Public Policy after Fifty Years*, vol. 1, *Economics and Policy* (New York, 1988), 66.

29. Hansen, "Keynes and the General Theory," 183, 185–87.

30. Alvin H. Hansen, notes on Harry G. Johnson, ca. early to mid-1960s, HUG (FP) 3.42, box 7, Hansen Papers; Alvin H. Hansen, "Stagnation and Under-employment Equilibrium," *Rostra Economica Amstelodamensia* (Nov. 1966): 7, HUG (FP) 3.42, box 7, offprint, Hansen Papers.

31. Hansen, notes on Harry G. Johnson.

32. Samuelson, "Hansen as a Creative Economic Theorist," 25; W. W. Rostow, *Theorists of Economic Growth from David Hume to the Present: With a Perspective on the Next Century* (New York, 1990), 297.

33. Musgrave, "Caring for the Real Problems," 6.

34. Stoneman, *Economic Analysis of the Great Depression*, 112, 115–16, 120–21; Allen M. Sievers, *Revolution, Evolution, and the Economic Order* (Englewood Cliffs, N.J., 1962), 23–24.

35. Hansen, "Keynes and the General Theory," 184; David McCord Wright, *The Creation of Purchasing Power: A Study in the Problem of Economic Stabilization* (Cambridge, Mass., 1942), 25.

36. Haberler, "Some Reminiscences," 12; Musgrave, "Caring for the Real Problems," 5; Tobin, "Hansen and Public Policy," 32–34; Robert Loring Allen, *Opening Doors: The Life and Work of Joseph Schumpeter*, vol. 2, *America* (New Brunswick, N.J., 1991), 65.

37. Nicholas Kaldor, review of *Full Recovery or Stagnation?* by Alvin H. Hansen, *Economic Journal* 49 (Mar. 1939): 91; "Harvard's Alvin H. Hansen: Prophet of a New Economics," *Fortune*, Nov. 1942, 130; Rothe, *Current Biography, 1945*, 265, 267.

CHAPTER FIVE

1. Alvin H. Hansen, "Economic Progress and Declining Population Growth," *American Economic Review* 29 (Mar. 1939): 3–4, 11; "Testimony of Alvin H. Hansen," May 1939, in *Hearings before the Temporary National Economic Committee*, part 9, *Savings and Investment* (Washington, D.C., 1939), 3502–3, 3514; Alvin H. Hansen, *Full Recovery or Stagnation?* (New York, 1938), 51, 117, 279–80; Alvin H. Hansen, *Fiscal Policy and Business Cycles* (New York, 1941), 44, 344–45, 347, 354.

2. "Testimony of Alvin H. Hansen," 3497; "Purchasing Power and Prosperity," *University of Chicago Round Table*, July 31, 1938, 5; Alvin H. Hansen, "We Can Pay the War Bill," *Atlantic Monthly*, Oct. 1942, 62.

3. "Seventh Series: Midday Club: The Spending Program," meeting, Oct. 5, 1938, 9, HUG (FP) 3.42, box 4, Alvin H. Hansen Papers, Harvard University Archives, Cambridge, Mass.; Hansen, "Economic Progress and Declining Population Growth," 10.

4. Hansen, *Full Recovery or Stagnation?* 279–82; Hansen, *Fiscal Policy and Business Cycles*, 297.

5. Alvin H. Hansen, "The Consequences of Reducing Expenditures," *Proceedings of the Academy of Political Science* 17 (Jan. 1938): 72; Hansen, *Full Recovery or Stagnation?* 7, 289; Hansen, *Fiscal Policy and Business Cycles*, 27–28, 353; "Testimony of Alvin H. Hansen," 3514.

6. Alvin H. Hansen, "Wesley Mitchell, Social Scientist and Social Counselor," *Review of Economics and Statistics* 31 (Nov. 1949): 245–46.

7. Hansen, *Full Recovery or Stagnation?* 50, 314; Simon Kuznets, review of *Fiscal Policy and Business Cycles*, by Alvin H. Hansen, *Review of Economic Statistics* 24 (Feb. 1942): 31, 35; David McCord Wright, *The Creation of Purchasing Power: A Study in the Problem of Economic Stabilization* (Cambridge, Mass., 1942), 224–25; Benjamin Higgins, "The Doctrine of Economic Maturity," *American Economic Review* 36 (Mar. 1946): 133; Benjamin Higgins, "Concepts and Criteria of Secular Stagnation," in Lloyd A. Metzler et al., *Income, Employment, and Public Policy: Essays in Honor of Alvin H. Hansen* (New York, 1948), 82, 90–91, 101; Benjamin Higgins, *Economic Development: Principles, Problems, and Policies*, rev. ed. (New York, 1968), 123.

8. Alvin H. Hansen, "Schumpeter's Contribution to Business Cycle Theory," *Review of Economics and Statistics* 33 (May 1951): 132.

9. Robert Aaron Gordon, *Business Fluctuations*, 2d ed. (New York, 1961), 240.

10. Hansen, *Full Recovery or Stagnation?* 288, 314–15; Hansen, *Fiscal Policy and Business Cycles*, 27–28, 32, 38–39, 41; "Testimony of Alvin H. Hansen," 3513–14; Hansen, "Consequences of Reducing Expenditures," 477–78; "Spending Program," 10.

11. William E. Stoneman, *A History of the Economic Analysis of the Great Depression in America* (New York, 1979), 198–99; Hansen, *Full Recovery or Stagnation?* 288, 328; Hansen, *Fiscal Policy and Business Cycles*, 41.

12. Alvin H. Hansen to David McCord Wright, July 30, 1945, 2, HUG (FP) 3.10, box 2, Hansen Papers.

13. Hansen, *Full Recovery or Stagnation?* 313; Hansen, *Fiscal Policy and Business Cycles*, 349; "Testimony of Alvin H. Hansen," 3503.

14. Alvin H. Hansen, "Some Notes on Terborgh's *The Bogey of Economic Maturity*," *Review of Economic Statistics* 28 (Feb. 1946): 13.

15. "Testimony of Alvin H. Hansen," 3503.

16. Ibid.

17. Hansen, *Full Recovery or Stagnation?* 298–99; Hansen, *Fiscal Policy and Business Cycles*, 42, 45–46, 350; Hansen, "Terborgh's *The Bogey of Economic Maturity*," 13.

18. Hansen, *Fiscal Policy and Business Cycles*, 42.

19. Ibid., 42, 45–46, 364; Alvin H. Hansen, "Extensive Expansion and Population Growth," *Journal of Political Economy* 48 (Aug. 1940): 585; "Testimony of Alvin H. Hansen," 3504, 3514; Hansen, "Terborgh's *The Bogey of Economic Maturity*," 14.

20. Hansen to Wright, July 30, 1945, 3.

21. Alvin H. Hansen, "Mr. Keynes on Underemployment Equilibrium," *Journal of Political Economy* 44 (Oct. 1936): 681.

22. "Testimony of Alvin H. Hansen," 3504; Hansen, "Economic Progress and Declining Population Growth," 4, 8–9; Hansen, *Fiscal Policy and Business Cycles*, 360; Alvin H. Hansen, "Stability and Expansion," in Paul T. Homan and Fritz Machlup, eds., *Financing American Prosperity: A Symposium of Economists* (New York, 1945), 202; Alvin H. Hansen, "Comments on Terborgh's Address at the National Industrial Conference Board, November 23, 1943, on 'Public and Private Investment after the War,'" 7–8, HUG (FP) 3.42, box 4, Hansen Papers.

23. Hansen, "Economic Progress and Declining Population Growth," 9–11; Hansen, *Fiscal Policy and Business Cycles*, 361–62, 364; "Testimony of Alvin H. Hansen," 3514; Alvin H. Hansen to D. H. Robertson, Sept. 29, 1939, 1, HUG (FP) 3.10, box 2, Hansen Papers; "Spending Program," 11.

24. Hansen, *Fiscal Policy and Business Cycles*, 46, 306.

25. Hansen, "Terborgh's *The Bogey of Economic Maturity*," 13; Paul A. Samuelson, "Alvin H. Hansen as a Creative Economic Theorist," *Quarterly Journal of Economics* 90 (Feb. 1976): 30; Alan R. Sweezy, "The Natural History of the Stagnation Thesis," in Joseph J. Spengler, ed., *Zero Population Growth: Implications* (Chapel Hill, 1975), 34, 36, 39.

26. Hansen, "Consequences of Reducing Expenditures," 72; Hansen, *Full Recovery or Stagnation?* 289–90; Hansen, "Stability and Expansion," 206–7; Alvin H. Hansen, "Four Outlets for Investment," *Survey Graphic* 32 (May 1943): 232; Alvin H. Hansen to John K. Jessup, Aug. 6, 1943, 5–7, HUG (FP) 3.10, box 1, Hansen Papers.

27. Hansen, *Full Recovery or Stagnation?* 273–74, 276–82; Hansen, "Consequences of Reducing Expenditures," 466–70, 472.

28. Hansen, *Full Recovery or Stagnation?* 121, 301–2; "The Economics of Pump Priming," *University of Chicago Round Table*, May 1, 1938, 7.

29. Hansen, "Economic Progress and Declining Population Growth," 12; "Spending Program," 13–14.

30. Hansen, *Full Recovery or Stagnation?* 329.

31. Hansen, *Fiscal Policy and Business Cycles*, 309, 346; Hansen, "Extensive Expansion and Population Growth," 585; "Testimony of Alvin H. Hansen," 3543, 3546, 3838–39.

32. Hansen, *Fiscal Policy and Business Cycles*, 306–7; Alvin H. Hansen, "The *General Theory* (2)," in Seymour E. Harris, ed., *The New Economics: Keynes' Influence on Theory and Public Policy* (New York, 1947), 139.

33. "Testimony of Alvin H. Hansen," 3838–39.

34. Ibid., 3558, 3838; Hansen, *Fiscal Policy and Business Cycles*, 309; "What Can We Do to Make Jobs for All?" *Independent Woman*, March 1940, 72.

35. Hansen, *Fiscal Policy and Business Cycles*, 307, 309.

36. Alvin H. Hansen, "Social Planning for Tomorrow," in Alvin H. Hansen et al., *The United States after War* (Ithaca, N.Y., 1945), 27; Hansen, "Four Outlets for Investment," 232; Alvin H. Hansen to Henry A. Wallace, May 6, 1941, box 31, Henry A. Wallace Papers, Franklin D. Roosevelt Library (hereafter FDRL), Hyde Park, N.Y.; Hansen to Wright, July 30, 1945, 13–15.

37. Alvin H. Hansen and Guy Greer, "Toward Full Use of Our Resources," *Fortune*, Nov. 1942, 162.

38. Alvin H. Hansen, "A Note on Fiscal Policy: A Clarification," *American Economic Review* 35 (June 1945): 410; Hansen, "Four Outlets for Investment," 232; Alvin H. Hansen, "Planning Full Employment," *Nation*, Oct. 21, 1944, 492.

39. Alvin H. Hansen, "Economic Problems of the Post-War World," in National Education Association, *Problems in American Life* (Washington, 1942), 11.

40. Alvin H. Hansen, "Notes on Mints' Paper on Monetary Policy," *Review of Economic Statistics* 28 (May 1946): 70.

41. Hansen, "Note on Fiscal Policy," 408.

42. James Tobin, "Hansen and Public Policy," *Quarterly Journal of Economics* 90 (Feb. 1976): 35–36.

43. Hansen to Wright, July 30, 1945, 15.

44. Ibid., 13; Hansen, *Fiscal Policy and Business Cycles*, 309; "What Can We Do to Make Jobs for All?" 72; Hansen to Robertson, Sept. 29, 1939, 1.

45. Hansen, "Terborgh's *The Bogey of Economic Maturity*," 17; "What Can We Do to Make Jobs for All?" 72.

46. Hansen, *Full Recovery or Stagnation?* 316–17; Hansen to Wright, July 30, 1945, 14; Hansen, "We Can Pay the War Bill," 62.

47. Hansen, *Full Recovery or Stagnation?* 145.

48. "Testimony of Alvin H. Hansen," 3545.

49. Hansen, "Four Outlets for Investment," 232; Alvin H. Hansen to Ralph E. Flanders, Apr. 20, 1938, 1–2, HUG (FP) 3.10, box 1, Hansen Papers; Hansen to Wright, July 30, 1945, 13; Alvin H. Hansen and Harvey Perloff, *Regional Resource Development*, National Planning Association Pamphlet no. 16 (Washington, D.C., Oct. 1942), 5.

50. Hansen, *Full Recovery or Stagnation?* 298–99; Hansen, *Fiscal Policy and Business Cycles*, 93.

51. Alvin H. Hansen, "The Postwar Economy," in Seymour E. Harris, ed., *Postwar Economic Problems* (New York, 1943), 14; Alvin H. Hansen, "Full Employment after the War," *American Federationist*, July 1944, 12.

52. Hansen, *Full Recovery or Stagnation?* 324–25.

53. Ibid., 311; Hansen, *Fiscal Policy and Business Cycles*, 74, 82; Alvin H. Hansen, "Keynes and the General Theory," *Review of Economic Statistics* 28 (Nov. 1946): 184–85.

54. Hansen, "Keynes and the General Theory," 186.

55. Alvin H. Hansen to Thomas Blaisdell Jr., Oct. 27, 1939, 1–2, box 11, Central Office Records of the National Resources Planning Board, RG 187, Papers of Thomas Blaisdell Jr., National Archives II, College Park, Md.

56. Alvin H. Hansen to Henry A. Wallace, Mar. 14, 1941, 1–2, box 24, Wallace Papers, FDRL.

57. Theodore Rosenof, *Patterns of Political Economy in America: The Failure to Develop a Democratic Left Synthesis, 1933–1950* (New York, 1983), 39–40.

58. George Terborgh, *The Bogey of Economic Maturity* (Chicago, 1945), 5, 16.

59. Alan Sweezy, "Secular Stagnation?" in Harris, *Postwar Economic Problems*, 67; John H.

Williams, "Free Enterprise and Full Employment," in Homan and Machlup, *Financing American Prosperity*, 346–47.

60. J. R. Hicks, *Value and Capital: An Inquiry into Some Fundamental Principles of Economic Theory*, 2d ed. (London, 1946), 302 n. 1.
61. William H. Beveridge, *Full Employment in a Free Society* (New York, 1945), 184, 186–87.
62. Luther Gulick to Mr. Eliot, memorandum, Jan. 30, 1942, 1–2, box 1, Records of the Post-War Agenda Section of the National Resources Planning Board, RG 187, entry 14, National Archives II, College Park, Md.; H. G. Moulton to Frederic A. Delano, June 8, 1943, 1–2, box 1847, Central Office Records of the National Resources Planning Board, RG 187, Public Finance and Monetary Policy, 765.
63. Albert Lepawsky, "The New Deal at Midpassage," *University of Chicago Magazine*, Summer 1975, 33.

CHAPTER SIX

1. Philip W. Warken, *A History of the National Resources Planning Board, 1933–1943* (New York, 1979), 190, 228–29; Frederic S. Lee and Warren J. Samuels, "Introduction: Gardiner C. Means, 1896–1988," in Lee and Samuels, eds., *The Heterodox Economics of Gardiner C. Means: A Collection* (Armonk, N.Y., 1992), xxvi.
2. "Summaries of Discussion between the Advisory Committee and the Industrial Committee, Sunday—June 5, 1938. I. (As It Appears to T. C. Blaisdell)," 3, box 7, Gardiner C. Means Papers, Franklin D. Roosevelt Library, Hyde Park, N.Y.; Frederic S. Lee, "From Multi-Industry Planning to Keynesian Planning: Gardiner C. Means, the American Keynesians, and National Economic Planning at the National Resources Committee," *Journal of Policy History* 2, no. 2 (1990): 203–4.
3. "Summaries of Discussion between the Advisory Committee and the Industrial Committee, Sunday—June 5, 1938. II. Summary of Same Meeting by Dr. Gardiner C. Means," 4, Box 7, Means Papers; United States National Resources Committee, *The Structure of the American Economy*, pt. 1, *Basic Characteristics: A Report Prepared by the Industrial Section under the Direction of Gardiner C. Means* (1939; New York, 1966).
4. Gardiner C. Means, "An Administrative Theory of Employment and Inflation," mid-1970s, P-3, box 91, Means Papers.
5. Gardiner C. Means to Industrial Committee, "Program for the Fiscal Year 1938–1939," memorandum, June 28, 1938, 3, box 7, Means Papers.
6. Gardiner C. Means to National Resources Planning Board, "Analyses to be Published with PART II of the Structure Report," memorandum, Nov. 20, 1939, 1, 3–5, box 7, Means Papers.
7. Gardiner C. Means to National Resources Planning Board, "Revised Part II of Structure Report," memorandum, Feb. 6, 1940, 1–2, box 7, Means Papers.
8. Gardiner C. Means to Frederic A. Delano, July 1, 1940, box 7, Means Papers; Gardiner C. Means to Paul G. Hoffman, July 21, 1943, 2, box 21, Means Papers; Lee, "Multi-Industry Planning to Keynesian Planning," 204, 206–7.
9. Gardiner C. Means to Hugh J. Kennedy Jr., Nov. 13, 1951, box 21, Means Papers.
10. Gardiner C. Means to Harriett Elliott, June 5, 1940, box 1849, Central Office Records of the National Resources Planning Board, RG 187, Public Finance and Monetary Policy, 765.3, National Archives II, College Park, Md.
11. Gardiner C. Means to Robert A. Brady, Jan. 8, 1944, box 20, Means Papers.
12. Alvin H. Hansen, *After the War—Full Employment* (Washington, 1943), 19; Alvin H.

Hansen, "Wesley Mitchell, Social Scientist and Social Counselor," *Review of Economics and Statistics* 31 (Nov. 1949): 252–53.

13. Alvin H. Hansen, *Full Recovery or Stagnation?* (New York, 1938), 298–99, 301; Alvin H. Hansen, *Fiscal Policy and Business Cycles* (New York, 1941), 46; Alvin H. Hansen, "Stability and Expansion," in Paul T. Homan and Fritz Machlup, eds., *Financing American Prosperity: A Symposium of Economists* (New York, 1945), 218 n. 23.

14. Hansen, *Fiscal Policy and Business Cycles*, 68.

15. Ibid., 315–17; Alvin H. Hansen, "Price Flexibility and Full Employment of Resources," in United States National Resources Committee, *The Structure of the American Economy*, pt. 2, *Toward Full Use of Resources: A Symposium* (Washington, D.C., 1940), 27–28.

16. Alvin H. Hansen to Thomas Blaisdell Jr., Oct. 27, 1939, 1, 3, box 11, in Central Office Records of the National Resources Planning Board, RG 187, Papers of Thomas Blaisdell Jr., National Archives II, College Park, Md.

17. Hansen, "Price Flexibility and Full Employment of Resources," 29–30, 33–34; Hansen, "Stability and Expansion," 208; Hansen, *Fiscal Policy and Business Cycles*, 317–18, 320, 325–26, 337; Alvin H. Hansen to Thomas C. Blaisdell, Dec. 26, 1939, box 1820, Central Office Records of the National Resources Planning Board, RG 187, The Structure of the American Economy, 751.

18. Hansen, *Fiscal Policy and Business Cycles*, 317.

19. Gottfried Haberler, *Prosperity and Depression: A Theoretical Analysis of Cyclical Movements*, 3d ed. (Lake Success, N.Y., 1946), 493 n. 5; John M. Blair, *Economic Concentration: Structure, Behavior, and Public Policy* (New York, 1972), 537, 542.

20. John M. Blair, "The Inverse Relationship between Price and Production Declines," 1958, 9–10, box 38, Means Papers.

21. Lee, "Multi-Industry Planning to Keynesian Planning," 205.

22. Gardiner C. Means, "Basic Structural Characteristics and the Problem of Full Employment," in United States National Resources Committee, *The Structure of the American Economy*, pt. 2, *Toward Full Use of Resources*, 7; Gardiner C. Means, "The Controversy over the Problem of Full Employment," in ibid., 10; Gardiner C. Means, "The Major Causes of the Depression," Oct. 15, 1935, 4, box 3, Means Papers.

23. Gardiner C. Means, "A Monetary Theory of Employment," 1947, I-3, box 32, Means Papers.

24. Alvin H. Hansen to Thomas C. Blaisdell, Jan. 17, 1940, Thomas C. Blaisdell to Alvin H. Hansen, Feb. 6, 1940, Alvin H. Hansen to Gardiner C. Means, Feb. 6, 1940, and Gardiner C. Means to Alvin H. Hansen, Feb. 9, 1940, all in box 1820, Central Office Records of the National Resources Planning Board, RG 187, The Structure of the American Economy, 751.

25. Gardiner C. Means, "Proposed Informal Economic Conference," undated memorandum in 1939 file, 4–5, box 7, Means Papers; Question-and-answer session following an address by Means at New York University, Nov. 3, 1943, 54, box 37, Means Papers; Gardiner C. Means, "The Veblen-Commons Award," *Journal of Economic Issues* 9 (June 1975): 153–54.

26. Gardiner C. Means to Frederic A. Delano, Jan. 6, 1938, 1–2, box 1849, Central Office Records of the National Resources Planning Board, RG 187, Public Finance and Monetary Policy, 766; Gardiner C. Means to Beardsley Ruml, Oct. 18, 1938, box 1820, Central Office Records of the National Resources Planning Board, RG 187, The Structure of the American Economy, 751; Gardiner C. Means, "Memorandum Prepared by GCM for Industrial Committee Meeting, 10/27/38," 2–4, box 6, Central Office Records of the National Resources Planning Board, RG 187, Blaisdell Papers.

27. Gardiner C. Means, "Which Was the True Keynesian Theory of Employment?" *Chal-*

lenge 19 (July/Aug. 1976): 61; Gardiner C. Means to John H. Hotson, Mar. 30, 1978, 2, box 69, Means Papers; Gardiner C. Means, "An Interview with Keynes," undated, 2, box 117, Means Papers.

28. Means to Hotson, Mar. 30, 1978, 2.

29. Means, "Keynesian Theory of Employment?" 61–62; Gardiner C. Means to Beardsley Ruml, Sept. 30, 1943, 6, box 22, Means Papers; Gardiner C. Means to Abba Lerner, Feb. 17, 1971, 2, box 70, Means Papers; Means, "Interview with Keynes," 3.

30. Gardiner C. Means, "Effect on Economic Activity of Shifts in Propensity to Consume and in Liquidity Preference," July 16, 1939, memorandum, 2–4, 7, box 6, Means Papers.

31. Gardiner C. Means, "Second Memorandum on: Effect on Economic Activity of Shifts in Propensity to Consume and in Liquidity Preference," July 22, 1939, 1–2, 11–12, box 6, Means Papers.

32. Gardiner C. Means to John M. Keynes, July 16, 1939, 2, box 117, Means Papers.

33. J. M. Keynes to Gardiner C. Means, July 31, 1939, 1–2, box 117, Means Papers.

34. Keynes's annotations are on a copy of Means's "Second Memorandum on: Effect on Economic Activity," box 117, Means Papers.

35. Keynes to Means, July 31, 1939, 2–3.

36. Gardiner C. Means, foreword to Blair, *Economic Concentration*, viii–ix.

37. Gardiner C. Means, "Neoclassical Economics and Employment," Jan. 5, 1950, 18, 20–21, box 24, Means Papers; Gardiner C. Means to Burton C. Hallowell, Apr. 22, 1957, 1–3, box 21, Means Papers; Gardiner C. Means to John R. Moore, July 23, 1957, box 21, Means Papers.

38. Gardiner C. Means to Gerhard Colm, Jan. 4, 1940, 10–11, box 1820, Central Office Records of the National Resources Planning Board, RG 187, The Structure of the American Economy, 751; Means to Ruml, Sept. 30, 1943, 7; Gardiner C. Means, "Preliminary Suggestions as to the Implications of the Economic Structure for the Problem of Full Use of Resources," May 24, 1939, 17–18, box 10, Means Papers; Gardiner C. Means, "After Discussion of Chapter 10, Structure Report," memorandum, May 1939, 2–6, box 7, Means Papers.

39. Means, "Neoclassical Economics and Employment," 19–20; Means to Hallowell, Apr. 22, 1957, 1–3; Means to Lerner, Feb. 17, 1971, 2; Gardiner C. Means to Beardsley Ruml, May 15, 1944, 2, box 22, Means Papers.

40. Gardiner C. Means to Alfred S. Eichner, Oct. 18, 1978, 3, box 68, Means Papers; Alfred S. Eichner to Gardiner C. Means, Nov. 2, 1978, box 68, Means Papers.

41. Gardiner C. Means, "Implications of the Corporate Revolution in Economic Theory," in Adolf A. Berle and Gardiner C. Means, *The Modern Corporation and Private Property* (New York, 1967), xxxi–xxxii.

42. Warren J. Samuels and Steven G. Medema, *Gardiner C. Means: Institutionalist and Post Keynesian* (Armonk, N.Y., 1990), 143, 170 n. 62.

43. J. R. Hicks, *Value and Capital: An Inquiry into Some Fundamental Principles of Economic Theory*, 2d ed. (London, 1946), 265–66.

44. Theodore Rosenof, *Patterns of Political Economy in America: The Failure to Develop a Democratic Left Synthesis, 1933–1950* (New York, 1983), 108–11.

45. Gardiner C. Means to Daniel Boorstin, Feb. 9, 1972, 1, 3, box 67, Means Papers.

CHAPTER SEVEN

1. Alexander Sachs to J. M. Keynes, May 27, 1939, box 39, Alexander Sachs Papers, Franklin D. Roosevelt Library (hereafter FDRL), Hyde Park, N.Y.

2. Franco Modigliani, review of *The Bogey of Economic Maturity*, by George Terborgh, *Social Research* 13 (Sept. 1946): 388; John T. Dunlop, "Sumner Huber Slichter," in Dunlop, ed., *Potentials of the American Economy: Selected Essays of Sumner H. Slichter* (Cambridge, Mass., 1961), xi–xiii; Richard M. Bissell Jr. to Alvin H. Hansen, Dec. 14, 1938, 3, HUG (FP), 3.10, box 1, Alvin H. Hansen Papers, Harvard University Archives, Cambridge, Mass.; Richard Bissell, "Postwar Industry and Public Spending," in Seymour E. Harris, ed., *Postwar Economic Problems* (New York, 1943), 86; Henry C. Simons, *Economic Policy for a Free Society* (Chicago, 1948), 193–94; Simon Kuznets, review of *Fiscal Policy and Business Cycles*, by Alvin H. Hansen, *Review of Economic Statistics* 24 (Feb. 1942): 34–35.

3. Alvin H. Hansen to David McCord Wright, July 30, 1945, 8, HUG (FP) 3.10, box 2, Hansen Papers.

4. Ibid., 3, 7–9; Alvin H. Hansen, "Comments on Terborgh's Address at the National Industrial Conference Board, November 23, 1943, on 'Public and Private Investment after the War,'" HUG (FP) 3.42, box 4, Hansen Papers; Alvin H. Hansen, "Some Notes on Terborgh's *The Bogey of Economic Maturity*," *Review of Economic Statistics* 28 (Feb. 1946): 15.

5. Alvin H. Hansen, *Economic Policy and Full Employment* (New York, 1947), 299–300; Hansen to Wright, July 30, 1945, 4–6; Hansen, "Comments on Terborgh's Address," 6–7.

6. Hansen, "Comments on Terborgh's Address," 7.

7. Ibid., 9; Hansen to Wright, July 30, 1945, 9.

8. Hansen, "Terborgh's *The Bogey of Economic Maturity*," 13.

9. Hansen to Wright, July 30, 1945, 12–13; Hansen, "Comments on Terborgh's Address," 2–3, 9–11.

10. Howard S. Ellis, "Monetary Policy and Investment," in Gottfried Haberler et al., eds., *Readings in Business Cycle Theory* (Philadelphia, 1944), 417; George Terborgh, *The Bogey of Economic Maturity* (Chicago, 1945), 173; William Fellner, "Employment Theory and Business Cycles," in Howard S. Ellis, ed., *A Survey of Contemporary Economics* (Philadelphia, 1948), 64, 89.

11. Kuznets, review of *Fiscal Policy and Business Cycles*, 32–33.

12. Alvin H. Hansen, "Brief Rejoinder," *Review of Economic Statistics* 29 (Nov. 1947): 268.

13. Harold G. Moulton, *The New Philosophy of Public Debt* (Washington, 1943), 24–25.

14. Alvin H. Hansen, "Report of the Director of Research," in *Report of the Commission of Inquiry into National Policy in International Economic Relations* (Minneapolis, 1934), 120; Alvin H. Hansen, *Full Recovery or Stagnation?* (New York, 1938), 7.

15. "Testimony of Alvin H. Hansen," May 1939, in *Hearings Before the Temporary National Economic Committee*, pt. 9, *Savings and Investment* (Washington, D.C., 1939), 3506.

16. Hansen, "Terborgh's *The Bogey of Economic Maturity*," 14; Alvin H. Hansen, *Fiscal Policy and Business Cycles* (New York, 1941), 45–46; Alvin H. Hansen, "Stability and Expansion," in Paul T. Homan and Fritz Machlup, eds., *Financing American Prosperity: A Symposium of Economists* (New York, 1945), 202.

17. Hansen, "Stability and Expansion," 202.

18. Hansen, "Comments on Terborgh's Address," 8.

19. Ibid., 8–9; Alvin H. Hansen, "Recovery—When?" *Education* 60 (Mar. 1940): 387.

20. Austin H. Spencer and Reuben Kyle, *The Administered Price Thesis: Reflections on Forty Years of Empirical Study*, Monograph ser. no. 7 (Murfreesboro: Business and Economic Research Center, Middle Tennessee State University, 1974), 54–55; John M. Blair, "The Price Inflexibility Controversy," ca. 1950, 14–15, box 38, Gardiner C. Means Pa-

pers, FDRL; Gardiner C. Means to John Blair, Aug. 10, 1971, 8–9, box 107, Means Papers; Ben W. Lewis, "Berle and Means on the Modern Corporation," *Journal of Political Economy* 43 (Aug. 1935): 549.

21. Gardiner C. Means to W. L. Crum, Oct. 16, 1933, 1–4, box 86, Means Papers.

22. Gardiner C. Means, "Big Business, Administered Prices, and the Problem of Full Employment," *Journal of Marketing* 55 (Apr. 1940): 373; Gardiner C. Means to Willford I. King, May 10, 1935, 4, box 4, Means Papers; Gardiner C. Means to George Stigler, Feb. 5, 1960, 1, box 126, Means Papers.

23. Edward S. Mason, "Price Inflexibility," *Review of Economic Statistics* 20 (May 1938): 64; Frederic S. Lee, "Gardiner C. Means and Administered Prices" (letters from economists; comments by Walter S. Salant), unpublished ms. in Lee's possession, chap. 2, 78–79; R. H. Whitman to Beardsley Ruml, Mar. 28, 1940, 1–2, box 1820, Central Office Records of the National Resources Planning Board, RG 187, The Structure of the American Economy, 751, National Archives II, College Park, Md.

24. D. G. Franzsen, "The Secular Stagnation-Thesis and the Problem of Economic Stability," *South African Journal of Economics* 10 (1942): 292; Oscar L. Altman, *Saving, Investment, and National Income*, Temporary National Economic Committee Monograph no. 37 (Washington, D.C., 1941), 100; Evsey D. Domar, "Investment, Losses, and Monopolies," in Lloyd A. Metzler et al., *Income, Employment, and Public Policy: Essays in Honor of Alvin H. Hansen* (New York, 1948), 51.

25. Richard V. Gilbert et al., *An Economic Program for American Democracy* (New York, 1938), 74–75.

26. John Maynard Keynes, *The General Theory of Employment, Interest, and Money* (New York, 1936), 268.

27. Hansen, *Economic Policy and Full Employment*, 247, 259–60; Hansen, "Stability and Expansion," 208; Alvin H. Hansen, "Postwar Employment Outlook," in Seymour E. Harris, ed., *Economic Reconstruction* (New York, 1946), 16–17.

28. Hansen, *Full Recovery or Stagnation?* 328.

29. Hansen, "Stability and Expansion," 208–9; Kenneth Boulding, *The Economics of Peace* (New York, 1945), 239–40; Arthur Smithies, "Federal Budgeting and Fiscal Policy," in Ellis, *Contemporary Economics*, 208.

30. Gerhard Colm, "Fiscal Policy in Economic Reconstruction," in Harris, *Economic Reconstruction*, 254; Arthur Smithies, "Schumpeter and Keynes," in Seymour E. Harris, ed., *Schumpeter: Social Scientist* (Cambridge, Mass., 1951), 140.

31. Sherwood M. Fine, *Public Spending and Postwar Economic Policy* (New York, 1944), 128–132; Joseph Rosenfarb, *Freedom and the Administrative State* (New York, 1948), 58–61; Otis L. Graham Jr., afterword to Rexford G. Tugwell, *To the Lesser Heights of Morningside: A Memoir* (Philadelphia, 1982), 254, 256.

32. Kuznets, review of *Fiscal Policy and Business Cycles*, 34–35.

33. Moses Abramowitz, review of *Economic Policy and Full Employment*, by Alvin H. Hansen, *American Economic Review* 37 (Sept. 1947): 681.

34. Fine, *Public Spending and Postwar Economic Policy*, 45–49, 64.

35. D. A. MacGibbon, "Fiscal Policy and Business Cycles," *Canadian Journal of Economics and Political Science* 9 (Feb. 1943): 81; Eugene V. Rostow, review of *Full Recovery or Stagnation?* by Alvin H. Hansen, *Yale Law Journal* 48 (Mar. 1939): 919–20; Kuznets, review of *Fiscal Policy and Business Cycles*, 35.

36. John D. Black to Paul Buck, Dec. 22, 1947, 5, box 70, John Kenneth Galbraith Papers, John F. Kennedy Library, Boston, Mass.

37. Fine, *Public Spending and Postwar Economic Policy*, 130–31; Dean L. May, *From New Deal to New Economics: The American Liberal Response to the Recession of 1937* (New York,

1981), 161; Michael A. Bernstein, *The Great Depression: Delayed Recovery and Economic Change in America, 1929–1939* (New York, 1987), 222.

38. Adolf A. Berle to Ralph E. Flanders, July 27, 1937, 2, box 7, Adolf A. Berle Papers, FDRL.

39. Stephen W. Baskerville, "Cutting Loose from Prejudice: Economists and the Great Depression," in Stephen W. Baskerville and Ralph Willet, eds., *Nothing Else to Fear: New Perspectives on America in the Thirties* (Manchester, England, 1985), 280–81.

40. Altman, *Saving, Investment, and National Income*, 10.

41. Alvin H. Hansen to Mordecai Ezekiel, May 21, 1941, 1, 3, box 6, Mordecai Ezekiel Papers, FDRL.

PART II

1. Books useful for understanding the period since World War II in relation to economic developments include Fred C. Allvine and Fred A. Tarpley Jr., *The New State of the Economy* (Cambridge, Mass., 1977); Michael A. Bernstein and David E. Adler, eds., *Understanding American Economic Decline* (New York, 1994); David P. Calleo, *The Imperious Economy* (Cambridge, Mass., 1982); Robert M. Collins, *The Business Response to Keynes, 1929–1964* (New York, 1981); Kim McQuaid, *Big Business and Presidential Power: From FDR to Reagan* (New York, 1982); Iwan W. Morgan, *Deficit Government: Taxing and Spending in Modern America* (Chicago, 1995); Hobart Rowen, *Self-Inflicted Wounds: From LBJ's Guns and Butter to Reagan's Voodoo Economics* (New York, 1994); Nicholas Spulber, *Managing the American Economy from Roosevelt to Reagan* (Bloomington, 1989); and Herbert Stein, *Presidential Economics: The Making of Economic Policy from Roosevelt to Reagan and Beyond* (New York, 1984).

CHAPTER EIGHT

1. Joseph A. Schumpeter to Gilbert Walker, May 19, 1937, 2, HUG (FP) 4.8, box 2, Joseph A. Schumpeter Papers, Harvard University Archives, Cambridge, Mass.; Alan W. Dyer, "Schumpeter as an Economic Radical: An Economic Sociology Assessed," *History of Political Economy* 20 (Spring 1988): 37; John E. Elliott, "Marx and Schumpeter on Capitalism's Creative Destruction: A Comparative Restatement," *Quarterly Journal of Economics* 95 (Aug. 1980): 55.

2. Joseph A. Schumpeter, *Capitalism, Socialism, and Democracy*, 3d ed. (New York, 1950), x, 31–32, 84; John E. Elliott, "Schumpeter's Theory of Economic Development and Social Change: Exposition and Assessment," *International Journal of Social Economics* 12, nos. 6/7 (1985): 18–19; Erich Schneider, *Joseph A. Schumpeter: Life and Work of a Great Social Scientist* (Lincoln, Neb., 1975), 32.

3. Schumpeter, *Capitalism, Socialism, and Democracy*, 131–33; Edward S. Mason, "Schumpeter on Monopoly and the Large Firm," in Seymour E. Harris, ed., *Schumpeter: Social Scientist* (Cambridge, Mass., 1951), 92–93; Arnold Heertje, "Schumpeter and Technical Change," in Horst Hanusch, ed., *Evolutionary Economics: Applications of Schumpeter's Ideas* (New York, 1988), 78, 80; Robert Loring Allen, *Opening Doors: The Life and Work of Joseph Schumpeter*, vol. 2, *America* (New Brunswick, N.J., 1991), 232.

4. Anne Mayhew, "Schumpeterian Capitalism versus the 'Schumpeterian Thesis,'" *Journal of Economic Issues* 14 (June 1980): 590; Martin Kessler, "The Synthetic Vision of Joseph Schumpeter," *Review of Politics* 23 (July 1961): 345, 347–48, 350, 355; Enrico

Santarelli and Enzo Pesciarelli, "The Emergence of a Vision: The Development of Schumpeter's Theory of Entrepreneurship," *History of Political Economy* 22 (Winter 1990): 685–86; Mark Blaug, "The Entrepreneur in Marx and Schumpeter," in Suzanne W. Helburn and David F. Bramhall, eds., *Marx, Schumpeter, Keynes: A Centenary Celebration of Dissent* (Armonk, N.Y., 1986), 176.

5. Jeffrey Young, "The Entrepreneur in Marx and Schumpeter: A Post-Keynesian Perspective," in Helburn and Bramhall, *Marx, Schumpeter, Keynes*, 184–85; Richard Swedberg, *Schumpeter: A Biography* (Princeton, N.J., 1991), 171, 173.

6. Richard V. Clemence, ed., *Essays of J. A. Schumpeter* (Cambridge, Mass., 1951), 218 n. 5, and 255; Joseph A. Schumpeter, *Business Cycles: A Theoretical, Historical, and Statistical Analysis of the Capitalist Process*, vol. 1 (New York, 1939), 223.

7. Wolfgang F. Stolper, "Aspects of Schumpeter's Theory of Evolution," in Helmut Frisch, ed., *Schumpeterian Economics* (New York, 1981), 35; Richard D. Coe and Charles K. Wilber, "Schumpeter Revisited: An Overview," in Coe and Wilber, eds., *Capitalism and Democracy: Schumpeter Revisited* (Notre Dame, Ind., 1985), 5–6; Akhtar A. Awan, "Marshallian and Schumpeterian Theories of Economic Evolution: Gradualism versus Punctualism," *Atlantic Economic Journal* 14 (Dec. 1986): 43.

8. Kessler, "Synthetic Vision of Joseph Schumpeter," 351–52; Elliott, "Schumpeter's Theory of Economic Development," 15, 18; "Statement of Dr. John M. Blair," U.S. Congress, Senate, *Economic Concentration: Hearings before the Subcommittee on Antitrust and Monopoly of the Committee on the Judiciary*, pt. 1, *Overall and Conglomerate Aspects*, 88th Cong., 2d sess., 1964, 207.

9. Nathan Rosenberg, "Schumpeter and Marx: How Common a Vision?" in Roy M. MacLeod, ed., *Technology and the Human Prospect* (Wolfeboro, N.H., 1986), 199.

10. Allen Oakley, *Schumpeter's Theory of Capitalist Motion: A Critical Exposition and Reassessment* (Brookfield, Vt., 1990), 14–15, 34.

11. Swedberg, *Schumpeter: A Biography*, 129.

12. C. E. Ayres, "Capitalism in Retrospect," *Southern Economic Journal* 9 (Apr. 1943): 294, 300–301; C. E. Ayres, "Foreword—1962," in *The Theory of Economic Progress: A Study of the Fundamentals of Economic Development and Cultural Change* (New York, 1962), xvi–xvii; H. H. Liebhafsky, "Institutions and Technology in Economic Progress," *American Journal of Economics and Sociology* 19, no. 2 (1960): 139–40, 142, 144, 146–48.

13. L. A. O'Donnell, "Rationalism, Capitalism, and the Entrepreneur: The Views of Veblen and Schumpeter," *History of Political Economy* 5 (Spring 1973): 205–6; Awan, "Marshallian and Schumpeterian Theories of Economic Evolution," 46; Nathan Rosenberg, "Problems in the Economist's Conceptualization of Technological Innovation," *History of Political Economy* 7 (Winter 1975): 463.

14. Schumpeter, *Capitalism, Socialism, and Democracy*, 110, 125; Clemence, *Essays of J. A. Schumpeter*, 193.

15. Allen M. Sievers, *Revolution, Evolution, and the Economic Order* (Englewood Cliffs, N.J., 1962), 51–52; Ayres, "Capitalism in Retrospect," 298–99; Paul A. Samuelson, "Schumpeter's *Capitalism, Socialism, and Democracy*," in Arnold Heertje, ed., *Schumpeter's Vision: "Capitalism, Socialism, and Democracy" after 40 Years* (New York, 1981), 13.

16. William E. Stoneman, *A History of the Economic Analysis of the Great Depression in America* (New York, 1979), 122, 151, 165; Lawrence R. Klein, *The Keynesian Revolution* (New York, 1961), 16, 62.

17. Clemence, *Essays of J. A. Schumpeter*, 155–56; Joseph A. Schumpeter, *Ten Great Economists: From Marx to Keynes* (New York, 1951), 274, 283, 286; Joseph A. Schumpeter, *History of Economic Analysis* (New York, 1954), 1174–75.

18. Stoneman, *Economic Analysis of the Great Depression*, 120, 168; Joseph A. Schumpeter to Paul M. McCracken, June 28, 1949, 2, HUG (FP) 4.8, box 4, Schumpeter Papers.

19. Joseph A. Schumpeter to David McCord Wright, Dec. 6, 1943, 2, HUG (FP) 4.8, box 3, Schumpeter Papers.

20. Schumpeter, *Capitalism, Socialism, and Democracy*, 49, 64, 70, 111; Joseph A. Schumpeter, "An Economic Interpretation of Our Time: The Lowell Lectures," in Richard Swedberg, ed., *Joseph A. Schumpeter: The Economics and Sociology of Capitalism* (Princeton, N.J., 1991), 350–52, 355; Joseph A. Schumpeter to Edna Lonegan, Feb. 16, 1942, in "Appendix III: Letters by Schumpeter," in Swedberg, *Schumpeter: A Biography*, 229.

21. Joseph A. Schumpeter, "Capitalism in the Postwar World," in Seymour E. Harris, ed., *Postwar Economic Problems* (New York, 1943), 117; Schumpeter, "Economic Interpretation of Our Time," 356–58; Gottfried Haberler, "Schumpeter's Theory of Interest," in Harris, ed., *Schumpeter: Social Scientist*, 75 n. 11; Sievers, *Revolution, Evolution, and the Economic Order*, 46–47.

22. Schumpeter, *Business Cycles*, 8–10; Schumpeter, *Capitalism, Socialism, and Democracy*, 72–73, 82–83, 109–10; Elizabeth Boody Schumpeter, foreword to Schumpeter, *Ten Great Economists*, viii–ix; Elliott, "Schumpeter's Theory of Economic Development," 12–13.

23. Schumpeter, *Ten Great Economists*, 283.

24. John Maynard Keynes, *The General Theory of Employment, Interest, and Money* (New York, 1936), 162.

25. Joseph A. Schumpeter, "Depressions," in Douglas V. Brown et al., *The Economics of the Recovery Program* (1934; New York, 1971), 14–16; Schumpeter, *Capitalism, Socialism, and Democracy*, 64–65, 419; Schumpeter, *History of Economic Analysis*, 1173 n. 3; Schumpeter, "Capitalism in the Postwar World," 118, 121.

26. Schumpeter to Walker, May 19, 1937, 1–2.

27. Stoneman, *Economic Analysis of the Great Depression*, 104–5; Allen, *Opening Doors*, 18.

28. Klas Eklund, "Long Waves in the Development of Capitalism?" *Kyklos* 33, no. 3 (1980): 392; Vincent J. Tarascio, "Kondratieff's Theory of Long Cycles," *Atlantic Economic Journal* 16 (Dec. 1988): 1, 3; Christopher Freeman, "Keynes or Kondratiev? How Can We Get Back to Full Employment?" in Pauline Marstrand, ed., *New Technology and the Future of Work and Skills* (Dover, N.H., 1984), 105.

29. Joseph A. Schumpeter to W. W. Rostow, Mar. 12, 1940, 3, HUG (FP) 4.8, box 3, Schumpeter Papers; Stoneman, *Economic Analysis of the Great Depression*, 105; Tarascio, "Kondratieff's Theory of Long Cycles," 8; Nathan Rosenberg and Claudio R. Frischtak, "Long Waves and Economic Growth: A Critical Appraisal," *American Economic Review: Papers and Proceedings* 73 (May 1983): 146.

30. Schumpeter to Rostow, Mar. 12, 1940, 1–2.

31. Joseph A. Schumpeter to Paul T. Homan, Apr. 2, 1938, HUG (FP) 4.8, box 2, Schumpeter Papers.

32. Gottfried Haberler, *Schumpeter's "Capitalism, Socialism, and Democracy" after Forty Years* (Kyoto, Japan, 1981), 23; François Chesnais, "Schumpeterian Recovery and the Schumpeterian Perspective—Some Unsettled Issues and Alternative Interpretations," in Herbert Giersch, ed., *Emerging Technologies: Consequences for Economic Growth, Structural Change, and Employment in Advanced Open Economies* (Tübingen, Germany, 1982), 49; Stoneman, *Economic Analysis of the Great Depression*, 106.

33. Nikolai Kondratieff, *The Long Wave Cycle* (1928; New York, 1984), 82–85, 92–93; W. W. Rostow, "Kondratieff, Schumpeter, and Kuznets: Trend Periods Revisited," *Journal of Economic History* 35 (Dec. 1975): 720; Rosenberg and Frischtak, "Long Waves and Economic Growth," 146.

34. George Garvy, "Kondratieff's Theory of Long Cycles," *Review of Economic Statistics* 25

(Nov. 1943): 219–20; Eklund, "Long Waves in the Development of Capitalism?" 394–96.

35. David McCord Wright, "Does the Business Cycle Exist?" ca. late 1940s, 2, HUG (FP) 4.7, box 9, Schumpeter Papers.

36. William Fellner to Joseph A. Schumpeter, Mar. 26, 1949, HUG (FP) 4.7, box 4, Schumpeter Papers.

37. Oscar L. Altman to Paul M. Sweezy. Nov. 2, 1940, box 1849, Central Office Records of the National Resources Planning Board, RG 187, Public Finance and Monetary Policy, 765.2, National Archives II, College Park, Md.

38. Christian Seidl, "Joseph Alois Schumpeter: Character, Life, and Particulars of His Graz Period," in Seidl, ed., *Lectures on Schumpeterian Economics: Schumpeter Centenary Memorial Lectures, Graz, 1983* (Berlin, 1984), 198; Wolfgang F. Stolper, "Joseph Alois Schumpeter—A Memoir," *Challenge* 21 (Jan./Feb. 1979): 69; Allen, *Opening Doors*, 2, 80–81.

39. Arthur Dahlberg, "Recovery Plans—An Analysis," in Temporary National Economic Committee, *Investigation of Concentration of Economic Power*, Monograph no. 25, *Recovery Plans* (Washington, 1940), 42; Oscar Lange, "Is the American Economy Contracting?" *American Economic Review* 29 (Sept. 1939): 513; Gunther Tichy, "Schumpeter's Business Cycle Theory and Its Importance for Our Time," in Seidl, ed., *Lectures on Schumpeterian Economics*, 88; Raymond S. Franklin, *American Capitalism: Two Views* (New York, 1977), 287; Chesnais, "Schumpeterian Recovery," 67–68.

40. Gerhard Mensch, *Stalemate in Technology: Innovations Overcome the Depression* (Cambridge, Mass., 1979), 51, 61.

41. W. W. Rostow, *Theorists of Economic Growth from David Hume to the Present: With a Perspective on the Next Century* (New York, 1990), 237.

CHAPTER NINE

1. Robert Lekachman, *The Age of Keynes* (New York, 1968), 254; Calvin B. Hoover, *The Economy, Liberty, and the State* (Garden City, N.Y., 1961), 239–42; Henry A. Villard, review of *The Corporate Revolution in America*, by Gardiner C. Means, *American Economic Review* 53 (Dec. 1963): 1119; Bernard Nossiter, "The World of Gardiner Means," *New Republic*, May 7, 1962, 18.

2. Gardiner C. Means to Raymond Rubicam, May 12, 1945, 1–2, box 22, Gardiner C. Means Papers, Franklin D. Roosevelt Library (hereafter FDRL), Hyde Park, N.Y.; U.S. Congress, Senate, "Statement of Gardiner C. Means," in *Administered Prices: Hearings before the Subcommittee on Antitrust and Monopoly of the Committee on the Judiciary*, 85th Cong., 1st sess., 1957, pt. 1, 87.

3. "Issue of the Week, November 13, 1946," transcript, 2, box 86, Means Papers.

4. Gardiner C. Means, "How May Business Enterprise Be Expanded after the War," in New York University Institute on Postwar Reconstruction, *Postwar Goals and Economic Reconstruction*, 2d ser., no. 5 (New York, Nov. 3, 1943), 111; "Statement of Gardiner C. Means," *Administered Prices* (1957), 86; U.S. Congress, Senate, "Statement of Dr. Gardiner C. Means," in *Economic Concentration: Hearings before the Subcommittee on Antitrust and Monopoly of the Committee on the Judiciary*, pt. 1, *Overall and Conglomerate Aspects*, 88th Cong., 2d sess., 1964, 21.

5. U.S. Congress, Senate, "Statement of Dr. Gardiner C. Means," in *Administered Prices: Hearings before the Subcommittee on Antitrust and Monopoly of the Committee on the Judiciary*, 88th Cong., 1st sess., 1963, pt. 29, 17989.

6. Gardiner C. Means to Maury Maverick, Feb. 29, 1944, 1–2, box 21, Means Papers; Gardiner C. Means to William Benton, June 14, 1944, 2, box 20, Means Papers; Gardiner C. Means to Donald K. David, Jan. 17, 1945, 2–3, box 21, Means Papers; Means to Rubicam, May 12, 1945, 1.

7. Gardiner C. Means to Beardsley Ruml, Sept. 30, 1943, 6–7, box 22, Means Papers; "Possible Footnote," enclosed in Gardiner C. Means to Beardsley Ruml, May 31, 1944, box 22, Means Papers; Gardiner C. Means, "Neoclassical Economics and Employment," Jan. 5, 1950, 18–19, 21, box 24, Means Papers.

8. Question-and-answer session following an address by Means at New York University, Nov. 3, 1943, transcript, 45, box 37, Means Papers.

9. Means to Rubicam, May 12, 1945, 1–2.

10. Gardiner C. Means, "A Monetary Theory of Employment," 1947, I-2, I-12, box 32, Means Papers; Frederic S. Lee and Warren J. Samuels, "Introduction: Gardiner C. Means, 1896–1988," in Lee and Samuels, eds., *The Heterodox Economics of Gardiner C. Means: A Collection* (Armonk, N.Y., 1992), xxviii.

11. Gardiner C. Means to Hugh J. Kelly, Oct. 9, 1946, box 21, Means Papers; Charles D. Anderson to Gardiner C. Means, June 30, 1947, box 70, Means Papers.

12. Critique of "A Monetary Theory of Employment," enclosed in Charles D. Anderson to Gardiner C. Means, July 1, 1947, 1–2, box 70, Means Papers.

13. Gardiner C. Means to Adolf A. Berle, June 1, 1962, 2, box 67, Means Papers.

14. Hyman P. Minsky, *John Maynard Keynes* (New York, 1975), 15–16.

15. William Guthrie and Vincent J. Tarascio, "Keynes on Economic Growth, Stagnation, and Structural Change: New Light on a 55-Year Controversy," *History of Political Economy* 24 (Summer 1992): 408–9.

16. Joseph S. Davis, "Our Changed Population Outlook and Its Significance," *American Economic Review* 42 (June 1952): 308, 323; William Fellner, *Trends and Cycles in Economic Activity: An Introduction to Problems of Economic Growth* (New York, 1956), 388–89; Herbert Stein, *The Fiscal Revolution in America* (Chicago, 1969), 169, 175–76; Raymond T. Bye, *Social Economy and the Price System: An Essay in Welfare Economics* (New York, 1950), 212–15; Robert Aaron Gordon, *Business Fluctuations*, 2d ed. (New York, 1961), 449.

17. Quoted in Michael G. Prime and David R. Henderson, "Schumpeter on Preserving Private Enterprise," *History of Political Economy* 7 (Fall 1975): 295.

18. Joseph A. Schumpeter to Paul M. McCracken, June 28, 1949, 2, HUG (FP) 4.8, box 4, Joseph A. Schumpeter Papers, Harvard University Archives, Cambridge, Mass.; Joseph A. Schumpeter to William Fellner, Mar. 22, 1949, 2, HUG (FP) 4.8, box 4, Schumpeter Papers.

19. Klas Eklund, "Long Waves in the Development of Capitalism?" *Kyklos* 33, no. 3 (1980): 399–401; Vincent J. Tarascio, "Kondratieff's Theory of Long Cycles," *Atlantic Economic Journal* 16 (Dec. 1988): 9.

20. Lekachman, *Age of Keynes*, 189–90; Paul M. Sweezy, "Discussion," in Robert V. Eagly, ed., *Events, Ideology, and Economic Theory: The Determinants of Progress in the Development of Economic Analysis* (Detroit, 1968), 148–49; Tibor Scitovsky, "Lerner's Contribution to Economics," *Journal of Economic Literature* 22 (Dec. 1984): 1560–61; David Colander, "Was Keynes a Keynesian or a Lernerian?" *Journal of Economic Literature* 22 (Dec. 1984): 1573.

21. John Kenneth Galbraith, *Economics in Perspective: A Critical History* (Boston, 1987), 235–36; James W. Dean, "The Dissolution of the Keynesian Consensus," *Public Interest*, special issue, 1980, 19–20; Athanasios Asimakopoulos, "The Role of the Short Pe-

riod," in J. A. Kregel, ed., *Distribution, Effective Demand, and International Economic Relations* (New York, 1983), 28.

22. Gordon, *Business Fluctuations*, 370; William E. Stoneman, *A History of the Economic Analysis of the Great Depression in America* (New York, 1979), 231; John Kenneth Galbraith, "The Causes of Economic Growth," 1956 statement, 6–7, box 104, John Kenneth Galbraith Papers, John F. Kennedy Library, Boston, Mass.

23. George Soule, "Macro-Economics," *New Republic*, Oct. 15, 1951, 20; Gordon, *Business Fluctuations*, 448 n. 37.

24. Alvin H. Hansen, "Needed: A Cycle Policy," in Seymour E. Harris, ed., *Saving American Capitalism: A Liberal Economic Program* (New York, 1948), 219–21; William Fellner, "Hansen on Full-Employment Policies," *Journal of Political Economy* 55 (June 1947): 254.

25. William H. Beveridge, *Full Employment in a Free Society* (New York, 1945), 26, 28–30, 99, 190–91, 205.

26. Alvin H. Hansen, "The Reports Prepared under the Employment Act," in Gerhard Colm, ed., *The Employment Act Past and Future: A Tenth Anniversary Symposium* (Washington, 1956), 93–94; Alvin H. Hansen, "Trends and Cycles in Economic Activity," *Review of Economics and Statistics* 39 (May 1957): 113–14; Alvin H. Hansen, *The American Economy* (New York, 1957), 31, 39; Alvin H. Hansen, *Economic Issues of the 1960s* (New York, 1960), 13, 209.

27. Richard A. Musgrave, "Hansen, Alvin," in John Eatwell et al., eds., *The New Palgrave: A Dictionary of Economics*, vol. 2 (New York, 1987), 591.

28. Sidney Weintraub, "Revision and Recantation in Hicksian Economics: A Review Article," *Journal of Economic Issues* 10 (Sept. 1976): 619; Warren Young, *Interpreting Mr. Keynes: The IS-LM Enigma* (Boulder, Colo., 1987), 115–17, 121, 173; Richard X. Chase, "Keynes's Principle(s) of Effective Demand: Redefining His Revolution," *Journal of Economic Issues* 26 (Sept. 1992): 874–75.

29. John H. Hotson, "The Fall of Bastard Keynesianism and the Rise of Legitimate Keynesianism," in Jesse Schwartz, ed., *The Subtle Anatomy of Capitalism* (Santa Monica, Calif., 1977), 329.

30. John H. Hotson, *Stagflation and the Bastard Keynesians* (Waterloo, Ontario, Canada, 1976), 8, 14, 17, 27.

31. Ibid., 12.

32. Alvin H. Hansen, *Monetary Theory and Fiscal Policy* (New York, 1949), 71 n. 1; Alvin H. Hansen, *A Guide to Keynes* (New York, 1953), 33.

33. Alvin H. Hansen to Mordecai Ezekiel, May 21, 1941, 3, box 6, Mordecai Ezekiel Papers, FDRL.

34. Gordon, *Business Fluctuations*, 367; W. Robert Brazelton, "Alvin Harvey Hansen: Economic Growth and a More Perfect Society," *American Journal of Economics and Sociology* 48 (Oct. 1989): 434.

35. Hansen, *American Economy*, 39.

36. Alvin H. Hansen, "Brief Rejoinder," *Review of Economic Statistics* 29 (Nov. 1947): 268.

CHAPTER TEN

1. Abba P. Lerner, "Keynesian Economics in the Sixties," in Robert Lekachman, ed., *Keynes' General Theory: Reports of Three Decades* (New York, 1964), 228; Kenneth K. Kurihara, "The Dynamic Impact of History on Keynesian Theory," in Robert V. Eagly,

ed., *Events, Ideology, and Economic Theory: The Determinants of Progress in the Development of Economic Analysis* (Detroit, 1968), 139–40.

2. Alfred E. Kahn, "Market Power Inflation: A Conceptual Overview," in Gardiner C. Means et al., *The Roots of Inflation: The International Crisis* (New York, 1975), 261; Frederic S. Lee amd Warren J. Samuels, "Introduction: Gardiner C. Means, 1896–1988," in Lee and Samuels, eds., *The Heterodox Economics of Gardiner C. Means: A Collection* (Armonk, N.Y., 1992), xxviii–xxix.

3. John M. Blair, *Economic Concentration: Structure, Behavior, and Public Policy* (New York, 1972), 420.

4. Gardiner C. Means, *Administrative Inflation and Public Policy* (Washington, 1959), 1, 36; U.S. Congress, Senate, "Statement of Gardiner C. Means," in *Administered Prices: Hearings before the Subcommittee on Antitrust and Monopoly of the Committee on the Judiciary*, 85th Cong., 1st sess., 1957, pt. 1, 88; Gardiner C. Means to William Benton, Feb. 5, 1958, 1, box 20, Gardiner C. Means Papers, Franklin D. Roosevelt Library, Hyde Park, N.Y.

5. Gardiner C. Means, "A General Formulation of Macro-Economic Equilibrium," Dec. 17, 1956, 36 n. 1, box 24, Means Papers.

6. Gardiner C. Means, "Monetary Institutions to Serve the Modern Economy," in Carey C. Thompson, ed., *Institutional Adjustment: A Challenge to a Changing Economy* (Austin, 1967), 160; Means to Benton, Feb. 5, 1958, 1; Gardiner C. Means to Walter Lippmann, July 10, 1957, box 21, Means Papers.

7. Bernard Nossiter, "The World of Gardiner Means," *New Republic*, May 7, 1962, 20.

8. Gardiner C. Means, "Pricing Power and the Public Interest," in U.S. Congress, Senate, *Administered Prices: A Compendium on Public Policy, Subcommittee on Antitrust and Monopoly of the Committee on the Judiciary*, 88th Cong., 1st sess., 1963, 232–33, 237.

9. Gardiner C. Means to Andre Schiffrin, Mar. 8, 1966, 1–2, box 105, Means Papers.

10. Gardiner C. Means, "The Problems and Prospects of Collective Capitalism," *Journal of Economic Issues* 3 (Mar. 1969): 28; Means to Schiffrin, Mar. 8, 1966, 1–2.

11. Gardiner C. Means, *Pricing Power and the Public Interest: A Study Based on Steel* (New York, 1962), xx; Donald Dewey, review of *Pricing Power and the Public Interest*, by Gardiner C. Means, *Political Science Quarterly* 77 (Dec. 1962): 601.

12. Gardiner C. Means to Adolf A. Berle, June 1, 1962, 1–2, box 67, Means Papers.

13. Adolf A. Berle to Gardiner C. Means, May 23, 1962, box 67, Means Papers.

14. Maxine Berg, "Historical Introduction," in Berg, ed., *Political Economy in the Twentieth Century* (Savage, Md., 1990), 9, 11, 14, 21; Malcolm C. Sawyer, *The Economics of Michal Kalecki* (Armonk, N.Y., 1985), 64; Paul M. Sweezy, "The First Quarter Century," in Lekachman, *Keynes' General Theory*, 309–10.

15. Joseph Steindl, *Maturity and Stagnation in American Capitalism* (1952; New York, 1976), 2, 125–26, 132–34, 137, 166, 168, 191–93, 223, 226.

16. Berg, "Historical Introduction," 11; Paul Sweezy, "Why Stagnation?" *Monthly Review* 34, no. 2 (1982): 4.

17. Ben B. Seligman, *Main Currents in Modern Economics: Economic Thought since 1870* (New York, 1962), 670; Harry K. Girvetz, *From Wealth to Welfare: The Evolution of Liberalism* (Stanford, 1950), 174, 177; Paul A. Samuelson, "Problems of the American Economy—Hard and Easy," in *The Collected Scientific Papers of Paul A. Samuelson*, ed. Robert C. Merton, vol. 3 (Cambridge, Mass., 1972), 732–33; Harold G. Vatter to Alvin H. Hansen, Apr. 27, 1965, 1–2, HUG (FP) 3.10, box 2, Alvin H. Hansen Papers, Harvard University Archives, Cambridge, Mass.

18. Alan R. Sweezy, "The Natural History of the Stagnation Thesis," in Joseph J. Spengler,

ed., *Zero Population Growth: Implications* (Chapel Hill, 1975), 40; Robert Aaron Gordon, *Business Fluctuations*, 2d ed. (New York, 1961), 213.

19. Daniel Hamberg, "Fiscal Policy and Stagnation since 1957," *Southern Economic Journal* 29 (Jan. 1963): 212 n. 2.

20. Alvin H. Hansen, *Economic Policy and Full Employment* (New York, 1947), 52, 210; Alvin H. Hansen, *Monetary Theory and Fiscal Policy* (New York, 1949), 152, 178–80; Alvin H. Hansen, *Business Cycles and National Income* (1951 [parts 1–4]; New York, 1964), 3–4, 56, 59–61, 64, 66, 71, 76, 131, 137, 308, 394–96, 399; Alvin H. Hansen, *A Guide to Keynes* (New York, 1953), 49–50; Alvin H. Hansen, "The Pigouvian Effect," *Journal of Political Economy* 59 (Dec. 1951): 535–36; Alvin H. Hansen, review of *Towards a Dynamic Economics*, by R. F. Harrod, *American Economic Review* 39 (Mar. 1949): 499; Alvin H. Hansen to Paul A. Samuelson, Apr. 20, 1954, 3, HUG (FP) 3.11, box 1, Hansen Papers.

21. Alvin H. Hansen, *The American Economy* (New York, 1957), 161, 162 n. 9.

22. Alvin H. Hansen, "Needed: A Cycle Policy," in Seymour E. Harris, ed., *Saving American Capitalism: A Liberal Economic Program* (New York, 1948), 218–19; Alvin H. Hansen, "Our Unstable Economy and What to Do About It," Nov. 17, 1948, speech transcript, 1–3, HUG (FP) 3.42, box 2, Hansen Papers.

23. Alvin H. Hansen, "Long-Run and Short-Run Adjustments," *Review of Economics and Statistics* 35 (Nov. 1953): 265; Alvin H. Hansen, "Growth or Stagnation in the American Economy," *Review of Economics and Statistics* 36 (Nov. 1954): 409.

24. Alvin H. Hansen, *The Postwar American Economy: Performance and Problems* (New York, 1964), vii, 1, 23; Alvin H. Hansen to [G.] Ackley, Apr. 23, 1963, 1, HUG (FP) 3.10, box 2, Hansen Papers; Alvin H. Hansen, "Keynes after Thirty Years," *Weltwirtschaftliches Archiv.* Bd. 98: 220, offprint, HUG (FP) 3.42, box 7, Hansen Papers.

25. Hansen, *Business Cycles and National Income*, 36; Alvin H. Hansen, "Trends and Cycles in Economic Activity," *Review of Economics and Statistics* 39 (May 1957): 114; Alvin H. Hansen, *Economic Issues of the 1960s* (New York, 1960), 209; Hansen, "Our Unstable Economy," 2.

26. "What Price Victory?" *Town Meeting*, Sept. 10, 1942, 6; Alvin H. Hansen, "We Can Pay the War Bill," *Atlantic Monthly*, Oct. 1942, 62.

27. Hansen, *Business Cycles and National Income*, 75–76; Hansen, "Growth or Stagnation," 412; Alvin H. Hansen, "Samuelson on Secular Stagnation," notes, Sept. 1961, 1–2, HUG (FP) 3.42, box 4, Hansen Papers.

28. Hansen, *Monetary Theory and Fiscal Policy*, 178–79, 182 n. 1; Alvin H. Hansen, "Commentary," *Review of Economics and Statistics* 45 (May 1963): 144.

29. Hansen, *Postwar American Economy*, 19, 35, 37; Alvin H. Hansen, "Appeal for a Dual Economy," *New York Times Magazine*, Mar. 12, 1961, 109; Alvin H. Hansen, "We Must Grow or Sink," *New York Times Magazine*, Mar. 18, 1962, 126.

30. Hansen to Ackley, Apr. 23, 1963, 2.

31. Hansen, *Economic Policy and Full Employment*, 197–99; Hansen, *Monetary Theory and Fiscal Policy*, 149; Alvin H. Hansen, "A Neglected Factor in Inflationary Pressures, 1955–1957," *Review of Economics and Statistics* 41 (May 1959): 184.

32. Alvin H. Hansen to Evsey Domar, Oct. 14, 1948, 1–3, HUG (FP) 3.10, box 1, Hansen Papers.

33. Alvin H. Hansen, "Stagnation and Under-employment Equilibrium," *Rostra Economica Amstelodamensia* (Nov. 1966): 8–9, offprint, HUG (FP) 3.42, box 7, Hansen Papers; Hansen, "Keynes after Thirty Years," 227–28.

34. Hansen, "Commentary," 144; Hansen, *Postwar American Economy*, 38; Hansen, *Economic Issues of the 1960s*, 204.

35. Hansen, "Needed: A Cycle Policy," 225.

36. Jesse J. Friedman, "Alvin H. Hansen's Economic Credo," *New York Times Book Review*, Jan. 12, 1947, 34; W. Robert Brazelton, "Alvin Harvey Hansen: Economic Growth and a More Perfect Society," *American Journal of Economics and Sociology* 48 (Oct. 1989): 435.

37. James F. Cusick, review of *The American Economy*, by Alvin H. Hansen, *American Economic Review* 48 (June 1958): 446.

38. Hansen, *Postwar American Economy*, 15.

39. Hansen to Ackley, Apr. 23, 1963, 3.

40. Hansen, *American Economy*, 146, 148; Hansen, *Economic Issues of the 1960s*, 47.

41. Alvin H. Hansen, "Post-Keynesian Economics," *American Economic Review* 45 (June 1955): 366.

42. Hansen, *Economic Policy and Full Employment*, 132–33; Hansen, *Monetary Theory and Fiscal Policy*, 177–78; Hansen, *Business Cycles and National Income*, 4, 376, 558–59, 569–70, 574–76; Hansen, "Growth or Stagnation," 409–14.

43. Hansen, *Business Cycles and National Income*, 574.

44. Alvin H. Hansen and Guy Greer, "Toward Full Use of Our Resources," *Fortune*, Nov. 1942, 170; Alvin H. Hansen, "Inflation," *Yale Review* 35 (June 1946): 709–10; Alvin H. Hansen, "Our Current Economic Dilemma," *Review of Economics and Statistics* 36 (Aug. 1954): 262; Hansen, "Post-Keynesian Economics," 369; Hansen, *Postwar American Economy*, 69–70; Hansen to Samuelson, Apr. 20, 1954, 1–3.

45. Hansen, *Economic Issues of the 1960s*, 13–14, 17–18, 22, 142.

46. Alvin H. Hansen, "Some Reflections on the Annual Report of the Council of Economic Advisers," *Review of Economics and Statistics* 44 (Aug. 1962): 338.

47. Means to Benton, Feb. 5, 1958, 1.

48. Gardiner C. Means to Adolf A. Berle, Aug. 2, 1958, box 67, Means Papers.

49. Alvin H. Hansen to J. K. Galbraith, Dec. 23, 1958, 1, box 33, John Kenneth Galbraith Papers, John F. Kennedy Library, Boston, Mass.; Alvin H. Hansen to "Dear Ken," draft of letter, undated (1969), 1, 5, HUG (FP) 3.10, box 1, Hansen Papers.

50. John Kenneth Galbraith to Alvin Hansen, May 27, 1969, HUG (FP) 3.10, box 1, Hansen Papers.

CHAPTER ELEVEN

1. Michael Harrington, *Decade of Decision: The Crisis of the American System* (New York, 1980), 55–56; Robert Sobel, *The Worldly Economists* (New York, 1980), 244; Raymond Vernon, "National Planning and the Multinational Enterprise: The U.S. Case," in Walter Goldstein, ed., *Planning, Politics, and the Public Interest* (New York, 1978), 88.

2. Ronald E. Muller, *Revitalizing America: Politics for Prosperity* (New York, 1980), 23, 63–64; Charles H. Ferguson, "From the People Who Brought You Voodoo Economics," *Harvard Business Review* 66 (May/June 1988): 59; Robert Aaron Gordon, "Rigor and Relevance in a Changing Institutional Setting," *American Economic Review* 66 (Mar. 1976): 6–7; William M. Dugger, *An Alternative to Economic Retrenchment* (New York, 1984), xii, 65.

3. Leon H. Keyserling et al., *Full Employment without Inflation* (Washington, D.C., 1975), 24; Mancur Olson, "An Evolutionary Approach to Inflation and Stagnation," in James H. Gapinski and Charles E. Rockwood, eds., *Essays in Post-Keynesian Inflation* (Cambridge, Mass., 1979), 146; Wallace C. Peterson, "Concluding Observations," in Peterson, ed., *Market Power and the Economy: Industrial, Corporate, Government, and Political Aspects* (Boston, 1988), 162.

4. Gardiner C. Means, "Corporate Power in the Marketplace," *Journal of Law and Economics* 26 (June 1983): 475, 480; Gardiner C. Means to Carliss Y. Baldwin, Feb. 4, 1983, 1, 4–5, box 67, Gardiner C. Means Papers, Franklin D. Roosevelt Library, Hyde Park, N.Y.; "Statement of Gardiner C. Means, Economist," in *Market Power, the Federal Trade Commission, and Inflation: Hearing before the Joint Economic Committee, Congress of the United States*, 93d Cong., 2d sess., Nov. 1974, 3–4; Richard Goode, "Gardiner C. Means on Administered Prices and Administrative Inflation," *Journal of Economic Issues* 28 (Mar. 1994): 177.

5. Gardiner C. Means, "Simultaneous Inflation and Unemployment: A Challenge to Theory and Policy," in Means et al., *The Roots of Inflation: The International Crisis* (New York, 1975), 30; Gardiner C. Means, "Administered Prices," in Douglas Greenwald, ed., *Encyclopedia of Economics* (New York, 1982), 14; "Statement of Gardiner C. Means, Economist," 3–4.

6. Gardiner C. Means, "How to Control Inflation in the United States: An Alternative to 'Planned Stagnation,'" *Wage-Price Law and Economics Review* 1 (Jan. 1975): 70–71, 74; Means, "Simultaneous Inflation and Unemployment," 29–30; "Statement of Gardiner C. Means, Economist," 5–6; Means, "Administered Prices," 14–15.

7. Means, "How to Control Inflation," 74.

8. Means, "Administered Prices," 14; "Statement of Gardiner C. Means, Economist," 7.

9. Sidney Weintraub, *Capitalism's Inflation and Unemployment Crisis: Beyond Monetarism and Keynesianism* (Reading, Mass., 1978), 166, 219; Marc R. Tool, *The Discretionary Economy: A Normative Theory of Political Economy* (Santa Monica, Calif., 1979), 124.

10. Alvin H. Hansen, "Monetary and Fiscal Policies for the 1970s," in Warren L. Smith and John M. Culbertson, eds., *Public Finance Stabilization Policy: Essays in Honor of Richard A. Musgrave* (New York, 1974), 235.

11. Gardiner C. Means to Dan Boorstin, Feb. 9, 1972, 3, box 67, Means Papers.

12. "Comments by Clark Warburton on Gardiner C. Means, 'Money, Employment, and Inflation,'" enclosed in Clark Warburton to Gardiner C. Means, Jan. 3, 1972, 2, box 104, Means Papers.

13. Tibor Scitovsky, "Can Capitalism Survive?—An Old Question in a New Setting," *American Economic Review* 70 (May 1980): 7–8; John Kenneth Galbraith, "On Post Keynesian Economics," *Journal of Post Keynesian Economics* 1 (Fall 1978): 10.

14. Robert Lekachman, *Economists at Bay: Why the Experts Will Never Solve Your Problems* (New York, 1976), 262; John Allet, *New Liberalism: The Political Economy of J. A. Hobson* (Toronto, 1981), 261; John F. Brothwell, "*The General Theory* after Fifty Years: Why Are We Not All Keynesians Now?" *Journal of Post Keynesian Economics* 8 (Summer 1986): 532, 539–40.

15. John Hicks, *Economic Perspectives: Further Essays on Money and Growth* (New York, 1977), xii.

16. Weintraub, *Capitalism's Inflation and Unemployment Crisis*, 194; Paul Davidson, "Reviving Keynes's Revolution," *Journal of Post Keynesian Economics* 6 (Summer 1984): 573–74; James E. Sawyer, *Why Reaganomics and Keynesian Economics Failed* (New York, 1987), 20–21.

17. Sidney Weintraub, "Revision and Recantation in Hicksian Economics: A Review Article," *Journal of Economic Issues* 10 (Sept. 1976): 619; Irwin Sobel, "Abba Lerner on Employment and Inflation: A Post-Keynesian Perspective," in Gapinski and Rockwood, *Post-Keynesian Inflation*, 277–78; Robert Sobel, *Worldly Economists*, 116.

18. Abba P. Lerner, "A Reluctant Keynesian," *Intermountain Economic Review* 7 (Fall 1976): 57; J. A. Kregel, review of *The Theory of Economic Breakdown*, by John Cornwall, *Journal of Economic Issues* 25 (Dec. 1991): 1177; Alfred S. Eichner, *Toward a New Eco-*

nomics: *Essays in Post-Keynesian and Institutionalist Theory* (Armonk, N.Y., 1985), 208–9.

19. Richard X. Chase, "Keynes and U.S. Keynesianism: A Lack of Historical Perspective and the Decline of the New Economics," *Journal of Economic Issues* 9 (Sept. 1975): 460; Leonard Silk, *The Economists* (New York, 1976), 141.

20. John Kenneth Galbraith, *Economics in Perspective: A Critical History* (Boston, 1987), 297; Richard McIntyre, "Economic Rhetoric and Industrial Decline," *Journal of Economic Issues* 23 (June 1989): 484, 486–87; Lawrence R. Klein, "The Neoclassical Tradition of Keynesian Economics and the Generalized Model," in George R. Feiwel, ed., *Samuelson and Neoclassical Economics* (Boston, 1982), 246.

21. Peter J. Reynolds, *Political Economy: A Synthesis of Kaleckian and Post Keynesian Economics* (New York, 1987), 5; Dugger, *Alternative to Economic Retrenchment*, 82–83; O. F. Hamouda, *John R. Hicks: An Intellectual Biography* (Cambridge, Mass., 1993), 221–22.

22. Paul A. Samuelson, "Comment," in David Worswick and James Trevithick, eds., *Keynes and the Modern World: Proceedings of the Keynes Centenary Conference, King's College, Cambridge* (Cambridge, England, 1983), 217.

23. James Tobin, "Keynesian Economics and Its Renaissance," in David A. Reese, ed., *The Legacy of Keynes* (San Francisco, 1987), 117; James Tobin, "A Revolution Remembered," *Challenge* 31 (July/Aug. 1988): 36–37.

24. John M. Blair to Walter W. Heller, Feb. 6, 1973, 1, box 67, Means Papers.

25. Marjorie S. Turner, "The Cambridge Keynesians and the 'Bastard Keynesians': A Comment on Economists and Their Understanding of the Inflationary Aspects of Keynesian Policy," *Journal of Economic Issues* 24 (Sept. 1990): 886, 888.

26. Silk, *Economists*, 169–70; W. Robert Brazelton, "Post-Keynesian Economics: An Institutional Compatibility?" *Journal of Economic Issues* 15 (June 1981): 538; Andrew Levison, *The Full Employment Alternative* (New York, 1980), 12–13, 68–69, 80; W. W. Rostow, *Why the Poor Get Richer and the Rich Slow Down: Essays in the Marshallian Long Period* (Austin, Tex., 1980), 119.

27. James R. Crotty, "Post-Keynesian Economic Theory: An Overview and Evaluation," *American Economic Review: Papers and Proceedings* 70 (May 1980): 20; Lorie Tarshis, "Post-Keynesian Economics: A Promise That Bounced?" *American Economic Review: Papers and Proceedings* 70 (May 1980): 10; Thomas Balogh, *The Irrelevance of Conventional Economics* (New York, 1982), 4–5, 159.

28. Reynolds, *Political Economy*, 8–10; Peter Kenyon, "Pricing," in Alfred S. Eichner, ed., *A Guide to Post-Keynesian Economics* (White Plains, N.Y., 1979), 35–36; Robert Neild, "The Wider World and Economic Methodology," in Peter Wiles and Guy Routh, eds., *Economics in Disarray* (New York, 1984), 45.

29. Irwin Sobel, "Abba Lerner on Employment and Inflation," 282; Galbraith, "On Post Keynesian Economics," 11; Joan Robinson and Francis Cripps, "Keynes Today," in Bernard S. Katz and Ronald E. Robbins, eds., *Modern Economic Classics: Evaluations through Time* (New York, 1988), 141.

30. Kenyon, "Pricing," 44; Allan G. Gruchy, *The Reconstruction of Economics: An Analysis of the Fundamentals of Institutional Economics* (New York, 1987), 149.

31. Allan G. Gruchy, "Planning in Contemporary Institutional Thought," *Journal of Economic Issues* 16 (June 1982): 373.

32. Kenyon, "Pricing," 44; Paul Davidson, "Natural Resources," in Eichner, *Guide to Post-Keynesian Economics*, 163–64.

33. Tarshis, "Post-Keynesian Economics," 14.

34. Warren J. Samuels and Steven G. Medema, "Gardiner C. Means's Institutional and

Post-Keynesian Economics," *Review of Political Economy* 1 (July 1989): 175; Frederic S. Lee and Warren J. Samuels, "Introduction: Gardiner C. Means, 1896–1988," in Lee and Samuels, eds., *The Heterodox Economics of Gardiner C. Means: A Collection* (Armonk, N.Y., 1992), xxviii, xxx.

35. Frederic S. Lee, "Gardiner C. Means and Administered Prices" (letters from economists), unpublished ms. in Lee's possession, chap. 1, 12.

36. Reynolds, *Political Economy*, 39; Malcolm C. Sawyer, *The Economics of Michal Kalecki* (Armonk, N.Y., 1985), 22.

37. Peter Wiles, "Whatever Happened to the Full-Cost Principle (UK)?" in Wiles and Routh, *Economics in Disarray*, 220; P. J. D. Wiles, "Administered Prices," in John Eatwell et al., eds., *The New Palgrave: A Dictionary of Economics*, vol. 1 (New York, 1987), 31.

38. Reynolds, *Political Economy*, 28, 230, 232; Malcolm C. Sawyer, "Towards a Post-Kaleckian Economics," in Philip Arestis and Thanos Skouras, eds., *Post Keynesian Economic Theory: A Challenge to Neo-Classical Economics* (Armonk, N.Y., 1985), 147.

39. Joan Robinson, "The Second Crisis of Economic Theory," *American Economic Review: Papers and Proceedings* 62 (May 1972): 4; Athanasios Asimakopoulos, "Kalecki and Robinson," in Mario Sebastiani, ed., *Kalecki's Relevance Today* (New York, 1989), 20.

40. Nina Shapiro, "The Revolutionary Character of Post-Keynesian Economics," *Journal of Economic Issues* 11 (Sept. 1977): 544–45, 549–51; George R. Feiwel, *The Intellectual Capital of Michal Kalecki: A Study in Economic Theory and Policy* (Knoxville, Tenn., 1975), 73–75, 88; Malcolm C. Sawyer, *Macro-Economics in Question: The Keynesian-Monetarist Orthodoxies and the Kaleckian Alternative* (Armonk, N.Y., 1982), 174.

41. Reynolds, *Political Economy*, 27.

42. Nicholas Kaldor, "Personal Recollections of Michal Kalecki," in Sebastiani, *Kalecki's Relevance Today*, 8.

43. Ibid., 4.

44. Malcolm C. Sawyer, *Economics of Michal Kalecki*, 22.

45. William Milberg and Bruce Emslie, "Technical Change in the Corporate Economy: A Vertically Integrated Approach," in Milberg, ed., *The Megacorp and Macrodynamics: Essays in Memory of Alfred Eichner* (Armonk, N.Y., 1992), 112; J. A. Kregel, "The Integration of Micro and Macroeconomics through Macrodynamic Megacorps: Eichner and the 'Post-Keynesians,'" *Journal of Economic Issues* 24 (June 1990): 527; Alfred S. Eichner, "Why Economics Is Not Yet a Science," in Eichner, ed., *Why Economics Is Not Yet a Science* (Armonk, N.Y., 1983), 221–22.

46. Alfred S. Eichner to Gardiner C. Means, Dec. 2, 1980, 2, box 68, Means Papers.

47. Alfred S. Eichner, *The Megacorp and Oligopoly: Micro Foundations of Macro Dynamics* (New York, 1976), 297 n. 6; Eichner, *Toward a New Economics*, 165–66; Alfred S. Eichner to Caroline Ware Means, Dec. 6, 1978, 2, box 68, Means Papers.

48. Eichner, *Megacorp and Oligopoly*, x, 38; Eichner, *Toward a New Economics*, 28; Johan Deprez and William S. Milberg, "Cycle and Trend in the Dynamics of Advanced Market Economies," *Journal of Economic Issues* 24 (June 1990): 514.

49. Eichner, *Megacorp and Oligopoly*, x, 2–3; Alfred S. Eichner, "A General Model of Investment and Pricing," in Edward J. Nell, ed., *Growth, Profits, and Prosperity: Essays in the Revival of Political Economy* (New York, 1980), 120; Kregel, "The Integration of Micro and Macroeconomics through Macrodynamic Megacorps," 524–25, 527.

50. Eichner, *Megacorp and Oligopoly*, x; Alfred S. Eichner, "The Micro Foundations of the Corporate Economy," *Managerial and Decision Economics* 4 (Nov. 1983): 136.

51. Eichner, *Megacorp and Oligopoly*, 190–91, 200–201.

52. Ibid., 2–3, 189–90; Eichner, "Why Economics Is Not Yet a Science," 218.

53. Eichner, *Megacorp and Oligopoly*, 190.

54. Ibid., 221–22.

55. Ibid., 250, 252, 254–56; Eichner, *Toward a New Economics*, 184.

56. Eichner, *Megacorp and Oligopoly*, 9.

57. Eichner, *Toward a New Economics*, 210.

58. Brazelton, "Post-Keynesian Economics," 538–40; Robert R. Keller, "Keynesian and Institutional Economics: Compatibility and Complementarity?" *Journal of Economic Issues* 17 (Dec. 1983): 1087–89, 1091–93.

59. Dudley Dillard, "A Monetary Theory of Production: Keynes and the Institutionalists," *Journal of Economic Issues* 14 (June 1980): 255, 271–72.

60. Wallace C. Peterson, "Institutionalism, Keynes, and the Real World," *Journal of Economic Issues* 11 (June 1977): 202; Peterson, "Concluding Observations," 168.

61. Allan G. Gruchy, "Institutional Economics: Its Development and Prospects," in Rolf Steppacher et al., eds., *Economics in Institutional Perspective: Memorial Essays in Honor of K. William Kapp* (Lexington, Mass., 1977), 11, 22; Philip A. Klein, "Power and Economic Performance: The Institutionalist View," *Journal of Economic Issues* 21 (Sept. 1987): 1342–44, 1358, 1361–62, 1364; Lee and Samuels, "Introduction," xxx.

62. Allan G. Gruchy, "Government Intervention and the Social Control of Business: The Neoinstitutionalist Position," *Journal of Economic Issues* 8 (June 1974): 242, 245, 247; Gruchy, *Reconstruction of Economics*, 141, 149.

63. Otis L. Graham Jr., *Toward a Planned Society: From Roosevelt to Nixon* (New York, 1976), 281.

64. Ibid., 68; Ellis W. Hawley, "Challenges to the Mixed Economy: The State and Private Enterprise," in Robert H. Bremner et al., eds., *American Choices: Social Dilemmas and Public Policy since 1960* (Columbus, Ohio, 1986), 166–67; Nicholas Spulber, *Managing the American Economy from Roosevelt to Reagan* (Bloomington, 1989), 93–94, 99, 104.

65. Quoted in Graham, *Planned Society*, 277.

66. Ibid.; Tool, *Discretionary Economy*, 157–58; Spulber, *Managing the American Economy*, 100; Kim McQuaid, *Uneasy Partners: Big Business in American Politics, 1945–1990* (Baltimore, 1994), 146.

67. Lester C. Thurow, *The Zero-Sum Society: Distribution and the Possibilities for Economic Change* (New York, 1980), 126; Graham, *Planned Society*, 282–83.

68. Wassily Leontief, "National Economic Planning: Methods and Problems," *Challenge* 19 (July/Aug. 1976): 7, 10–11; Robert Lekachman, "Managing Inflation in a Full Employment Society," *Annals of the American Academy of Political and Social Science* 418 (Mar. 1975): 85.

69. Harrington, *Decade of Decision*, 71.

70. Wassily Leontief, "What an Economic Planning Board Should Do," *Challenge* 17 (July/Aug. 1974): 35.

71. Spulber, *Managing the American Economy*, 104–6; McIntyre, "Economic Rhetoric and Industrial Decline," 484, 486; Lee Smith et al., *The Cuomo Commission Report: A New American Formula for a Strong Economy* (New York, 1988), 132; Bruce Bartlett, "Commentaries," in Claude E. Barfield and William A. Schambra, eds., *The Politics of Industrial Policy* (Washington, 1986), 274; Paul Krugman, *The Age of Diminished Expectations: U.S. Economic Policy in the 1990s* (Cambridge, Mass., 1990), 15–16; Otis L. Graham Jr., *Losing Time: The Industrial Policy Debate* (Cambridge, Mass., 1992), 237.

CHAPTER TWELVE

1. J. J. van Duijn, *The Long Wave in Economic Life* (London, 1983), 105, 223; Christopher Freeman, "Innovation and the Process of Economic Growth," in Herbert Giersch, ed., *Emerging Technologies: Consequences for Economic Growth, Structural Change, and Employment in Advanced Open Economies* (Tübingen, Germany, 1982), 1–2; Tom Bottomore, "J. A. Schumpeter," in Maxine Berg, ed., *Political Economy in the Twentieth Century* (Savage, Md., 1990), 116, 129.

2. Alfred Kleinknecht, *Innovation Patterns in Crisis and Prosperity: Schumpeter's Long Cycle Revisited* (New York, 1987), 203; Nathan Rosenberg, "Schumpeter and Marx: How Common a Vision?" in Roy M. MacLeod, ed., *Technology and the Human Prospect* (Wolfeboro, N.H., 1986), 197; Kurt W. Rothschild, "Discussion," in Horst Hanusch, ed., *Evolutionary Economics: Applications of Schumpeter's Ideas* (New York, 1988), 90.

3. Herbert Giersch, "The Age of Schumpeter," *American Economic Review: Papers and Proceedings* 74 (May 1984): 103; Gunnar Eliasson, "Schumpeterian Innovation, Market Structure, and the Stability of Industrial Development," in Hanusch, *Evolutionary Economics*, 159.

4. Richard Goodwin, "My Life and Times in the Shadow of Keynes," in Omar F. Hamouda and John N. Smithin, eds., *Keynes and Public Policy after Fifty Years*, vol. 1, *Economics and Policy* (New York, 1988), 145.

5. Giersch, "Age of Schumpeter," 105, 107; Gerhard Mensch, *Stalemate in Technology: Innovations Overcome the Depression* (Cambridge, Mass., 1979), 32–33, 212–13; Christopher Freeman, "Keynes or Kondratiev? How Can We Get Back to Full Employment?" in Pauline Marstrand, ed., *New Technology and the Future of Work and Skills* (Dover, N.H., 1984), 113.

6. Bruce Williams, "Technical Change and Fluctuations in Employment," in MacLeod, *Technology and the Human Prospect*, 186; Peter F. Drucker, "Toward the Next Economics," in Daniel Bell and Irving Kristol, eds., *The Crisis in Economic Theory* (New York, 1981), 11.

7. Mensch, *Stalemate in Technology*, 61, 212–13.

8. Freeman, "Keynes or Kondratiev?" 113.

9. R. D. Norton, "Industrial Policy and American Renewal," *Journal of Economic Literature* 24 (Mar. 1986): 1–2.

10. Peter Schachner-Blazizek, "The Current Relevance of Schumpeter's Theory of the Decay of Capitalism," in Christian Seidl, ed., *Lectures on Schumpeterian Economics: Schumpeter Centenary Memorial Lectures, Graz, 1983* (Berlin, 1984), 118.

11. Giersch, "Age of Schumpeter," 107.

12. Tibor Scitovsky, "Can Capitalism Survive?—An Old Question in a New Setting," *American Economic Review* 70 (May 1980): 5–6.

13. Christian Seidl, "Schumpeter versus Keynes: Supply-Side Economics or Demand Management?" in Seidl, *Lectures on Schumpeterian Economics*, 150.

14. Christopher Freeman et al., *Unemployment and Technical Innovation: A Study of Long Waves and Economic Development* (Westport, Conn., 1982), 20; Freeman, "Innovation and the Process of Economic Growth," 5.

15. Robert Heilbroner, "Analysis and Vision in the History of Modern Economic Thought," *Journal of Economic Literature* 28 (Sept. 1990): 1103–4, 1108.

16. Giersch, "Age of Schumpeter," 105–8; Richard R. Nelson and Sidney G. Winter, "The Schumpeterian Tradeoff Revisited," *American Economic Review* 72 (Mar. 1982): 114.

17. Arnold Heertje, preface to Heertje, ed., *Schumpeter's Vision: "Capitalism, Socialism, and*

Democracy" after 40 Years (New York, 1981), x; Edwin Harwood, "The Entrepreneurial Renaissance and Its Promoters," *Society*, Mar./Apr. 1979, 27–28; Arnold Heertje, "Schumpeter and Technical Change," in Hanusch, *Evolutionary Economics*, 88.

18. Chaitram J. Talele, *Keynes and Schumpeter: New Perspectives* (Brookfield, Vt., 1991), 75–76.

19. John D. Sterman, "The Economic Long Wave: Theory and Evidence," in Tibor Vasko, ed., *The Long-Wave Debate* (New York, 1987), 153.

20. Gerhard Mensch et al., "Changing Capital Values and the Propensity to Innovate," in Christopher Freeman, ed., *Long Waves in the World Economy* (Dover, N.H., 1984), 31.

21. Kleinknecht, *Innovation Patterns in Crisis and Prosperity*, 123–24, 210–11; David L. McKee, *Schumpeter and the Political Economy of Change* (New York, 1991), 65.

22. Mensch, *Stalemate in Technology*, 11, 32–33.

23. François Chesnais, "Schumpeterian Recovery and the Schumpeterian Perspective— Some Unsettled Issues and Alternative Interpretations," in Giersch, *Emerging Technologies*, 43, 67–68; Kleinknecht, *Innovation Patterns in Crisis and Prosperity*, 123–24, 167, 209–12; Christopher Freeman, "Structural Crises of Adjustment, Business Cycles, and Investment Behaviour," in Giovanni Dosi et al., eds., *Technical Change and Economic Theory* (New York, 1988), 61.

24. Freeman, "Keynes or Kondratiev?" 106, 110–12, 119.

25. Alfred Kleinknecht, "Post-1945 Growth as a Schumpeter Boom," *Review (F. Braudel Center)* 12 (Fall 1989): 437, 453–54; Sterman, "Economic Long Wave," 151–52; R. W. Coombs, "Innovation, Automation, and the Long-Wave Theory," in Freeman, ed., *Long Waves in the World Economy*, 116.

26. Kleinknecht, "Post-1945 Growth as a Schumpeter Boom," 453; Myron H. Ross, *A Gale of Creative Destruction: The Coming Economic Boom, 1992–2020* (New York, 1988), 6, 33.

27. Freeman, "Innovation and the Process of Economic Growth," 6; F. M. Scherer, *Innovation and Growth: Schumpeterian Perspectives* (Cambridge, Mass., 1984), 263–64.

28. Sterman, "Economic Long Wave," 152–53.

29. John Cornwall, "Macrodynamics," in Alfred S. Eichner, ed., *A Guide to Post-Keynesian Economics* (White Plains, N.Y., 1979), 26–27; Joan Robinson, *What Are the Questions? and Other Essays: Further Contributions to Modern Economics* (Armonk, N.Y., 1981), 53.

30. W. W. Rostow, *Theorists of Economic Growth from David Hume to the Present: With a Perspective on the Next Century* (New York, 1990), 457; Edwin Mansfield, "Long Waves and Technological Innovation," *American Economic Review* 73 (May 1983): 141; Massimo Di Matteo, "Relative Prices and Technical Change: A Suggested Approach to Long Waves," in Vasko, *Long-Wave Debate*, 326.

31. Mensch et al., "Changing Capital Values," 36; W. W. Rostow, "Kondratieff, Schumpeter, and Kuznets: Trend Periods Revisited," *Journal of Economic History* 35 (Dec. 1975): 749; Jay W. Forrester, "An Alternative Approach to Economic Policy: Macrobehavior from Microstructure," in Nake M. Kamrany and Richard H. Day, eds., *Economic Issues of the Eighties* (Baltimore, 1979), 103.

32. Klas Eklund, "Long Waves in the Development of Capitalism?" *Kyklos* 33, no. 3 (1980): 401, 405–7; W. W. Rostow, *The Barbaric Counter-Revolution: Cause and Cure* (Austin, Tex., 1983), 8, 11–13; Michael Harrington, *The Twilight of Capitalism* (New York, 1976), 328–29.

33. Jay W. Forrester, "Business Structure, Economic Cycles, and National Policy," *Cycles* 27 (Feb./Mar. 1976): 39; Leonard Silk, *The Economists* (New York, 1976), 246–47; Michael Harrington, *Decade of Decision: The Crisis of the American System* (New York, 1980), 56–57.

34. Rostow, *Barbaric Counter-Revolution*, 11–12; Rostow, *Theorists of Economic Growth*, 257.

35. W. W. Rostow, "Cycles in the Fifth Kondratieff Upswing," in *The Business Cycle and Public Policy, 1929–80: A Compendium of Papers Submitted to the Joint Economic Committee, Congress of the United States* (Washington, D.C., 1980), 61; Rostow, *Theorists of Economic Growth*, 257.

36. Rostow, *Theorists of Economic Growth*, 256; W. W. Rostow, "A Rejoinder," *Intermountain Economic Review* 7 (Fall 1976): 61; W. W. Rostow, "Economic Growth and the Diffusion of Power," *Challenge* 29 (Sept./Oct., 1986): 32, 34.

37. Rostow, "Economic Growth and the Diffusion of Power," 37; W. W. Rostow, "Caught by Kondratieff," *Wall Street Journal*, Mar. 8, 1977, 20.

38. Eklund, "Long Waves in the Development of Capitalism?" 407; Rostow, "Caught by Kondratieff," 20, and "Rejoinder," 63–64.

39. Rostow, "Rejoinder," 64; Rostow, "Cycles in the Fifth Kondratieff Upswing," 64; Rostow, "Caught by Kondratieff," 20.

40. Di Matteo, "Relative Prices and Technical Change," 326; Rainer Metz, "Kondratieff and the Theory of Linear Filters," in Vasko, *Long-Wave Debate*, 390.

41. Kleinknecht, *Innovation Patterns in Crisis and Prosperity*, 13.

42. Eklund, "Long Waves in the Development of Capitalism?" 412–14.

CHAPTER THIRTEEN

1. Paul M. Sweezy, "Why Stagnation?" *Monthly Review* 34 (June 1982): 4–10; Michael A. Lebowitz, "Paul M. Sweezy," in Maxine Berg, ed., *Political Economy in the Twentieth Century* (Savage, Md., 1990), 140, 143, 146.

2. Ernest Mandel, *Long Waves of Capitalist Development: The Marxist Interpretation* (New York, 1980), viii, 9, 20–22, 24–25, 87–88, 126; Paul A. Attewell, *Radical Political Economy since the Sixties: A Sociology of Knowledge Analysis* (New Brunswick, N.J., 1984), 190–92; Klas Eklund, "Long Waves in the Development of Capitalism?" *Kyklos* 33, No. 3 (1980): 405.

3. J. J. van Duijn, *The Long Wave in Economic Life* (London, 1983), 55; Anthony Scaperlanda, "Hansen's Secular Stagnation Thesis Once Again," *Journal of Economic Issues* 11 (June 1977): 224; W. Robert Brazelton, "Alvin Harvey Hansen: Economic Growth and a More Perfect Society," *American Journal of Economics and Sociology* 48 (Oct. 1989): 437.

4. W. W. Rostow, *Theorists of Economic Growth from David Hume to the Present: With a Perspective on the Next Century* (New York, 1990), 462.

5. Leonard Silk, "The 'Secular Slowdown' Thesis," *New York Times*, Oct. 21, 1976, 55.

6. R. D. Norton, "Industrial Policy and American Renewal," *Journal of Economic Literature* 24 (Mar. 1986): 7.

7. Scaperlanda, "Hansen's Secular Stagnation Thesis," 230–31.

8. Ibid., 228; Vincent J. Tarascio, "Keynes on the Sources of Economic Growth," *Journal of Economic History* 31 (June 1971): 444.

9. Clarence L. Barber, "On the Origins of the Great Depression," *Southern Economic Journal* 44 (Jan. 1978): 442–43, 445, 453–55.

10. Charles P. Kindleberger, *The World in Depression, 1929–1939*, rev. ed. (Berkeley, 1986), 191.

11. George Stigler, lecture, 1985, in William Breit and Roger W. Spencer, eds., *Lives of the Laureates: Ten Nobel Economists*, 2d ed. (Cambridge, Mass., 1990), 93.

12. Harold G. Vatter, "The Atrophy of Net Investment and Some Consequences for the U.S. Mixed Economy," *Journal of Economic Issues* 16 (Mar. 1982): 243, 245, 249; Brazelton, "Alvin Harvey Hansen," 437–38.

13. Silk, "'Secular Slowdown' Thesis," 55.
14. Van Duijn, *Long Wave in Economic Life*, 103.
15. Christopher Freeman, "Innovation and the Process of Economic Growth," in Herbert Giersch, ed., *Emerging Technologies: Consequences for Economic Growth, Structural Change, and Employment in Advanced Open Economies* (Tübingen, Germany, 1982), 6.
16. Gordon A. Fletcher, *The Keynesian Revolution and Its Critics: Issues of Theory and Policy for the Monetary Production Economy* (New York, 1987), 305.
17. Richard X. Chase, "Keynes and U.S. Keynesianism: A Lack of Historical Perspective and the Decline of the New Economics," *Journal of Economic Issues* 9 (Sept. 1975): 446–48, 451, 460.

CHAPTER FOURTEEN

1. Herbert Stein, *Presidential Economics: The Making of Economic Policy from Roosevelt to Reagan and Beyond* (New York, 1984), 261; Paul Craig Roberts, *The Supply-Side Revolution: An Insider's Account of Policymaking in Washington* (Cambridge, Mass., 1984), 5; Teresa Amott, "The Politics of Reaganomics," in Edward Nell, ed., *Free Market Conservatism: A Critique of Theory and Practice* (London, 1984), 165.
2. Roberts, *Supply-Side Revolution*, 25, 31, 71, 224; Amott, "Politics of Reaganomics," 165; George Gilder, *Wealth and Poverty* (New York, 1981), 76–78, 202, 218; Paul Krugman, *Peddling Prosperity: Economic Sense and Nonsense in the Age of Diminished Expectations* (New York, 1994), 93; Leonard Silk, *Economics in the Real World* (New York, 1984), 171.
3. Roberts, *Supply-Side Revolution*, 76.
4. Lester C. Thurow, *Dangerous Currents: The State of Economics* (New York, 1983), xv; John M. Culbertson, "American Economics: 100 Years in a Rut," *New York Times*, Jan. 12, 1986, sec. 3, F3.
5. Leonard Silk, "Economic Scene," *New York Times*, June 19, 1985, D2; Lester C. Thurow, *The Zero-Sum Solution: Building a World-Class American Economy* (New York, 1985), 12; Archibald L. Gillies, "Start Planning for Post-Reagan America," *New York Times*, Mar. 5, 1986, A27; Paul Davidson, *Post Keynesian Macroeconomic Theory: A Foundation for Successful Economic Policies for the Twenty-First Century* (Brookfield, Vt., 1994), 154–55.
6. Wolfgang F. Stolper, "A 'Real' Supply-Sider Views Reagan's Legacy," *New York Times*, Nov. 29, 1987, E16.
7. Basil J. Moore, "Why Investment Determines Saving," *Challenge* 33 (May/June 1990): 55–56; Iwan W. Morgan, *Deficit Government: Taxing and Spending in Modern America* (Chicago, 1995), 172, 195.
8. Michael Barker, "The End of the Reagan Boom," *New Republic*, July 1, 1985, 21; Wallace C. Peterson, "The Macroeconomic Legacy of Reaganomics," *Journal of Economic Issues* 22 (Mar. 1988): 14.
9. Wallace C. Peterson, "What Is to Be Done?" *Journal of Economic Issues* 26 (June 1992): 338.
10. Allen Sinai, "What's Wrong with the Economy?" *Challenge* 35 (Nov./Dec. 1992): 6; Peter Passell, "Light at the End of the Elevator Shaft," *New York Times*, Sept. 8, 1991, E1.
11. Sinai, "What's Wrong with the Economy?" 6; Benjamin M. Friedman, "Financial Roadblocks on the Route to Economic Prosperity," *Challenge* 35 (Mar./Apr. 1992): 25–26.
12. John Kenneth Galbraith, "Recessions? Why Worry?" *New York Times*, May 12, 1993, A19; James Tobin, "Thinking Straight about Fiscal Stimulus and Deficit Reduction,"

Challenge 36 (Mar./Apr. 1993): 16; Robert L. Heilbroner, "Where Is Capitalism Going?" *Challenge* 35 (Nov./Dec. 1992): 45–46.

13. Louis Uchitelle, "Business Scene," *New York Times*, Nov. 5, 1991, D2; Louis Uchitelle, "Cutback in Military Spending: No Help for Ailing Economy," *New York Times*, Aug. 12, 1992, A1.

14. David A. Levy, "1990s: A Contained Depression," *Challenge* 34 (July/Aug. 1991): 35–36, 38; Floyd Norris, "If Banks Don't Lend, Credit Is Not Easy," *New York Times*, Sept. 15, 1991, F1; Peterson, "What Is to Be Done?" 339.

15. Levy, "1990s: A Contained Depression," 38.

16. Ibid., 35; Heilbroner, "Where Is Capitalism Going?" 45; Louis Uchitelle, "Even Words Fail in This Economy," *New York Times*, Sept. 8, 1992, D2.

17. Jeff Madrick, "The Slow-Growth Monster," *New York Times*, Dec. 11, 1991, A27; Levy, "1990s: A Contained Depression," 40.

18. Levy, "1990s: A Contained Depression," 36–37.

19. Sinai, "What's Wrong with the Economy?" 5; Louis Uchitelle, "Limited Menu," *New York Times*, Nov. 24, 1991, sec. 4, 1; Louis Uchitelle, "Old Idea Gains New Respect: Spending Way Out of Slump," *New York Times*, Oct. 8, 1992, A1.

20. Allan G. Gruchy, *The Reconstruction of Economics: An Analysis of the Fundamentals of Institutional Economics* (New York, 1987), 99, 103; Henry M. Trebing, "Some Thoughts on the Future of Economic Planning: The Gruchy/Institutional Contribution," *Journal of Economic Issues* 25 (June 1991): 411; Robert Reich, *The Work of Nations: Preparing Ourselves for Twenty-First-Century Capitalism* (New York, 1991), 70.

21. John Kenneth Galbraith, "A Look Back: Affirmation and Error," *Journal of Economic Issues* 23 (June 1989): 414; John Kenneth Galbraith, "Ideology and Economic Reality," *Challenge* 32 (Nov./Dec. 1989): 7.

22. Lee Smith et al., *The Cuomo Commission Report: A New American Formula for a Strong Economy* (New York, 1988), 113–14, 193; Robert B. Reich, *The Next American Frontier* (New York, 1983), 18–20; Robert Eisner, "Tax Tinkering Won't Help the Economy," *New York Times*, Sept. 3, 1989, sec. 4, E12.

23. Alicia H. Munnell, "Why Has Productivity Growth Declined? Productivity and Public Investment," *New England Economic Review* (Jan./Feb. 1990): 14, 20; David Alan Aschauer, "Is Public Expenditure Productive?" *Journal of Monetary Economics* 23 (Mar. 1989): 195, 197; David Alan Aschauer, *Public Investment and Private Sector Growth: The Economic Benefits of Reducing America's "Third Deficit"* (Washington, D.C., 1990), 4, 11.

24. Levy, "1990s: A Contained Depression," 41; Heilbroner, "Where Is Capitalism Going?" 46–47; John H. Cushman Jr., "While President Bush Is Satisfied on Public Works Spending, Opponents Call for More," *New York Times*, Oct. 19, 1992, A12; Robert Eisner, "Debunking the Conventional Wisdom in Economic Policy," *Challenge* 33 (May/ June 1993): 11; Peter Applebome, "Study Ties Educational Gains to More Productivity Growth," *New York Times*, May 14, 1995, 22.

25. Aschauer, *Public Investment and Private Sector Growth*, 25.

26. Steven Greenhouse, "President Gambles on Spending," *New York Times*, Feb. 15, 1993, D1.

27. Smith et al., *Cuomo Commission Report*, 182, 192–93.

28. Alan S. Blinder, "The Fall and Rise of Keynesian Economics," *Economic Record* 64 (Dec. 1988): 278; Alan S. Blinder, "A Keynesian Restoration Is Here," *Challenge* 35 (Sept./Oct. 1992): 18.

29. Thomas Karier, "The Heresies of John Kenneth Galbraith," *Challenge* 36 (July/Aug. 1993): 23, 27.

30. Blinder, "A Keynesian Restoration Is Here," 14.

31. Quoted in Thomas L. Friedman, "Clinton's Aides Search for Options and Offices," *New York Times*, Nov. 16, 1992, A14.

32. Warren E. Leary, "4% Rise Sought in Science Budget," *New York Times*, Feb. 8, 1994, C5; Laura D'Andrea Tyson, "From Stagnation to Renewed Growth," *Challenge* 37 (May/June 1994): 20; Bob Woodward, *The Agenda: Inside the Clinton White House* (New York, 1994), 324; John B. Judis, "Sleazy Genius," *New Republic*, May 15, 1995, 24.

33. Nicholas Spulber, *Managing the American Economy from Roosevelt to Reagan* (Bloomington, 1989), 106–7; John Holusha, "States Try New Routes to Reviving Industries," *New York Times*, Nov. 30, 1985, 8.

34. Gillies, "Start Planning for Post-Reagan America," A27; Smith et al., *Cuomo Commission Report*, 109.

35. Robert Kuttner, "Facing Up to Industrial Policy," *New York Times Magazine*, Apr. 19, 1992, 22.

36. Otis L. Graham Jr., *Losing Time: The Industrial Policy Debate* (Cambridge, Mass., 1992), 197, 237.

37. Louis Uchitelle, "An Old Liberal, a New Sermon," *New York Times*, Apr. 12, 1990, D5.

38. Robert B. Reich, *The Resurgent Liberal (and Other Unfashionable Prophecies)* (1989; New York, 1991), 57–59, 256–57.

39. Keith Bradsher, "U.S. to Aid Industry in Computer Battle with the Japanese," *The New York Times*, Apr. 27, 1994, A1, D5; Todd Schafer and Paul Hyland, "Technology Policy in the Post–Cold War World," *Journal of Economic Issues* 28 (June 1994): 600–601, 604; David E. Sanger, "G.O.P. Finds Commerce Dept. Is Hard to Uproot," *New York Times*, Sept. 20, 1995, B8.

40. Quoted in Matthew L. Wald, "Government Dream Car," *New York Times*, Sept. 30, 1993, D7.

EPILOGUE

1. Mark Blaug, "Recent Biographies of Keynes," *Journal of Economic Literature* 32 (Sept. 1994): 1211–12.

2. George J. Stigler and Claire Friedland, "The Literature of Economics: The Case of Berle and Means," in Bernard S. Katz and Ronald E. Robbins, eds., *Modern Economic Classics: Evaluations through Time* (New York, 1988), 234.

3. Harold G. Vatter et al., "The Onset and Persistence of Secular Stagnation in the U.S. Economy: 1910–1990" (paper presented at meeting of Association for Evolutionary Economics, 1995), 28–30, 32–34, a shorter version of which appears in *Journal of Economic Issues* (June 1995); Wolfgang Streeck, "On the Institutional Conditions of Diversified Quality Production," in Egon Matzner and Wolfgang Streeck, eds., *Beyond Keynesianism: The Socio-Economics of Production and Full Employment* (Brookfield, Vt., 1991), 47–48; Malcolm C. Sawyer, "Reflections on the Nature and Role of Industrial Policy," *Metroeconomica* 43, nos. 1/2 (1992): 51.

4. Christopher Freeman, "Schumpeter's *Business Cycles* Revisited," in Arnold Heertje and Mark Perlman, eds., *Evolving Technology and Market Structure: Studies in Schumpeterian Economics* (Ann Arbor, 1990), 19.

5. James K. Galbraith, "Economic Report of the President: A Review," *Challenge* 38 (May/June 1995): 9.

6. Quoted in Bob Woodward, *The Agenda: Inside the Clinton White House* (New York, 1994), 90.

7. Ibid., 74, 77, 95, 108, 133, 140, 155–56, 161–62, 211, 225, 238.

8. Alan S. Blinder, "A Keynesian Restoration Is Here," *Challenge* 35 (Sept./Oct. 1992): 14.

9. Elizabeth Drew, *On the Edge: The First Year of the Clinton Presidency* (New York, 1994), 167.

10. Woodward, *Agenda*, 225.

11. Paul Krugman, *The Age of Diminished Expectations: U.S. Economic Policy in the 1990s* (Cambridge, Mass., 1990), xi.

12. Robert Kuttner, "Postwar Economics," *New York Times Magazine*, pt. 2, *The Business World*, Mar. 24, 1991, 10.

13. L. Randall Wray, "A New Year's Keynesian Wish: Advice to Clinton in the Aftermath of November 1994," *Journal of Economic Issues* 29 (June 1995): 602.

14. E. J. Dionne, *They Only Look Dead: Why Progressives Will Dominate the Next Political Era* (New York, 1996), 268.

Index